PYTHON
BASICS

PYTHON BASICS

H. Bhasin

MERCURY LEARNING AND INFORMATION
Dulles, Virginia
Boston, Massachusetts
New Delhi

Publisher: David Pallai
MERCURY LEARNING AND INFORMATION
22841 Quicksilver Drive
Dulles, VA 20166
info@merclearning.com
www.merclearning.com
1-800-232-0223

H. Bhasin. *Python Basics*.
ISBN: 978-1-683923-53-4

Library of Congress Control Number: 2018962670

19202132   Printed on acid-free paper in the United States of America.

To
My Mother

CONTENTS

## CHAPTER 1

INTRODUCTION TO PYTHON

After reading this chapter, the reader will be able to

- Understand the chronology of Python
- Appreciate the importance and features of Python
- Discover the areas in which Python can be used
- Install Anaconda

1.1 INTRODUCTION

Art is an expression of human creative skill, hence programming is an art. The choice of programming language is, therefore, important. This book introduces Python, which will help you to become a great artist. A. J. Perlis, who was a professor at the Purdue University, and who was the recipient of the first Turing award, stated

> *"A language that doesn't affect the way you think about programming is not worth knowing."*

Python is worth knowing. Learning Python will not only motivate you to do highly complex tasks in the simplest manners but will also demolish the myths of conventional programming paradigms. It is a language which will change the way you program and hence look at a problem.

Python is a strong, procedural, object-oriented, functional language crafted in the late 1980s by Guido Van Rossum. The language is named after Monty Python, a comedy group. The language is currently being used in diverse application domains. These include software development, web development, Desktop GUI development, education, and scientific applications. So, it spans almost all the facets of development. Its popularity is primarily owing to its simplicity and robustness, though there are many other factors too which are discussed in the chapters that follow.

There are many third party modules for accomplishing the above tasks. For example Django, an immensely popular Web framework dedicated to clean and fast development, is developed on Python. This, along with the support for HTML, E-mails, FTP, etc., makes it a good choice for web development.

Third party libraries are also available for software development. One of the most common examples is Scions, which is used for build controls. When joined with the inbuilt features and support, Python also works miracles for GUI development and for developing mobile applications, e.g., Kivy is used for developing multi-touch applications.

Python also finds its applications in scientific analysis. SciPy is used for Engineering and Mathematics, and IPython is used for parallel computing. Those of you working in statistics and machine learning would find some of these libraries extremely useful and easy to use. SciPy provides MATLAB like features and can be used for processing multidimensional arrays. Figure 1.1 summarizes the above discussion.

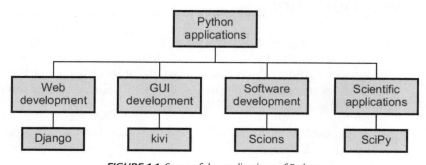

FIGURE 1.1 Some of the applications of Python

This chapter introduces the Python programming language. The chapter has been organized as follows. Section 1.2 discusses the features of Python, Section 1.3 discusses the paradigms and Section 1.4 discusses the development and uses. The installation of Anaconda has been introduced in Section 1.5. The last section concludes the chapter.

1.2   FEATURES OF PYTHON

As stated earlier, Python is a simple but powerful language. Python is portable. It has built-in object types, many libraries and is free. This section briefly discusses the features and strengths of Python.

1.2.1   Easy

Python is easy to learn and understand. As a matter of fact, if you are from a programming background you will find it elegant and uncluttered. The removal of braces and parentheses makes the code short and sweet. Also, some of the tasks in Python are pretty easy. For example, swapping numbers in Python is as easy as writing `(a, b)= (b, a)`.

It may also be stated here that learning something new is an involved and intricate task. However, the simplicity of Python makes it almost a cake walk. Moreover, learning advanced features in Python is a bit intricate, but is worth the effort. It is also easy to understand a project written in Python. The code, in Python, is concise and effective and therefore understandable and manageable.

1.2.2   Type and Run

In most projects, testing something new requires scores of changes and therefore recompilations and re-runs. This makes testing of code a difficult and time consuming task. In Python, a code can be run easily. As a matter of fact, we run scripts in Python.

As we will see later in this chapter, Python also provides the user with an interactive environment, in which one can run independent commands.

1.2.3   Syntax

The syntax of Python is easy; this makes the learning and understanding process easy. According to most of authors, the three main features which make Python attractive are that it's simple, small, and flexible.

1.2.4   Mixing

If one is working on a big project, with perhaps a large team, it might be the case that some of the team members are good in other programming languages.

This may lead to some of the modules in some other languages wanting to be embedded with the core Python code. Python allows and even supports this.

1.2.5 Dynamic Typing

Python has its own way of managing memory associated with objects. When an object is created in Python, memory is dynamically allocated to it. When the life cycle of the object ends, the memory is taken back from it. This memory management of Python makes the programs more efficient.

1.2.6 Built in Object Types

As we will see in the next chapter Python has built in object types. This makes the task to be accomplished easy and manageable. Moreover, the issues related to these objects are beautifully handled by the language.

1.2.7 Numerous Libraries and Tools

In Python, the task to be accomplished becomes easy—really easy. This is because most of the common tasks (as a matter of fact, not so common tasks too) have already been handled in Python. For example, Python has libraries which help users to develop GUI's, write mobile applications, incorporate security features and even read MRI's. As we will see in the following chapters, the libraries and supporting tools make even the intricate tasks like pattern recognition easy.

1.2.8 Portable

A program written in Python can run in almost every known platform, be it Windows, Linux, or Mac. It may also be stated here that Python is written in C.

1.2.9 Free

Python is not propriety software. One can download Python compilers from among the various available choices. Moreover, there are no known legal issues involved in the distribution of the code developed in Python.

1.3 THE PARADIGMS

1.3.1 Procedural

In a procedural language, a program is actually a set of statements which execute sequentially. The only option a program has, in terms of manageability, is dividing the program into small modules. "C," for example, is a procedural language. Python supports procedural programming. The first section of this book deals with procedural programming.

1.3.2 Object-Oriented

This type of language primarily focuses on the instance of a class. The instance of a class is called an object. A class is a real or a virtual entity that has an importance to the problem at hand, and has sharp physical boundaries. For example in a program that deals with student management, "student" can be a class. Its instances are made and the task at hand can be accomplished by communicating via methods. Python is object-oriented. Section 2 of this book deals with the object-oriented programming.

1.3.3 Functional

Python also supports functional programming. Moreover, Python supports immutable data, tail optimization, etc. This must be music to the ears for those from a functional programming background. Here it may be stated that functional programming is beyond the scope of this book. However, some of the above features would be discussed in the chapters that follow.

So Python is a procedural, object-oriented and functional language.

1.4 CHRONOLOGY AND USES

Having seen the features, let us now move onto the chronology and uses of Python. This section briefly discusses the development and uses of Python and will motivate the reader to bind with the language.

1.4.1 Chronology

Python is written in C. It was developed by Guido Van Rossum, who is now the Benevolent Director for Life of Python. The reader is expected to take note of the fact that Python has got nothing to do with pythons or snakes. The name of the language comes from the show *"Monty Python's Flying Circus,"* which was one of the favorite shows of the developer, Guido van Rossum. Many people attribute the fun part of the language to the inspiration.

Python is easy to learn as the core of the language is pretty concise. The simplicity of Python can also be attributed to the desire of the developers to make a language that was very simple, easy to learn but quite powerful.

The continuous betterment of the language has been possible because of a dedicated group of people, committed to supporting the cause of providing the world with an easy yet powerful language. The growth of the language has given rise to the creation of many interest groups and forums for Python. A change in the language can be brought about by what is generally referred to as the PEP (Python Enhancement Project). The PSF (Python Software Foundation) takes care of this.

1.4.2   Uses

Python is being used to accomplish many tasks, the most important of which are as follows:

- Graphical User Interface (GUI) development
- Scripting web pages
- Database programming
- Prototyping
- Gaming
- Component based programming

If you are working in Unix or Linux, you don't need to install Python. This is because in Unix and Linux systems, Python is generally pre-installed. However, if you work in Windows or Mac then you need to download Python. Once you have decided to download Python, look for its latest version. The reader is requested to ensure that the version he/she intends to download is not an alpha or a beta version. Reference 1 at the end of the book gives a brief overview of distinctions between two of the most famous versions. The next section briefly discusses the steps for downloading Anaconda, an open source distribution software.

Many development environments are available for Python. Some of them are as follows:

1. PyDev with Eclipse

2. Emacs

3. Vim

4. TextMate

5. Gedit

6. Idle

7. PIDA (Linux)(VIM based)

8. NotePad++ (Windows)

9. BlueFish (Linux)

There are some more options available. However, this book uses IDLE and Anaconda. The next section presents the steps involved in the installation of Anaconda.

1.5   INSTALLATION OF ANACONDA

In order to install Anaconda, go to *https://docs.continuum.io/anaconda/install* and select the installer (Windows or Mac OS or Linux). This section presents the steps involved in the installation of Anaconda on the Windows Operating System.

First of all, one must choose the installer (32 bit or 64 bit). In order to do so, click on the selected installer and download the .exe file. The installer will ask you to install it on the default location. You can provide a location that does not contain any spaces or Unicode characters. It may happen that during the installation you might have to disable your anti-virus software. Figures 1.2(a) to 1.2(g) take the reader through the steps of installation.

FIGURE 1.2(a) The welcome screen of the installer, which asks the user to close all running applications and then click Next

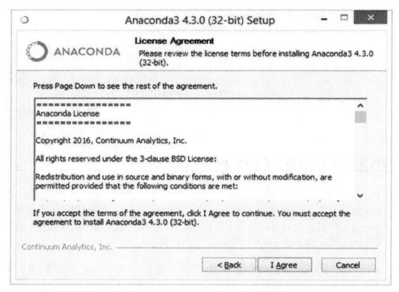

FIGURE 1.2(b) The license agreement to install Anaconda3 4.3.0 (32 bit)

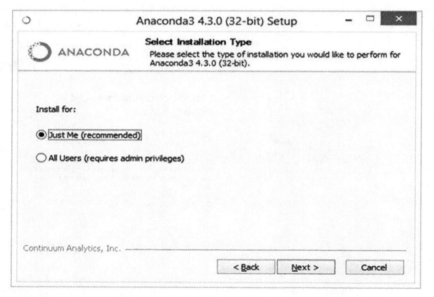

FIGURE 1.2(c) In the third step, the user is required to choose whether he wants to install Anaconda for a single user or for all the users

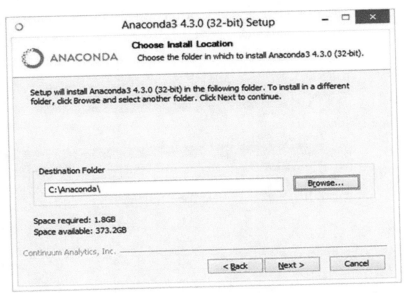

FIGURE 1.2(d) The user then needs to select the folder in which it will install

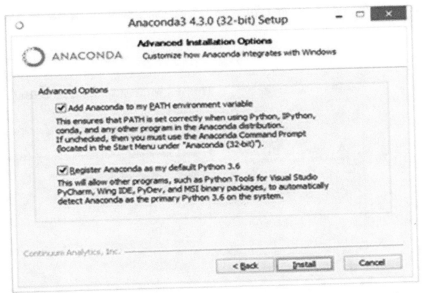

FIGURE 1.2(e) The user then must decide whether he wants to add Anaconda to path environment variable and whether to register Anaconda as the default Python 3.6

The installation then starts. After installation, the following screen will appear:

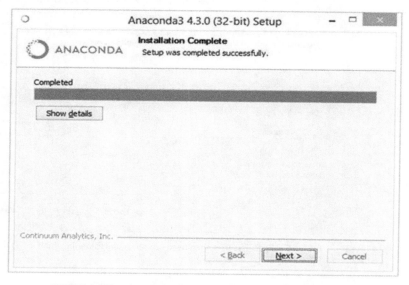

FIGURE 1.2(f) When the installation is complete, this screen appears

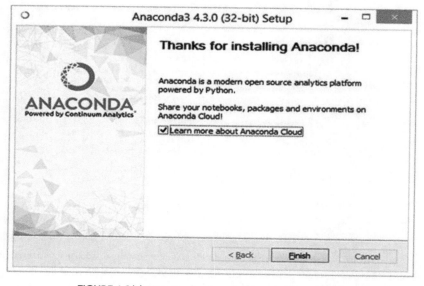

FIGURE 1.2(g) You can also share your notebooks on cloud

Once Anaconda is installed, you can open Anaconda and run your scripts. Figure 1.3 shows the Anaconda navigator. From the various options available you can choose the appropriate option for you. For example, you can open the QTConsole and run the commands/ scripts. Figure 1.4 shows the snapshot of QTConsole. The commands written may appear gibberish at this point, but will become clear in the chapters that follow.

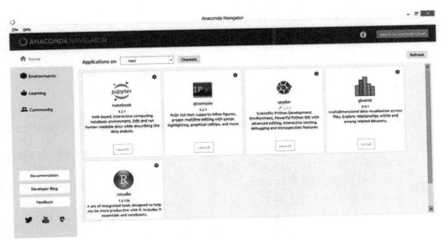

FIGURE 1.3 The Anaconda navigator

```
                        Jupyter QtConsole                  _ □ ×

 File   Edit   View   Kernel   Window   Help

Jupyter QtConsole 4.2.1
Python 3.6.0 |Anaconda 4.3.0 (32-bit)| (default, Dec 23 2016, 12:06:52) [MSC v.
1900 32 bit (Intel)]
Type "copyright", "credits" or "license" for more information.

IPython 5.1.0 -- An enhanced Interactive Python.
?         -> Introduction and overview of IPython's features.
%quickref -> Quick reference.
help      -> Python's own help system.
object?   -> Details about 'object', use 'object??' for extra details.

In [1]: a=10

In [2]: b=5

In [3]: a+b
Out[3]: 15

In [4]: L=[1,2,3]

In [5]: for i in L:
   ...:     print(i)
   ...:
1
2
3

In [6]:
```

FIGURE 1.4 The QtConsole

1.6   CONCLUSION

Before proceeding any further, the reader must take note of the fact that some things in Python are different when compared to any other language. The following points must be noted to avoid any confusion.

- In Python, statements do not end with any special characters. Python considers the newline character as an indication of the fact that the statement has ended. If a statement is to span more than a single line, the next line must be preceded with a (\).
- In Python, indentation is used to detect the presence of loops. The loops in Python do not began or end with delimiters or keywords.
- A file in Python is generally saved with a .py extension.
- The shell can be used as a handy calculator.
- The type of a variable need not to be mentioned in a program.

Choice at every step is good but can also be intimidating. As stated earlier, Python's core is small and therefore it is easy to learn. Moreover, there are some things like (if/else), loops and exception handling which are used in almost all the programs.

The chapter introduces Python and discusses the features of Python. One must appreciate the fact that Python supports all three paradigms: procedural, object-oriented, and functional. This chapter also paves the way for the topics presented in the following chapters. It may also be stated that the codes presented in this book will run on versions 3.X.

GLOSSARY

PEP: Python Enhancement Project

PSF: Python Software Foundation

POINTS TO REMEMBER

- Python is a strong procedural, object-oriented, functional language crafted in late 1980s by Guido Van Rossum.
- Python is open source.

- The applications of Python include software development, web development, desktop GUI development, education and scientific applications.
- Python is popular due to its simplicity and robustness.
- It is easy to interface with C++ and Java.
- SciPy is used for engineering and mathematics, IPython for parallel computing etc., Scions is used for build control.
- The various development environments for Python are PyDev with Eclipse, Emacs, Vim, TextMate, Gedit, Idle, PIDA (Linux)(VIM Based), NotePad++ (Windows), and BlueFish (Linux).

RESOURCES

- To download Python, visit *www.python.org*
- The documentation is available at *www.python.org/doc/*

EXERCISES

MULTIPLE CHOICE QUESTIONS

1. Python can subclass a class made in
   (a) Python only
   (b) Python, C++
   (c) Python, C++, C#, Java
   (d) None of the above

2. Who created Python?
   (a) Monty Python
   (b) Guido Van Rossum
   (c) Dennis Richie
   (d) None of the above

3. Monty Python was
   (a) Creator of Python Programming Language
   (b) British Comedy Group
   (c) American Band
   (d) Brother of Dosey Howser

4. In Python, libraries and tools
   (a) Not supported
   (b) Supported but not encouraged
   (c) Supported and encouraged
   (d) Supported (only that of PSF's)

5. Python has
    (*a*) Built in object types   (*b*) Data types
    (*c*) Both   (*d*) None of the above

6. Python is a
    (*a*) Procedural language   (*b*) object-oriented Language
    (*c*) Functional   (*d*) All of the above

7. There is no data type, so a code in Python is applicable to whole range of Objects. This is called
    (*a*) Dynamic Binding   (*b*) Dynamic Typing
    (*c*) Dynamic Leadership   (*d*) None of the above

8. Which of the following is automatic memory management?
    (*a*) Automatically assigning memory to objects
    (*b*) Taking back the memory at the end of life cycle
    (*c*) Both
    (*d*) None of the above

9. PEP is
    (*a*) Python Ending Procedure   (*b*) Python Enhancement proposal
    (*c*) Python Endearment Project   (*d*) none of the above

10. PSF is
    (*a*) Python Software Foundation   (*b*) Python Selection Function
    (*c*) Python segregation function   (*d*) None of the above

11. What can be done in Python
    (*a*) GUI   (*b*) Internet scripting
    (*c*) Games   (*d*) All of the above

12. What can be done using Python?
    (*a*) System programming
    (*b*) Component based programming
    (*c*) Scientific programming
    (*d*) All of the above

13. Python is used in
    (*a*) Google
    (*b*) Raspberry Pi
    (*c*) Bit Torrent
    (*d*) All of the above

14. Python is used in
    (*a*) App Engine
    (*b*) YouTube sharing
    (*c*) Real time programming
    (*d*) All of the above

15. Which is faster?
    (*a*) PyPy
    (*b*) IDLE
    (*c*) Both are equally good
    (*d*) depends on the task

THEORY

1. Write the names of three projects which are using Python.

2. Explain a few applications of Python.

3. What type of language is Python? (Procedural, object-oriented or functional)

4. What is PEP?

5. What is PSF?

6. Who manages Python?

7. Is Python open source or proprietary?

8. What languages can be supported by Python?

9. Explain the chronology of the development of Python.

10. Name a few editors for Python.

11. What are the features of Python?

12. What is the advantage of using Python over other languages?

13. What is Dynamic Typing?

14. Does Python have data types?

15. How is Python different from Java?

## CHAPTER 2

PYTHON OBJECTS

After reading this chapter, the reader will be able to

- Understand the meaning and importance of variables, operators, keywords, and objects
- Use numbers and fractions in a program
- Appreciate the importance of strings
- Understand slicing and indexing in strings
- Use of lists and tuples
- Understand the importance of tuples

2.1 INTRODUCTION

To be able to write a program in Python the programmer can use Anaconda, the installation of which was described in the previous chapter—or you can use IDLE, which can be downloaded from the reference given at the end of the Chapter 1. IDLE has an editor specially designed for writing a Python program.

As stated earlier Python is an interpreted language, so one need not to compile every piece of code. The programmer can just write the command and see the output at the command prompt. For example, when writing 2+3 on the command line we get

```
>>2+3
5
```

As a matter of fact you can add, subtract, multiply, divide and perform exponentiation in the command line. Multiplication can be done using the

* operator, the division can be performed using the / operator, the exponentiation can be done using the ** operator and the modulo can be found using the % operator. The modulo operator finds the remained if the first number is greater than the other, otherwise it returns the first number as the output. The results of the operations have been demonstrated as follows:

```
>>> 2*3
6
>>> 2/3
0.6666666666666666
>>> 2**3
8
>>> 2%3
2
>>> 3%2
1
>>>
```

In the above case, the Python interpreter is used to execute the commands. This is referred to as a **script mode**. This mode works with small codes. Though simple commands can be executed on the command line, the complex programs can be written in a file. A file can be created as follows:

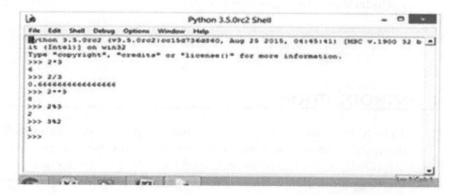

Step 1. Go to FILE→NEW

Step 2. Save the file as calc.py

Step 3. Write the following code in the file

```
print(2+3)
print(2*3)
print(2**3)
```

```
print(2/3)
print(2%3)
print(3/2)
```

Step 4. Go to debug and run the program. The following output will be displayed.

```
>>>
============= RUN C:/Python/Chapter 2/calc.py =============
5
6
8
0.6666666666666666
2
1.5
>>>
```

Conversely, the script can be executed by writing Python calc.py on the command prompt. In order to exit IDLE go to FILE->EXIT or write the exit() function at the command prompt.

In order to store values, we need **variables**. Python empowers the user to manipulate variables. These variables help us to use the values later. As a matter of fact, everything in Python is an **object**. This chapter focuses on objects. Each object has **identity**, a **type**, and a **value** (given by the user / or a default value). The identity, in Python, refers to the address and does not change. The type can be any of the following.

None: This represents the absence of a value.

Numbers: Python has three types of numbers:

- **Integer:** It does not have any fractional part
- **Floating Point:** It can store number with a fractional part
- **Complex:** It can store real and imaginary parts

Sequences: These are ordered collections of elements. There are three types of sequences in Python:

- String
- Tuples
- Lists

These types have been discussed in the sections that follow.

Sets: This is an un-ordered collection of elements.

Keywords: These are words having special meanings and are understood by the interpreter. For example, `and`, `del`, `from`, `not`, `while`, `as`, `elif`, `global`, `else`, `if`, `pass`, `Yield`, `break`, `except`, `import`, `class`, `raise`, `continue`, `finally`, `return`, `def`, `for`, and `try` are some of the keywords which have been extensively used in the book. For a complete list of keywords, the reader may refer to the Appendix.

Operators: These are special symbols which help the user to carry out operations like addition, subtraction, etc. Python provides following type of operators:

- **Arithmetic operators:** +, −, *, /, %, ** and //.
- **Assignment operators:** =, + =, − =, *=, /=, %=, **= and //=
- **Logical operators:** `or`, `and`, and `not`
- **Relational operators:** <, <=, >, >=, != or < > and ==.

This chapter deals with the basic data types in Python and their uses. The chapter has been organized as follows: Section 2 of this chapter deals with the introduction to programming in Python and basic data types, and Section 3 deals with strings. Section 4 deals with lists and tuples. The last section of this chapter concludes the chapter. The readers are advised to go through the references at the end of this book for comprehensive coverage of the topic.

2.2   BASIC DATA TYPES REVISITED

The importance of data types has already been discussed. There is another reason to understand and to be able to deal with built-in data types, which is that they generally are an intrinsic part of the bigger types which can be developed by the user.

The data types provided by Python are not only powerful but also can be nested within others. In the following discussion the concept of nested lists has been presented, which is basically a list within a list. The power of data types can be gauged by the fact that Python provides the user with dictionaries, which makes mapping easy and efficient.

Numbers are the simplest data types. Numbers comprise of integers, floats, decimals, and complexes in Python. The type of numbers and their explanations have been summarized in Table 2.1. The operators supported by numbers have been presented in Table 2.2.

Table 2.1 Numbers

Numbers	Explanation
Integers	Which do not have any fractional part
Floating point numbers	That do have a fractional part
Complex numbers	The numbers having a real and an imaginary part
Decimal	Those having fixed precision
Rational	Those having a numerator and a denominator
Sets	Abstraction of a mathematical set

Table 2.2 Operators supported in numbers

+	Addition
−	Subtraction
*	Multiplication
**	Power
%	Modulo

In addition to the above, Python is practically free from the problems of C and C++ and can calculate very, very large integers. Let us now have a look at how to use these operators. For example if one needs to calculate the square root of a number, then importing `math` and using `math.sqrt()` is a solution. Some of the most important functions have been explained in the following sneak peek.

Sneak Peek

1. **Ceil:** The ceiling of a given number is the nearest integer greater than or equal to that number. For example, the ceiling of 2.678 is 3.

```
>>> import math
>>>math.ceil(2.678)
3
That of 2 is 2.
>>>math.ceil(2)
2
>>>
```

2. **Copy sign:** The sign of the second argument is returned along with the result on the execution of this function.

```
math.copysign(x, y)
Return x with the sign of y.
```

On a platform that supports signed zeros, copy sign $(1.0, -0.0)$ returns -1.0.

3. **Fabs:** The absolute value of a number is its positive value; that is if the number is positive then the number itself is returned. If, on the other hand, the number is negative then it is multiplied by –1 and returned.

$$\text{Absolute}(x) = \begin{cases} x, & x \geq 0 \\ -x, & x < 0 \end{cases}$$

In Python, this task is accomplished with the function fabs (x).

The fabs(x) returns the absolute value of x.

```
>>>math.fabs(-2.45)
2.45
>>>math.fabs(x)
Return the absolute value of x.
```

4. **Factorial:** The factorial of a number x is defined as the continued product of the numbers from 1 to that value. That is:

```
Factorial(x) = 1 × 2 × 3 × ... × n.
```

In Python, the task can be accomplished by the factorial function `math.factorial(x)`.

It returns the factorial of the number x. Also if the given number is not an integer or is negative, then an exception is raised.

5. **Floor:** The floor of a given number is the nearest integer smaller than or equal to that number. For example the floor of 2.678 is 2 and that of 2 is also 2.

```
>>> import math
>>>math.floor(2.678)
2
>>>math.floor(2)
2
>>>
```

2.2.1 Fractions

Python also provides the programmer the liberty to deal with fractions. The use of fractions and decimals has been shown in the following listing.

Listing

```
from fractions import Fraction
print(Fraction(128, -26))
print(Fraction(256))
```

```
print(Fraction())
print(Fraction('2/5'))
print(Fraction(' -5/7'))
print(Fraction('2.675438 '))
print(Fraction('-32.75'))
print(Fraction('5e-3'))
print(Fraction(7.85))
print(Fraction(1.1))
print(Fraction(2476979795053773, 2251799813685248))
from decimal import Decimal
print(Fraction(Decimal('1.1')))
>>>
```

Output

```
========== RUN C:/Python/Chapter 2/Fraction.py ==========
-64/13
256
0
2/5
-5/7
1337719/500000
-131/4
1/200
4419157134357299/562949953421312
2476979795053773/2251799813685248
2476979795053773/2251799813685248
11/10
>>>
```

2.3   STRINGS

In Python a string is a predefined object which contains characters. The string in Python is non-mutable; that is, once defined the value of a string cannot be changed. However, as we proceed further, the exceptions to the above premise will be discussed. To begin with, let us consider a string containing value "Harsh," that is:

```
name = 'Harsh'
```

The value of this string can be displayed simply by typing the name of the object (name in this case) into the command prompt.

```
>>>name
Harsh
```

The value can also be printed by using the print function, explained previously.

```
print(name)
```

The value at a particular location of a string can be displayed using indexing. The syntax of the above is as follows.

```
<name of the String>[index]
```

It may be stated here that the index of the first location is 0. So, name[0] would print the first letter of the string, which is "H."

```
print(name[0])
H
```

Negative indexing in a string refers to the character present at the nth position beginning from the end. In the above case, name[-2] would generate "s."

```
print(name[-2])
s
```

The length of a string can be found by calling the len function. `len(str)` returns the length of the string "str." For example, `len(name)` would return 5, as `'harsh'` has 5 characters.

The last character of a given string can also be printed using the following.

```
print(name[len(name)-1])
```

The + operator concatenates, in the case of a string. For example "harsh" + "arsh" would return "Harsharsh," that is

```
name = name + 'arsh'
print(name)
Harsharsh
```

After concatenation, if the first and the second last characters are to be printed then the following can be used.

```
print(name[0])
print(name[-2])
print(name)[len(name)-1-2]
H
S
s
```

The * operator, of string, concatenates a given string the number of times, given as the first argument. For example, 3*name would return "harsharsh-harsharsh." The complete script as follows:

Listing

```
name = 'Harsh'
print(name)
print(name[0])
print(name[-2])
print(name[len(name)-1])
name = name + 'arsh'
print(name)
print(name[0])
print(name[-2])
print(name[len(name)-1])
>>>
```

Output

```
=========== RUN C:/Python/Chapter 2/String.py ===========
Harsh
H
s
h
Harsharsh
H
s
h
>>>
```

Slicing: Slicing, in strings, refers to removing some part of a string. For example:

```
>>>name = 'Sonam'
>>>name
'Sonam'
```

Here, if we intend to extract the portion after the first letter we can write [1:].

```
>>> name1=name[1:]
>>> name1
'onam'
```

In the same way the portion of the string after the first two letters can be extracted as follows.

```
>>>name = name[2:]
>>>name
'nam'
```

Now, we modify the string by adding "man man"

```
>>>name = "man"+name
>>>name
'mannam'
```

It may be noted that the last two characters cannot be removed in the same way as the first two. Observe the following output in order to understand the concept.

```
>>>name = name[:2]
>>>name
'ma'
>>>name = "man manam"
```

In order to accomplish the above task, negative indexing ought to be used.

```
>>>name
'manmanam'
>>> name2 = name[:-2]
>>> name2
'man man'
>>>
```

Immutability of Strings

It may be noted that when we write

```
name = 'Hello' + name
```

we don't actually change the string; as a matter of fact we create a new string having the value `'Hello'` concatenated with the value stored in `name`. The concept can be understood by the fact that when we try to change the value of a particular character in a string, an error crops up.

```
>>>name='Anupam'
>>>name
'Anupam'
>>>name[2]='p'
```

```
Traceback (most recent call last):
File "<pyshell#17>", line 1, in <module>
name[2]='p'
TypeError: 'str' object does not support item assignment
>>>
```

2.4   LISTS AND TUPLES

2.4.1   List

A list, in Python, is a collection of objects. As per Lutz *"It is the most general sequence provided by the language."* Unlike strings, lists are mutable. That is, an element at a particular position can be changed in a list. A list is useful in dealing with homogeneous and heterogeneous sequences.

A list can be one of the following:

- A list can be a collection of similar elements (homogeneous), for example [1, 2, 3]
- It can also contain different elements (heterogeneous), like [1, "abc," 2.4]
- A list can also be empty ([])
- A list can also contain a list (discussed in Chapter 4, of this book)

For example, the following list of authors has elements "Harsh Bhasin," "Mark Lutz," and "Shiv." The list can be printed using the usual print function. In the following example, the second list in the following listing contains a number, a string, a float, and a string. "list 3" is a null list and list-of-list contains list as its elements.

Listing

```
authors = ['Harsh Bhasin', 'Mark Lutz', 'Shiv']
print(authors)
combined =[1, 'Harsh', 23.4, 'a']
print(combined)
list3= []
print(list3)
listoflist = [1, [1,2], 3]
print(listoflist)
>>>
```

Output

```
============ RUN C:/Python/Chapter 2/Lists.py ===========
['Harsh bhasin', 'Mark Lutz', 'Shiv']
[1, 'Harsh', 23.4, 'a']
[]
[1, [1, 2], 3]
>>>
```

An element of a list can be accessed by indexing; for example if list 1 contains [1, 2, 3], then list 1[1] contains "2" and list 1[-1] contains "3."

Listing

```
list1 = [1, 2, 3]
print(list1[1])
print(list1[-1])
>>>
```

Output

```
============ RUN C:/Python/Chapter 2/list2.py ============
2
3
>>>
```

A list can also contain list(s). The topic has been discussed in Chapter 4. Lists also support slicing.

2.4.2 Tuples

A tuple contains elements which can be treated individually or as a group. A tuple (say (x, y)) can be printed using the standard print( ) function. The elements of a **tuple** can be accessed by assigning it to a tuple, as shown in the following listing. A tuple may also contain heterogeneous elements. For example, in the following listing, tup2 and tup3 contain a string and an integer.

Listing

```
tup1= (2, 3)
print(tup1)
(a, b) = tup1
print('The first element is ',a)
print('The second element is ',b)
```

```
tup2=(101, 'Hari')
tup3=(102,'Shiv')
(code1, name1)=tup1
(code2, name2)=tup2
print('The code of ', name1,' is ',code1,'\nThe code
of ',name2, ' is ',code2)
>>>
```

Output

```
=========== RUN C:/Python/Chapter 2/tuple.py ============
(2, 3)
The first element is 2
The second element is 3
The code of 3 is 2
The code of Hari is 101
>>>
```

Tuples are extremely useful in operations like swapping etc. Swapping in Python is as simple as assigning (a, b) to (b, a). The program for swapping two numbers using tuples has been given as follows.

Illustration 2.1: Write a program to swap two numbers using tuples.

Solution:

```
print('Enter the first number\t:')
num1= int(input())
print('Enter the second number\t:')
num2= int(input())
print('\nThe numbers entered are ',num1,' & ', num2)
(num1, num2) = (num2, num1)
print('\nThe numbers now are ',num1,' & ', num2)
>>>
```

Output

```
============ RUN C:/Python/Chapter 2/swap.py ============
Enter the first number  :
2
Enter the second number :
3
The numbers entered are 2& 3
The numbers now are 3& 2
>>>
```

2.4.3 Features of Tuples

- Tuples are immutable—an element of a tuple cannot be assigned a different value once it has been set. For example,
```
tup1 = (2, 3)
tup1[1] = 4
would raise an exception.
```

- The "+" operator in a tuple concatenates two tuples. For example,
```
>>> tup1= (1,2)
>>> tup2=(3,4)
>>> tup3= tup1+tup2
>>> tup3
(1, 2, 3, 4)
>>>
```

2.5 CONCLUSION

In a program, instructions are given to a computer to perform a task. To be able to do so, the operators operate on what are referred to as "objects." This chapter explains the various types of objects in Python and gives a brief overview of the operators that act upon them. The objects can be built in or user defined. As a matter of fact, everything that will be operated upon is an object.

The first section of this chapter describes various built-in objects in Python. The readers familiar with "C" must have an idea as to what a procedural language is. In "C," for example, a program is divided into manageable modules, each of which performs a particular task. The division of bigger tasks into smaller parts makes parts manageable and the tracking of bugs easy. There are many more advantages of using modules, some of which have been stated in Chapter 1.

These modules contain a set of statements, which are equivalent to instructions (or no instruction, *e.g.* in case of a comment). The statements may contain expressions, in which objects are operated upon by operators. As stated earlier, Python gives its user the liberty to define their own objects. This will be dealt with in the chapter on classes and objects. This chapter focuses on the built in objects.

In C (or for that matter C++), one needs to be careful not only about the built-in type used but also about the issues relating to the allocation of memory and data structures. However, Python spares the user of these problems and can therefore focus on the task at hand. The use of built-in data types makes things easy and efficient.

GLOSSARY

None: This represents the absence of value.

Numbers: Python has three types of numbers: integers, floating point, complex.

Sequences: These are ordered collections of elements. There are three types of sequences in Python:

- String
- Tuples
- Lists

POINTS TO REMEMBER

- In order to store values, we need **variables**.
- Everything in Python is an **object**.
- Each object has **identity**, a **type**, and a **value**.

EXERCISES

MULTIPLE CHOICE QUESTIONS

1.
```
>>> a = 5
>>> a + 2.7
>>> a
```
(*a*) a + 2.7

(*b*) 7

(*c*) None of the above

(*d*) An exception is raised

2.
```
>>> a = 5
>>> b = 2
>>> a/b
```
(*a*) 2   (*b*) 2.5

(*c*) 3   (*d*) None of the above

3.
```
>>> a = 5
>>> b = 2
>>> c = float (a)/b
>>> c
```
(*a*) 2   (*b*) 2.5

(*c*) 3   (*d*) An exception is raised

4.
```
>>> a = 2
>>> b = 'A'
>>> c = a + b
>>> c
```
(*a*) 67   (*b*) 60

(*c*) None of the above   (*d*) An exception is raised

5.
```
>>> a = 'A'
>>> 2*A
```
(*a*) 'AA'   (*b*) 2A

(*c*) A2   (*d*) None of the above

6.
```
>>> a = 'A'
>>> b = 'B'
>>> a + b
```
(*a*) A + B   (*b*) AB

(*c*) BA   (*d*) None of the above

7.
```
>>> (a, b) = (2, 5)
>>> (a, b) = (b, a)
>>> (a, b)
```
(*a*) (2, 5)   (*b*) (5, 2)

(*c*) (5, 5)   (*d*) None of the above

8.
```
>>> a = 5
>>> b = 2
>>> a = a + b
>>> b = a - b
>>> a = a - b
>>> a
```
(*a*) 5

(*c*) None of the above

(*b*) 2

(*d*) An exception is raised

9.
```
>>> a = 5
>>> b * b = a
>>> b
```
(*a*) 2.7

(*c*) None of the above

(*b*) 25

(*d*) An exception is raised

10.
```
>>> (a, b) = (2, 3)
>>> (c, d) = (4, 5)
>>> (a, b) + (c, d)
```
(*a*) (6, 8)

(*c*) (8, 6)

(*b*) (2, 3, 4, 5)

(*d*) None of the above

11. In the above question what would $(a, b) - (c, d)$ generate

(*a*) (6, 8)

(*c*) (8, 6)

(*b*) (2, 3, 4, 5)

(*d*) None of the above

12. In the above question what would $(a, b) * (c, d)$ generate

(*a*) (6, 8)

(*c*) (8, 6)

(*b*) (2, 3, 4, 5)

(*d*) None of the above

13.
```
>>> a = 'harsh'
>>> b = a[1: len(a)]
>>> b
```
(*a*) arsh

(*c*) harsh

(*b*) hars

(*d*) None of the above

14.
```
>>>a = 'harsh'
>>>b = [-3, len (a)]
```
  (*a*) a[-3: len(a)]   (*b*) arsh

  (*c*) harsh   (*d*) None of the above

15.
```
>>>b
>>>a = 'tar'
>>>b = 'rat'
>>>2*(a + b) is
```
  (*a*) tarrattarrat   (*b*) rattarrattar

  (*c*) tarratrattar   (*d*) None of the above

PROGRAMS

1. Write a program to swap two numbers.

2. Ask the user to enter the coordinates of a point and find the distance of the point from the origin.

3. Ask the user to enter two points (*x* and *y* coordinates) and find the distance between them.

4. Ask the user to enter three points and find whether they are collinear.

5. In the above question, if the points are not collinear then find the type of triangle formed by them (equilateral, isosceles or scalene).

6. In the above question, check if the triangle is right angled.

7. In question number 4, find the angles of the triangle.

8. Ask the user to enter two points and find if they are at equal distances from the origin.

9. In question number 8, find the angle between the line joining the points and the origin.

10. Ask the user to enter 4 points and arrange them in order of their distances from the origin.

11. In question 10, arrange the above points in order of their *x* co-ordinates.

CHAPTER 3

CONDITIONAL STATEMENTS

After reading this chapter, the reader will be able to

- Use conditional statements in programs
- Appreciate the importance of the `if-else` construct
- Use the `if-elif-else` ladder
- Use the ternary operator
- Understand the importance of & and |
- Handle conditional statements using the get construct

3.1 INTRODUCTION

The preceding chapters presented the basic data types and simple statements in Python. The concepts studied so far are good for the execution of a program which has no branches. However, a programmer would seldom find a problem solving approach devoid of branches.

Before proceeding any further let us spare some time contemplating life. Can you move forward in life without making decisions? The answer is NO. In the same way the problem solving approach would not yield results until the power of decision making is incorporated. This is the reason one must understand the implementation of decision making and looping. This chapter describes the first concept. This is needed to craft a program which has branches. Decision making empowers us to change the control-flow of the program. In C, C++, Java, C#, etc., there are two major ways to accomplish the above task. One is the 'if' construct and the other is 'switch'. The 'if' block in a program is executed if the 'test' condition is true otherwise it is not executed. Switch is used to implement a scenario in which there are many 'test' conditions, and the corresponding block executes in case a particular test condition is true.

The chapter introduces the concept of conditional statements, compound statements, the if-elif ladder and finally the get statement. The chapter assumes importance as conditional statements are used in every aspect of programming, be it client side development, web development, or mobile application development.

The chapter has been organized as follows. The second section introduces the 'if' construct. Section 3.3 introduces 'if-elif' ladder. Section 3.4 discusses the use of logic operators. Section 3.5 introduces ternary operators. Section 3.6 presents the get statement and the last section concludes the chapter. The reader is advised to go through the basic data types before proceeding further.

3.2 IF, IF-ELSE, AND IF-ELIF-ELSE CONSTRUCTS

Implementing decision making gives the power to incorporate branching in a program. As stated earlier, a program is a set of instructions given to a computer. The instructions are given to accomplish a task and any task requires making decisions. So, conditional statements form an integral part of programming. The syntax of the construct is as follows:

General Format

1. **if**
```
if <test condition>:
     <block if the test condition is true>
```

2. **if-else**
```
if <test condition>:
     <block if the test condition is true>
else:
     <block if the test condition is not true>
. . .
```

3. **If else ladder (discussed in the next section)**

```
if <test condition>:
        <block if the test condition is true>
elif <test 2>:
        <second block>
elif <test 3>:
        <third block>
else:
        <block if the test condition is true>
```

Note that indentation is important, as Python recognizes a block through indentation. So, make sure that the `'if (<condition>):'` is followed by a block, each statement of which is at the same alignment. In order to understand the concept, let us consider a simple example. A student generally clears a university exam in India if he scores more than 40%. In order to implement the logic, the user is asked to enter the value of the percentage. If the percentage entered is more than 40 then "exam cleared" is printed, otherwise "failed" is printed. The situation has been depicted in the following figure (Figure 3.1).

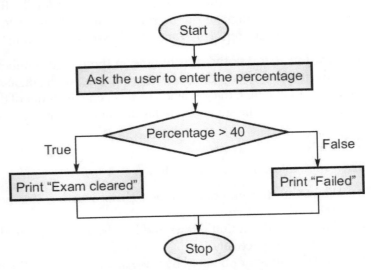

FIGURE 3.1 Flow chart for example 1

Illustration 3.1: Ask the user to enter the marks of a student in a subject. If the marks entered are greater than 40 then print "pass," if they are lower print "fail."

Program

```
>>>a = input("Enter marks : ")
if int(a)> 40:
    print('Pass')
else:
    print('Fail')
...
```

Output 1

```
Enter Marks : 50
    Pass
```

Output 2

```
Enter Marks : 30
    Fail
```

Let us have a look at another example. In the problem, the user is asked to enter a three digit number to find the number obtained by reversing the order of the digits of the number; then find the sum of the number and that obtained by reversing the order of the digits and finally, find whether this sum contains any digit in the original number. In order to accomplish the task, the following steps (presented in Illustration 3.2) must be carried out.

Illustration 3.2: Ask the user to enter a three digit number. Call it `num`. Find the number obtained by reversing the order of the digits. Find the sum of the given number and that obtained by reversing the order of the digits. Finally, find if any digit in the sum obtained is the same as that in the original number.

Solution:

The problem can be solved as follows:

- When the user enters a number, check whether it is between 100 and 999, both inclusive.
- Find the digits at unit's, ten's and hundred's place. Call them `u`, `t` and `h` respectively.
- Find the number obtained by reversing the order of the digits (say, 'rev') using the following formula.
- Number obtained by reversing the order of the digits, `rev = h + t × 10 + u × 100`
- Find the sum of the two numbers.
  `Sum = rev + num`
- The sum may be a three digit or a four digit number. In any case, find the digits of this sum. Call them `u1`, `t1`, `h1` and `th1` (if required).

- Set 'flag=0'.
- Check the following condition. If any one is true, set the value of flag to 1. If "sum" is a three digit number

  $u == u1$
  $u == t1$
  $u == h1$
  $t == u1$
  $t == t1$
  $t == h1$
  $h == u1$
  $h == t1$
  $h == h1$

- If "sum" is a four digit number the above conditions need to be checked along with the following conditions:

  $u == th1$
  $h == th1$
  $t == th1$

- The above conditions would henceforth be referred to as "set 1." If the value of "flag" is 1, then print 'true' else print 'false'.
- The above process has been depicted in the following figure (Figure 3.2).

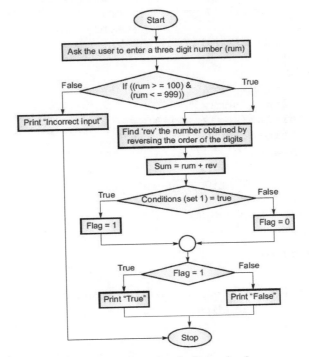

FIGURE 3.2 Flow chart for Illustration 2

Program

```
num=int(input('Enter a three digit number\t:'))
if ((num<100) | (num>999)):
    print('You have not entered a number between 100 and 999')
else:
    flag=0
    o=num%10
    t=int(num/10)%10
    h=int(num/100)%10
    print('o\t:',str(o),'t\t:',str(t),'h\t:',str(h))
    rev=h+t*10+o*100
    print('Number obtained by reversing the order of the
                                digits\t:',str(rev))
    sum1=num+rev
    print('Sum of the number and that obtained by
                reversing the order of digits\t:',str(sum1))
    if sum1<1000:
      o1=sum1%10
      t1=int(sum1/10)%10
      h1=int(sum1/100)%10
      print('o1\t:',str(o1),'t1\t:',str(t1),'h1\t:',str(h1))
    if ((o==o1)|(o==t1)|(o==h1)|(t==o1)|(t==t1)|
                        (t==h1)|(h==o1)|(h==t1)|(h==h1)):
      print('Condition true')
      flag==1
    else:
      o1=sum1%10
      t1=int(sum1/10)%10
      h1=int(sum1/100)%10
      th1=int(sum1/1000)%10
      print('o1\t:',str(o1),'t1\t:',str(t1),'h1\
                            t:',str(h1),'t1\t:',str(t1))
    if ((o==o1)|(o==t1)|(o==h1)|(o==th1)|(t==o1)|(t==t1)|
          (t==h1)|(t==th1)|(h==o1)|(h==t1)|(h==h1)|(h==th1)):
      print('Condition true')
      flag==1
```

Output: First run

```
>>>
========= RUN C:/Python/Conditional/Problem 2.py =========
Enter a three digit number :4
You have not entered a number between 100 and 999
>>>
```

Output: Second run

```
>>>
========= RUN C:/Python/Conditional/Problem 2.py =========
Enter a three digit number :343
o : 3 t : 4 h : 3
Number obtained by reversing the order of the digits : 343
No digit of the sum is same as the original number
>>>
```

Output: Third run

```
>>>
========= RUN C:/Python/Conditional/Problem 2.py =========
Enter a three digit number : 435
o : 5 t : 3 h : 4
Number obtained by reversing the order of the digits : 534
No digit of the sum is same as the original number
>>>
```

Output: Fourth run

```
>>>
========= RUN C:/Python/Conditional/Problem 2.py =========
Enter a three digit number :121
o : 1 t : 2 h : 1
Number obtained by reversing the order of the digits : 121
Sum of the number and that obtained by reversing the
                                order of digits : 242
o1 : 2 t1 : 4 h1 : 2
Condition true
>>>
.
```

Tip

One must be careful regarding the indentation, failing which the program would not compile. The indentation decides the beginning and ending of a particular block in Python. It is advisable not to use a combination of spaces and tabs in indentation. Many versions of Python may treat this as a syntax error.

The `if-elif` ladder can also be implemented using the get statement, explained later in the chapter. The important points regarding the conditional statements in Python are as follows:

- The if <test> is followed by a colon.

- There is no need of parentheses for this test condition. Though enclosing test in parentheses will not result in an error.
- The nested blocks in Python are determined by indentation. Therefore, proper indentation in Python is essential. As a matter of fact, an inconsistent indentation or no indentation will result in errors.
- An if can have any number of if's nested within.
- The test condition in if must result in a True or a False.

Illustration 3.3: Write a program to find the greatest of the three numbers entered by the user.

Solution: First of all, three variables (say num1, num2, and num3) are needed. These variables will get their values from the user. This input will be followed by the condition checking as depicted in the following program. Finally, the greatest number will be displayed. The listing is given as follows:

Program

```
>>>num1 = input('Enter the first number\t:')
...num2 = input('Enter the second number\t:')
...num3 = input('Enter the third number\t:')
...if int(num1)> int(num2):
...  if int(num1) > int(num3):
...        big= int(num1)
...  else:
...        big = int(num2)
...
...else:
...  if int(num2)> int(num3)
...        big= num2
...  else:
...        big = num3
...
...
...print(big)
```

3.3 THE IF-ELIF-ELSE LADDER

If there are multiple conditions and the outcomes decide the action, then an if- elif- else ladder can be used. This section discusses the construct and presents the concept using relevant examples. The syntax of this construct is as follows:

Syntax

```
if <test condition 1>:
    # The task to be performed if the condition 1 is true
elif <test condition 2>:
    # The task to be performed if the condition 2 is true
elif <test condition 3>:
    # The task to be performed if the condition 1 is true
else:
    # The task to be performed if none of the above
                                    condition is true
```

The flow of the program can be managed using the above construct. Figure 3.3 shows the diagram depicting the flow of the program which uses the above constructs.

In the figure, the left edge depicts the scenario where the condition C is true and the right edge depicts the scenario where the condition is false. In the second graph, conditions C1, C2, C3, and C4 lead to different paths [*Programming in C#*, Harsh Bhasin, 2014].

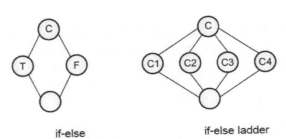

if-else   if-else ladder

FIGURE 3.3 The flow graph of if and elif ladder

The following section has programs that depict the use of the `elif` ladder. It may be noted that if there are multiple `else` statements, then the second `else` is taken along with the nearest `if`.

3.4 LOGICAL OPERATORS

In many cases the execution of a block depends on the truth value of more than one statement. In such cases the operators "and" ("&") and "or" ("|") come to our rescue. The first ('and') is used when the output is 'true', when both the conditions are 'true'. The second ('or') is used if the output is 'true', if any of the conditions are 'true'.

The truth table of `'and'` and `'or'` is given as follows. In the tables that follow "T" stands for "true" and "F" stands for "false."

Table 3.1 Truth table of a&b

a	b	a&b
t	T	T
t	F	F
F	T	F
F	F	F

Table 3.2 Truth table of a|b

a	b	a|b
t	T	T
t	F	T
F	T	T
F	F	F

The above statement helps the programmer to easily handle compound statements. As an example, consider a program to find the greatest of the three numbers entered by the user. The numbers entered by the user are (say) `'a'`, `'b'`, and `'c'`, then `'a'` is greatest if `(a > b)` and `(a > c)`. This can be written as follows:

```
if((a>b)&(a>c))
    print('The value of a greatest')
```

In the same way, the condition of '*b*' being greatest can be crafted. Another example can be that of a triangle. If all the three sides of a triangle are equal, then it is an equilateral triangle.

```
if((a==b) or (b==c) or (c==a))
    //The triangle is isosceles;
```

3.5   THE TERNARY OPERATOR

The conditional statements explained in the above section are immensely important to write any program that contains conditions. However, the code can still be reduced further by using the ternary statements provided by Python. The ternary operator performs the same task as the if-else construct. However, it has the same disadvantage as in the case of C or C++. The problem is that each part caters to a single statement. The syntax of the statement is given as follows.

Syntax

```
<Output variable> = <The result when the condition is
                                                true>
if <condition> else <The result when the condition is not
                                                true>
```

For example, the conditional operator can be used to check which of the two numbers entered by the user is greater.

```
great = a if (a>b) else b
```

Finding the greatest of the three given numbers is a bit intricate. The following statement puts the greatest of the three numbers in "great."

```
great = a if (a if (a > b) else c)) else(b if (b>c) else c))
```

The program that finds the greatest of the three numbers entered by the user using a ternary operator is as follows.

Illustration 3.4: Find the greatest of three numbers entered by the user, using a ternary operator.

Program

```
a = int(input('Enter the first number\t:'))
b = int(input('Enter the second number\t:'))
c = int(input('Enter the third number\t:'))
big = (a if (a>c) else c) if (a>b) else (b if (b>c) else c)
print('The greatest of the three numbers is '+str(big))
>>>
```

Output

```
========== RUN C:/Python/Conditional/big3.py ==========
Enter the first number   2
Enter the second number  3
Enter the third number   4
The greatest of the three numbers is 4
>>>
```

3.6   THE GET CONSTRUCT

In C or C++ (even in C# and Java) a switch is used in the case where different conditions lead to different actions. This can also be done using the 'if-elif' ladder, as explained in the previous sections. However, the get construct greatly eases this task in the case of dictionaries.

In the example that follows there are three conditions. However, in many situations there are many more conditions. The contact can be used in such cases. The syntax of the construct is as follows:

Syntax

```
<dictionary name>.get('<value to be searched>',
                                    'default value>')
```

Here, the expression results in some value. If the value is value 1, then block 1 is executed. If it is value 2, block 2 is executed, and so on. If the value of the expression does not match any of the cases, then the statements in the default block are executed. Illustration 5 demonstrates the use of the get construct.

Illustration 3.5: This illustration has a directory containing the names of books and the corresponding year they were published. The statements that follow find the year of publication for a given name. If the name is not found the string (given as the second argument, in get) is displayed.

Program

```
hbbooks = {'programming in C#': 2014, 'Algorithms': 2015,
                                    'Python': 2016}
print(hbbooks.get('Programming in C#', 'Bad Choice'))
print(hbbooks.get('Algorithms', 'Bad Choice'))
print(hbbooks.get('Python', 'Bad Choice'))
print(hbbooks.get('Theory Theory, all the way', 'Bad
                                    Choice'))
```

Output

```
>>>
========== RUN C:/Python/Conditional/switch.py ==========
Bad Choice
2015
2016
Bad Choice
>>>
```

Note that in the first case the "P" of "Programming" is capital, hence "Bad Choice" is displayed. In the second and the third cases, the get function is able to find the requisite value. In the last case the value is not found and so the second argument of the get function appears. Note that it is similar to the default of the "C" type `switch` statement. The flow diagram given in Figure 3.4 shows a program that has many branches.

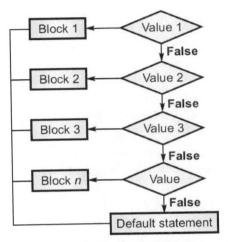

FIGURE 3.4 A program having multiple conditional statements

Observation

In Python, dictionaries and lists form an integral part of the language basics. The use of the get construct was not explained in Chapter 2 of this book, as it implements the concept of conditional selection. It may be noted that this construct greatly reduces the problems of dealing with the situations where mapping is required and is therefore important.

3.7   EXAMPLES

The 'if' condition is also used for input validation. The process will be explained in the following sections of this book. However, the idea has been used in the example that follows. The program asks the user to enter a character and checks whether its ASCII value is greater a certain value.

Illustration 3.6: Ask the user to enter a number and check whether its ASCII value is greater than 80.

Program

```
inp = input('Enter a character :')
if ord(inp) > 80:
    print('ASCII value is greater than 80')
else:
    print('ASCII value is less than 80')
Output 1:
>>>Enter a character: A
ASCII value is less than 80
...
```

Output 2

```
>>>Enter a character: Z
ASCII value is greater than 80
>>>
```

The construct can also be used to find the value of a multi-valued function. For example, consider the following function:

$$f(x) = \begin{cases} x^2 + 5x + 3, \text{ if } x > 2 \\ x + 3, \text{ if } x \le 2 \end{cases}$$

The following example asks the user to enter the value of x and calculates the value of the function as per the given value of x.

Illustration 3.7: Implement the above function and find the values of the function at $x = 2$ and $x = 4$.

Program

```
fx = """
f(x) = x^2 + 5x + 3 , if x > 2
     = x + 3 , if x <= 2
"""
x = int (input('Enter the value of x\t:'))
if x > 2:
    f = ((pow(x,2)) + (5*x) + 3)
else:
    f = x + 3
print('Value of function f(x) = %d' % f )
```

Output

```
========== RUN C:\Python\Conditional\func.py ==========
Enter the value of x :4
```

```
Value of function f(x) = 39
>>>
========== RUN C:\Python\Conditional\func.py ==========
Enter the value of x :1
Value of function f(x) = 4
>>>
```

The 'if-else' construct, as stated earlier, can be used to find the outcome based on certain conditions. For example two lines are parallel if the ratio of the coefficients of x's is same as that of those of y's.

For $a_1x + b_1y + c_1 = 0$ and $a_2x + b_2y + c_2 = 0$. Then the condition of lines being parallel is:

$$\frac{a_1}{a_2} = \frac{b_1}{b_2}$$

The following program checks whether two lines are parallel or not.

Illustration 3.8: Ask the user to enter the coefficients of $a_1x + b_1y + c_1 = 0$ and $a_2x + b_2y + c_2 = 0$ and find out whether the two lines depicted by the above equations are parallel or not.

Program

```
print('Enter Coefficients of the first equation [a₁x + b₁y
                                              + c₁ = 0]\n')
r₁ = input('Enter the value of a₁: ')
a₁ = int (r₁)
r₁ = input('Enter the value of b₁: ')
b₁ = int (r₁)
r₁ = input('Enter the value of c₁: ')
c₁ = int (r₁)
print('Enter Coefficients of second equation [a₂x + b₂y +
                                              c₂ = 0]\n')
r₁ = input('Enter the value of a₂: ')
a₂ = int (r₁)
r₁ = input('Enter the value of b₂: ')
b₂ = int (r₁)
r₁ = input('Enter the value of c₂: ')
c₂ = int (r₁)
if (a₁/a₂) == (b₁/b₂):
        print('Lines are parallel')
else:
        print('Lines are not parallel')
```

Output

```
>>>
========== RUN C:\Python\Conditional\parallel.py ==========
Enter Coefficients of the first equation [a₁x + b₁y + c₁ = 0]
Enter the value of a₁: 2
Enter the value of b₁: 3
Enter the value of c₁: 4
Enter Coefficients of second equation [a₂x + b₂y + c₂ = 0]

Enter the value of a₂: 4
Enter the value of b₂: 6
Enter the value of c₂: 7
Lines are parallel
>>>
```

The above program can be extended to find whether the lines are intersecting or overlapping: two lines intersect if the following condition is true.

$a_1x + b_1y + c_1 = 0$ and $a_2x + b_2y + c_2 = 0$. Then the lines intersect if:

$$\frac{a_1}{a_2} \neq \frac{b_1}{b_2}$$

And the two lines overlap if:

$$\frac{a_1}{a_2} = \frac{b_1}{b_2} = \frac{c_1}{c_2}$$

The following flow-chart shows the flow of control of the program (Figure 3.5).

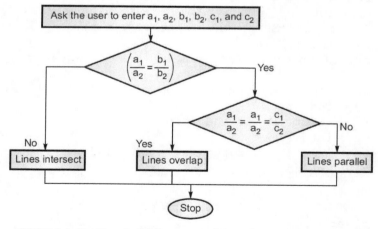

FIGURE 3.5 Checking whether lines are parallel, overlapping, or if they intersect

The following program implements the above logic.

Illustration 3.9: Ask the user to enter the values of a_1, a_2, b_1, b_2, c_1, and c_2 and find whether the lines are parallel, or if they overlap or intersect.

Program

```
print('Enter Coefficients of the first equation [a₁x +
                              b₁y + c₁ = 0]\n')
r₁ = input('Enter the value of a₁: ')
a₁ = int (r₁)
r₁ = input('Enter the value of b₁: ')
b₁ = int (r₁)
r₁ = input('Enter the value of c₁: ')
c₁ = int (r₁)
print('Enter Coefficients of second equation [a₂x + b₂y +
                              c₂ = 0 ]\n')
r₁ = input('Enter the value of a₂: ')
a₂ = int (r₁)
r₁ = input('Enter the value of b₂: ')
b₂ = int (r₁)
r₁ = input('Enter the value of c₂: ')
c₂ = int (r₁)
if ((a₁/a₂) == (b₁/b₂))&((a₁/a₂)==(c₁/c₂)):
    print('Lines overlap')
elif (a₁/a₂)==(b₁/b₂):
    print('Lines are parallel')
else:
    print('Lines intersect')
```

Output

```
>>>
========= RUN C:/Python/Conditional/Lines.py ==========
Enter Coefficients of the first equation [a₁x + b₁y + c₁ = 0]

Enter the value of a₁: 2
Enter the value of b₁: 3
Enter the value of c₁: 4
Enter Coefficients of second equation [a₂x + b₂y + c₂ = 0]

Enter the value of a₂: 1
Enter the value of b₂: 2
Enter the value of c₂: 3
Lines intersect
>>>
```

3.8   CONCLUSION

As stated in the first chapter, we write a program with a purpose. The purpose to be accomplished by a program generally requires making decisions. This decision making capacity also empowers a programmer to write a code that requires branching. Python greatly reduces unnecessary clutter when compared to C or C++. In a Python code there is hardly a need for braces, or for that matter handling obvious conditions. Python also provides us with a switch-like construct to handle multiple conditions. This chapter discusses the basics of conditional statements and presents ample illustrations to make things clear. These conditional statements are used everywhere; from a basic program to decision support systems and expert systems. The reader is required to go through the points to remember, and implement the problems given in the exercise for better understanding of this. One must also understand that the conditional statements are the first step towards programming. However understanding conditional statements, though essential, is just the beginning. Your journey of becoming a programmer has just started.

GLOSSARY

1.   The syntax of "if" is as follows.
```
if <test condition>:
        <block if the test condition is true>
```

2.   The "if else" construct is written as follows.
```
if <test condition>
        <block if the test condition is true>
else:
        <block if the test condition is not true>
...
```

3.   The syntax of the "if else ladder"
```
if <test condition>:
        <block if the test condition is true>
elif <test 2>:
        <second block>
elif <test 3>:
        <third block>
else:
        <block if the test condition is true>
```

POINTS TO REMEMBER

- The `'if'` statement implements conditional branching.
- The test condition is a Boolean expression which results in a `true` or a `false`.
- The block of `'if'` executes if the test condition it `true`.
- The `else` part executes if the test condition is `false`.
- Multiple branches can be implemented using the `if-elif` ladder.
- Any number of `if-elif` can be nested.
- A ternary `if` can be implemented in Python.
- Logical operators can be used in implementing conditional statements.

EXERCISES

MULTIPLE CHOICE QUESTIONS

1. What will be the output of the following?
```
if 28:
  print('Hi')
else:
  print('Bye')
```
   (*a*) Hi
   (*b*) Bye
   (*c*) None of the above
   (*d*) The above snippet will not compile

2.
```
a = 5
b = 7
c = 9
if a>b:
   if b>c:
      print(b)
   else:
      print(c)
else:
   if b>c:
      print(c)
   else:
      print(b)
```
   (*a*) 7
   (*b*) 9
   (*c*) 34
   (*d*) None of the following

3.
```
a = 34
b = 7
c = 9
if a>b:
    if b>c:
        print(b)
    else:
        print(c)
else:
    if b>c:
        print(c)
    else:
        print(b)
```
(*a*) 7

(*b*) 9

(*c*) None of the above

(*d*) The code will not compile

4.
```
a = int(input('First number\t:'))
b = int(input('Second number\t'))
c = int(input('Third number\t:'))
if ((a>b) & (a>c)):
    print(a)
elif ((b>a) &(b>c)):
    print(b)
else:
    print(c)
```
(*a*) The greatest of the three numbers entered by the user

(*b*) The smallest of the three numbers entered by the user

(*c*) None

(*d*) The code will not compile

5.
```
n = int(input('Enter a three digit number\t:'))
if (n%10)==(n//100):
    print('Hi')
else:
    print('Bye')
    # The three digit number entered by the user is 453
```
(*a*) Hi

(*b*) Bye

(*c*) None of the above

(*d*) The code will not compile

6. In the above question, if the number entered is 545, what would the answer be?

    (*a*) Hi   (*b*) Bye

    (*c*) None of the above   (*d*) The code will not compile

7.
```
hb1 = ['Programming in C#','Oxford University Press', 2014]
hb2 = ['Algorithms', 'Oxford University Press', 2015]
if hb1[1]==hb2[1]:
    print('Same')
else:
     print('Different')
```

    (*a*) same   (*b*) Different

    (*c*) No output   (*d*) The code would not compile

8.
```
hb1 = ['Programming in C#','Oxford University Press', 2014]
hb2 = ['Algorithms', 'Oxford University Press', 2015]
if (hb1[0][3]==hb2[0][3]):
     print('Same')
else:
      print('Different')
```

    (*a*) Same   (*b*) Different

    (*c*) No output   (*d*) The code will not compile

9. In the snippet given in question 8, the following changes are made. What will the output be?
```
hb1 = ['Programming in C#','Oxford University Press', 2014]
hb2 = ['Algorithms', 'Oxford University Press', 2015]
if (str(hb1[0][3])==str(hb2[0][3])):
     print('Same')
else:
      print('Different')
```

    (*a*) Same   (*b*) Different

    (*c*) No output   (*d*) The code will not compile

10. Finally, the code in question 8 is changed to the following. What will the output be?
```
hb1 = ['Programming in C#','Oxford University Press', 2014]
hb2 = ['Algorithms', 'Oxford University Press', 2015]
```

```
if (char(hb1[0][3])==char(hb2[0][3])):
    print('Same')
else:
    print('Different')
```

(a) Same   (b) Different

(c) No output   (d) The code will not compile

PROGRAMMING EXERCISE

1. Ask the user to enter a number and find the number obtained by reversing the order of the digits.

2. Ask the user to enter a four digit number and check whether the sum of the first and the last digits is same as the sum of the second and the third digits.

3. In the above question if the answer is true then obtain a number in which the second and the third digit are one more than that in the given number.
    Example: Number 5342, sum of the first and the last digit = 7 that of the second and the third digit = 7. New number: 5452

4. Ask the user to enter the concentration of hydrogen ions in *a* given solution (C) and find the PH of the solution using the following formula.
    $$PH = \log_{10} C$$

5. If the PH is <7 then the solution is deemed acidic, else it is deemed as basic. Find if the given solution is acidic.

6. In the above question find whether the solution is neutral. (A solution is neutral if the PH is 7)

7. The centripetal force acting on a body (mass m), moving with a velocity v, in a circle of radius r, is given by the formula mv^2/r. The gravitational force on the body is given by the formula $(GmM)/R^2$, where m and M are the masses of the body and earth and R is the radius of the earth. Ask the user to enter the requisite data and find whether the two forces are equal or not.

8. Ask the user to enter his salary and calculate the TADA, which is 10% of the salary; the HRA, which is 20% of the salary and the gross income, which is the sum total of the salary, TADA and the HRA.

9. In the above question find whether the net salary is greater than $300,000.

10. Use the Tax Tables of the current year to find the tax on the above income (question number 8), assuming that the savings are $100,000.

11. Find whether a number entered by the user is divisible by 3 and 13.

12. Find whether the number entered by the user is a perfect square.

13. Ask the user to enter a string and find the alphanumeric characters from the string.

14. In the above question find the digits in the strings.

15. In question 13, find all the components of the string which are not digits or alphabets.

CHAPTER 4

LOOPING

After reading this chapter, the reader will be able to

- Understand the importance and use of loops
- Appreciate the importance of the `while` and `for`
- Use `range`
- Process list of lists
- Understand nesting of loops and design patterns

4.1 INTRODUCTION

When we were young, we were taught tables of numbers. The table of a number had a pattern. Writing a table in an examination required writing, say, "$n\times$" followed by "i" (i varying from 1 to n) and then the result of calculations (that is $n \times 1, n \times 2$ and so on). Many such situations require us to repeat a given task many times. This repetition can be used to calculate the value of a function, to print a pattern or to simply repeat something. This chapter discusses loops and iterations, which are an integral part of procedural programming. Looping means repeating a set of statements until a condition is true. The number of times this set is repeated depends on the test condition. Also, what is to be repeated needs to be chalked out with due deliberation. In general, repeating a block requires the following (Figure 4.1).

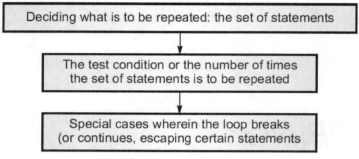

FIGURE 4.1 Looping

Python provides two types of loops: `for` and `while` (Figure 4.2).

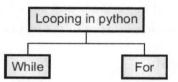

FIGURE 4.2 Loops in Python

`While` loop is one of the most general constructs in any programming language. If you come from a "C" background, you must be equipped with the above construct. `While` loop retains most of its features in Python as well, however, there are notable differences too.

The `while` loop repeats a block, identified by indentation, until the test condition remains true. As we will see in the following discussion, one can come out of the loop using `break` and `continue`. Also, to decide if the loop repeats as per the test condition after which the `else` condition executes. This is an additional feature in Python.

The use of `for` in Python is a bit different to "C"-like languages. The `for` construct in Python is generally used for lists, tuples, strings, etc. The chapter presents `range`, which will help the programmer to select a value from a given range. The reader is advised to go through the discussion of lists and tuples presented in Chapter 2 of this book before starting with the `for` loop.

The chapter has been organized as follows. Section 4.2 of this chapter presents the basics of the `while` loop. Section 4.3 uses looping to create patterns. Section 4.4 introduces the concept of nesting and presents the processing of lists and tuples using `for` loops. The last section concludes the chapter.

4.2 WHILE

In Python, the `while` loop is the most commonly used construct for repeating a task over and over again. The task is repeated until the test condition remains true, after which the loop ends and if the exit occurs without a `break`, then the `else` part of the construct executes. The syntax of the loop is as follows:

Syntax

```
while test:
        ...
        ...
else:
        ...
```

It may be stated here that the body of the loop is determined by indentation. This is the reason why you must be extremely careful with indentation. Also, the `else` part is an addition in Python when compared to "C"-like languages. In order to understand the concept, let us go through the following illustrations.

Illustration 4.1: Ask the user to enter a number and calculate its factorial.

Solution: The factorial of a number n is defined as follows.

$$\text{factorial} = 1 \times 2 \times 3 \times \ldots \times n$$

That is the factorial of a number, n, is the product of n terms starting from 1. To calculate the factorial of a given number, first of all the user is asked to input a number. The number is then converted into an integer. This is followed by the initialization of "`factorial`" by 1. Then a `while` loop successively multiplies i to `'factorial'` (note that after each iteration the value of i increases by 1). The following program calculates the factorial of a number entered by the user.

Program

```
n = input('Enter number whose factorial is required')#ask
                               user to enter number
m = int(n)#convert the input to an integer
factorial = 1#initialize
i=1# counter
while i<=m:
    factorial =factorial*i
    i=i+1
print('\factorial of '+str(m)+' is '+str(factorial))
```

Output

```
>>>
RUN C:/Users/ACER ASPIRE/AppData/Local/Programs/Python/
                 Python35-32/Tools/scripts/factorial.py
Enter number whose factorial is required6
Factorial of 6 is 720
```

Illustration 4.2: Ask the user to enter two numbers "*a*" and "*b*" and calculate "*a*" to the power of "*b*."

Solution: "*a*" raised to the power of "*b*" can be defined as follows.

$$\text{power} = a \times a \times a \times .. \times a \ (b \text{ times})$$

That is, the power of a number "*a*" raised to "*b*" is the product of the number "*a*," "*b*" times. To calculate the power, first of all the user is asked to input two numbers. The numbers are then converted into integers. This is followed by the initialization of 'power' by 1. Then a while loop successively multiplies 'a' to 'power' (note that after each iteration the value of i increases by 1). The following program implements the above logic.

Program

```
>>>
a = int(input('Enter the first number'))
b = int(input('Enter the second number'))
power=1
i = 1
while i < = b:
    power = power*a
    i=i+1
else:
    print(str(a)+' to the power of '+str(b)+' is '+str(power))
```

Output

```
>>>
RUN C:/Users/ACER ASPIRE/AppData/Local/Programs/Python/
                 Python35-32/Tools/scripts/power.py
Enter the first number4
Enter the second number5
4 to the power of 5 is 1024
>>>
```

Illustration 4.3: The arithmetic progression is obtained by adding the common difference "*d*" to the first term "*a*," successively. The ith term of the arithmetic progression is given by the following formula:

$$T\,(i) = a + (i-1) \times d$$

Ask the user to enter the value of "*a*," "*d*," and "*n*" (the number of terms), and find all the terms of the AP. Also, find the sum of all the terms.

Solution: The following program asks the user to enter the values of "*a*," "*d*," and "*n*." Note that the input is converted into integers. Also, since all the terms are to be calculated, this evaluation is done inside a loop. The 'sum' is initialized to 0 and the terms are added to 'sum' in each iteration.

Program

```
>>>
a = int(input('Enter the first term of the Arithmetic
                                 Progression\t:'))
d = int(input('Enter the common
difference\t:')) n = int(input('Enter the number of
                                 terms\t:')) i = 1
sum = 0#initialize
while i<=n:
    term = a +(i-1)*d
    print('The '+str(i)+'th term is '+str(term))
    sum = sum + term
    i=i+1
else:
    print('The sum of '+str(n)+' terms is\t:'+str(sum))
```

Output

```
RUN C:/Users/ACER ASPIRE/AppData/Local/Programs/Python/
                        Python35-32/Tools/scripts/AP.py
Enter the first term of the Arithmetic Progression    :5
Enter the common difference    :6
Enter the number of terms    :7
The 1th term is 5
The 2th term is 11
The 3th term is 17
The 4th term is 23
The 5th term is 29
The 6th term is 35
The 7th term is 41
The sum of 7 terms is    :161
```

Illustration 4.4: The geometric progression is obtained by multiplying the common ratio 'r' to the first term 'a', successively. The ith term of the progression is given by the following formula. $T(i) = a \times r^{i-1}$

Ask the user to enter the value of 'a', 'r', and 'n' (the number of terms), and find all the terms of the GP. Also, find the sum of all the terms.

Solution: The following program asks the user to enter the values of 'a', 'r', and 'n'. Since all the terms are to be calculated, this evaluation is done inside a loop. The 'sum' is initialized to 0 and the terms are added to 'sum' in each iteration.

Program

```
>>>
a = int(input('Enter the first term of the Geometric
                                      Progression\t:'))
r = int(input('Enter the common ratio\t:'))
n = int(input('Enter the number of terms\t:'))
i = 1
sum = 0#initialize
while i<=n:
    term = a * (r**(i-1))
    print('The '+str(i)+'th term is '+str(term))
    sum = sum + term
    i=i+1
else:
    print('The sum of '+str(n)+' terms is\t:'+str(sum))
```

Output

```
>>>
RUN C:/Users/ACER ASPIRE/AppData/Local/Programs/Python/
                        Python 35-32/Tools/scripts/GP.py
Enter the first term of the Arithmetic Progression    :5
Enter the common ratio  3
Enter the number of terms       5
The 1th term is 5
The 2th term is 15
The 3th term is 45
The 4th term is 135
The 5th term is 405
The sum of 5 terms is     605
>>>
```

4.3 PATTERNS

Have you ever wondered why quizzes and riddles form an integral part of any intelligence test? The following incident will help the reader to understand the importance of patterns. During World War II, the British were striving hard to break Enigma, the machine used by the Germans for encrypting their messages. The army somehow recruited Alan Turing, who was never in his lifetime recognized, for the above task. He wanted a team to help him, for which he conducted an exam. Many of you would be amazed to know what he asked in that exam which would determine the destiny of a country! He asked the candidates to solve the given puzzles in a given time. This incident underlines the importance of comprehending patterns. What happened thereafter is history. Decoding patterns and solving puzzles helps to judge the intellect of a person. This is much more important than learning a formula. This section presents the designing of patterns using loops to help the reader understand the concept of nesting. Moreover, this book also intends to inculcate the problem solving approach in the reader. Therefore this section becomes all the more important.

The following illustrations show how to assign values to the counters of the inner and the outer loops to carry out the given task. The patterns, as such, may not be very useful. However, doing the following program would help the reader to comprehend the concept of nesting. The methodology of making a pattern has been explained in each of the following programs.

Illustration 4.5: Write a program to generate the following pattern in Python.

```
*
* *
* * *
* * * *
```

The number of rows would be entered by the user.

Solution: The number of rows n, will determine the value of the counter (from 0 to n). The value of i denotes the row number in the following program. In each row, the number of stars is equal to the row number. The values of j, in each iteration, denotes the number of stars in each row. This loop is therefore nested. Also, note that after the inner loop ends a new line is printed using the print() function.

Program

```
>>>
n = input('Enter the number of rows')
m = int(n)
*k=1
for i in range(m):
    for j in range(1, i+2):
        print('*', end=" ")
    print()
```

Output

```
RUN C:/Users/ACER ASPIRE/AppData/Local/Programs/Python/
                        Python35-32/Tools/scripts/loop2.py
Enter the number of rows 5
*
* *
* * *
* * * *
```

Illustration 4.6: Write a program to generate the following pattern in Python.

```
1
2 2
3 3 3
4 4 4 4
```

The number of rows would be entered by the user.

Solution: The number of rows will determine the value of the counter i, (from 0 to n). The value of i denotes the row number in the following program. In each row, the number of elements is equal to the row number. The values of j in each iteration denote the number of elements in each row. This loop is therefore nested. The element printed is the value of $i+1$. Also, note that after the inner loop ends a new line is printed using the print() function.

Program

```
>>>
n = input('Enter the number of rows')
m = int(n)
k=1
```

```
for i in range(m):
    for j in range(1, i+2):
      print(i+1, end=" ")
    print()
```

Output

```
RUN C:/Users/ACER ASPIRE/AppData/Local/Programs/Python/
                        Python35-32/Tools/scripts/loop2.py
Enter the number of rows5
1
2 2
3 3 3
4 4 4 4
5 5 5 5 5
```

Illustration 4.7: Write a program to generate the following pattern in Python.

```
2
2 3
2 3 4
2 3 4 5
```

The number of rows would be entered by the user.

Solution: The number of rows, entered by the user, will determine the value of i (from 0 to n). The value of i denotes the row number in the following program. In each row, the number of elements is equal to the row number. The values of j in each iteration denote the number of elements in each row. This loop is therefore nested. The element printed is the value of j+1. Also note that after the inner loop ends a new line is printed using the print() function.

Program

```
>>>
n = input('Enter the number of rows')
m = int(n)
k=1
for i in range(m):
    for j in range(1, i+2):
      print(j+1, end=" ")
    print()
```

Output

```
>>>
RUN C:/Users/ACER ASPIRE/AppData/Local/Programs/Python/
                    Python35-32/Tools/scripts/loop3.py
Enter the number of rows5
2
2 3
2 3 4
2 3 4 5
2 3 4 5 6
```

Illustration 4.8: Write a program to generate the following pattern in Python.

```
1
2 3
4 5 6
7 8 9 10
```

The number of rows would be entered by the user.

Solution: The value of i denotes the row number in the following program. In each row, the number of elements is equal to the row number. The values of i in each iteration will denote the number of elements in each row. This loop is therefore nested. The element printed is the value of k, which starts from 1 and incrementally increases in each iteration. Also note that after the inner loop ends a new line is printed using the print() function.

Program

```
>>>
n = input('Enter the number of rows')
m = int(n)
k=1
for i in range(m):
    for j in range(1, i+2):
      print(k, end=" ")
      k=k+1
    print()
```

Output

```
>>>
RUN C:\Users\ACER ASPIRE\AppData\Local\Programs\Python\
                    Python35-32\Tools\scripts\loop1.py
```

```
Enter the number of rows7
1
2 3
4 5 6
7 8 9 10
11 12 13 14 15
16 17 18 19 20 21
22 23 24 25 26 27 28
```

Illustration 4.9: Write a program to generate the following pattern in Python.

```
        *
       ***
      *****
     *******
    *********
```

The number of rows would be entered by the user.

Solution: The value of i denotes the row number in the following program. In each row, the number of stars is equal to the row number. The values of k in each iteration denote the number of stars in each row, which ranges from 0 to (2*i +1). This loop is therefore nested. The leading spaces are governed by the value of j, which ranges from 0 to (m-i-1). This is because if the value of i is 0, the number of spaces should be 4 (if the value of n is 5). In case the value of i is 1, the number of spaces should be 3 and so on. Also note that after the inner loop ends a new line is printed using the print() function.

Program

```
n = input('Enter the number of rows')
m = int(n)
for i in range(m):
    for j in range(0, (m-i-1)):
        print(' ', end="")
    for k in range(0, 2*i+1):
        print('*',end="")
    print()

>>>
```

Output

```
RUN C:/Users/ACER ASPIRE/AppData/Local/Programs/Python/
                        Python35-32/Tools/scripts/loop5.py
Enter the number of rows 6
                    *
                  * * *
                * * * * *
              * * * * * *
            * * * * * * * *
```

4.4 NESTING AND APPLICATIONS OF LOOPS IN LISTS

Nested loops can be used to generate matrices. In order to do this, the outer loop is designed to govern the rows and the inner loop to govern each element of a particular row. The following illustration shows the generation of a matrix having i^{th} element given by the following formula:

$$a_{i,j} = 5 \times (i + j)^2$$

Note that in the following illustration, two loops have been used. The outer loop runs n times where n is the number of rows, and the inner loop runs m times where m is the number of columns. The number of columns can be perceived as the number of elements in each row.

The inner loop has one statement, which calculates the element. At the end of each iteration (of the outer loop) a new line is printed using the `print()` function.

Illustration 4.10: Generate a n × m, matrix, wherein each element (a_{ij}), is given by

$$a_{i,j} = 5 \times (i + j)^2$$

Solution: The concept has been explained in the above discussion. There will be two loops; the outer loop for the number of rows and the inner loop for the number of columns.

Program

```
n = int(input('Enter the number of rows'))
m = int(input('Enter the number of columns'))
```

```
for i in range (n):
   for j in range(m):
     element = 5*(i+j)*(i+j)
     print(element, sep=' ', end= ' ')
   print() >>>
```

Output

```
RUN C:/Users/ACER ASPIRE/AppData/Local/Programs/Python/
            Python35-32/Tools/scripts/matrixgeneartion.py
Enter the number of rows3
Enter the number of columns3
0 5 20
5 20 45
20 45 80
>>>
```

It may be noted that in the following chapters, this nesting is used to deal with most of the operations of matrices. As a matter of fact addition and subtraction of two matrices requires two levels of nesting, whereas multiplication of two matrices requires three levels of nesting.

Illustration 4.11: Handling list of lists: Note that in the following program the first list's second element is itself a list. Its first element can be accessed by writing hb[0][1] and the first letter of the first element of the nested list would be hb[0][1][0].

Program

```
>>>
hb=["Programming in C#",["Oxford University Press", 2015]]
rm=["SE is everything",["Obscure Publishers", 2015]]
authors=[hb, rm]
print(authors)
print("List:\n"+str(authors[0])+"\n"+str(authors[1])+"\n")
print("Name of books\n"+str(authors[0][0])+"\n"+
                                str(authors[1][0])+"\n")
print("Details of the books\n"+str(authors[0][1])+"\n"+
                                str(authors[1][1])+"\n")
print("\nLevel 3 Publisher 1\t:"+str(authors[0][1][0]))
>>>
```

Output

```
RUN C:\Users\ACER ASPIRE\AppData\Local\Programs\Python\
                Python35-32\Tools\scripts\listoflist.py
[['Programming in C#', ['Oxford University Press', 2015]],
      ['SE is everything', ['Obscure Publishers', 2015]]]
List:
['Programming in C#', ['Oxford University Press', 2015]]
['SE is everything', ['Obscure Publishers', 2015]]

Name of books
Programming in C#
SE is everything
Details of the books
['Oxford University Press', 2015]
['Obscure Publishers', 2015]
Level 3 Publisher 1     :Oxford University Press
>>>
```

The following two illustrations handle the list of lists using nested loops. Kindly note the output and the corresponding mappings.

Illustration 4.12: Handling list of lists using loops: The elements of nested lists can also be dealt with using nested loops as shown in this illustration.

Program

```
hb=["Programming in C#",["Oxford University Press", 2015]]
rm=["SE is everything",["Obscure Publishers", 2015]
authors=[hb, rm]
print(authors)
for i in range(len(authors)):
   for j in range(len(authors[i])):
     print(str(i)+" "+str(j)+" "+str(authors[i][j])+"\n")
   print()

>>>
```

Output

```
RUN C:/Users/ACER ASPIRE/AppData/Local/Programs/Python/
                Python35-32/Tools/scripts/listfor.py
[['Programming in C#', ['Oxford University Press', 2015]],
      ['SE is everything', ['Obscure Publishers', 2015]]]
```

```
0 0 Programming in C#
0 1 ['Oxford University Press', 2015]
1 0 SE is everything
1 1 ['Obscure Publishers', 2015]

>>>
```

Illustration 4.13: Another illustration of the use of loops in processing nested lists. The user is expected to observe the output and infer what happened.

Program
```
hb=["Programming in C#",["Oxford University Press", 2015]]
rm=["SE is everything",["Obscure Publishers", 2015]]
authors=[hb, rm]
print(authors)
for i in range(len(authors)):
   for j in range(len(authors[i])):
     for k in range(len(authors[i][j])):
       print(str(i)+" "+str(j)+" "+str(k)+"
   "+str(authors[i][j][k])+"\n")
print()
```

Output
```
RUN C:/Users/ACER ASPIRE/AppData/Local/Programs/Python/
                  Python35-32/Tools/scripts/listfor.py
[['Programming in C#', ['Oxford University Press', 2015]],
      ['SE is everything', ['Obscure Publishers', 2015]]]
0 0 0 P
0 0 1 r
0 0 2 o
0 0 3 g
0 0 4 r
0 0 5 a
0 0 6 m
0 0 7 m
0 0 8 i
0 0 9 n
0 0 10 g
0 0 11
0 0 12 i
0 0 13 n
```

```
0 0 14
0 0 15 C
0 0 16 #
0 1 0 Oxford University Press
0 1 1 2015
1 0 0 S
1 0 1 E
1 0 2
1 0 3 i
1 0 4 s
1 0 5
1 0 6 e
1 0 7 v
1 0 8 e
1 0 9 r
1 0 10 y
1 0 11 t
1 0 12 h
1 0 13 i
1 0 14 n
1 0 15 g
1 1 0 Obscure Publishers
1 1 1 2015
```

4.5   CONCLUSION

Repeating a task is an immensely important job. This is needed in a whole variety of situations to accomplish different tasks. This chapter introduces the two most important looping constructs in Python. The chapter demonstrated the use of these looping constructs by showing simple examples. Having a loop within a loop is called nesting. The nesting of loops has been explained using patterns and lists of lists. Chapter 6 revisits one of the constructs and compares the use of iterators and generators. The reader is expected to solve the problems given at the end of the chapter for better understanding. However, Python provides us with other constructs which greatly simplify program writing. At the moment try various permutations and combinations, observe the outputs and learn.

GLOSSARY

1. Looping means repeating a task a certain number of times.

2. Syntax of for loop
```
for i in range(n):
    ...
    ...
OR
for i in range(n, m):
    ...
    ...
OR
for i in (_, _,...)
    ...
    ...
    ...
```

3. Syntax of while loop
```
while <test condition>:
    ...
```

POINTS TO REMEMBER

- In order to repeat a set of statements a certain number of times looping is used.
- Looping in Python can be implemented using while and for.
- 'while' is the most common looping construct in Python.
- The statements in the while block executes until the test condition remains true.
- The else part executes if the loop ends without a break.
- 'for' can be used for all the purposes for which a 'while' is used.
- 'for' is generally used for processing lists, tuples, matrices, etc.
- range (n) means values from 0 to $(n-1)$.
- range (m, n) means all the values from m to $(n-1)$.
- A loop can be nested in a loop.
- There can be any number of nestings, although this is undesirable.

EXERCISES

MULTIPLE CHOICE QUESTIONS

1. What will be the output of the following?
    ```
    a=8
    i=1
    while a:
      print(a)
      i=i+1
      a=a-i
    print(i)
    ```
    (a) 8, 6, 3   (b) 8, 6, 3, 1

    (c) 8, 6, 3, –1, ...   (d) None of the above

2.
    ```
    a=8
    i=1
    while a:
            print(a)
            i=i+1
            a=a/2
            print(i)
    ```
    (a) 8, 4, 2, 1   (b) 8, 4, 2, 1, 0

    (c) 8, 4, 2, 1, 0.5   (d) Infinite loop

3. How many times will the following loop execute?
    ```
    n = int(input('Enter number'))
    i = n
    while (i>0):
            print(n)
            i=i+1
            n = int(n/2)
            print(i)
    ```
    #The value of n entered by the user is 10

    (a) 4   (b) 5

    (c) Infinite   (d) The code will not compile

4. Which loop can be used when the number of iterations is not known?

(*a*) while   (*b*) for

(*c*) both   (*d*) None of the above

5. How many levels of nesting are possible in for?

(*a*) 2   (*b*) 3

(*c*) Any number   (*d*) Depends on environment

6.
```
n = int(input('Enter number'))
for i in (0,7):
print('i is '+str(i))
i = i+1;
else:
print('bye')
```
How many values would be printed?

(*a*) 2   (*b*) 3

(*c*) 6   (*d*) None of the above

7.
```
n = int(input('Enter number'))
for i in range(n, 1, -1):
for j in range(i):
print(i, j)
#value entered by the user is 5
```

(*a*) (5, 0), (5, 1), ...(2, 1)   (*b*) (5, 1), (5,2),...(2, 0)

(*c*) (0, 1), (0, 2), ...(5, 2)   (*d*) None of the above

8. In order to print the elements of a given matrix which of the following is essential?

(*a*) Nested loops   (*b*) Single loop

(*c*) if-else   (*d*) None of the above

9. What is meant by `range (5)`?

(*a*) Integers from 0 to 4   (*b*) Integers from 0 to 5

(*c*) Integers from 1 to 4   (*d*) Integers from 1 to 5

10. What is meant by `range (3, 8)`?

(*a*) 3, 4, 5, 6, 7, 8   (*b*) 3, 4, 5, 6, 7

(*c*) 1, 2, 4, 5, 6, 7, 8   (*d*) 8, 8, 8

PROGRAMMING

1.   Ask the user to enter a number and find whether it is a prime number.

2.   Ask the user to enter a number and find all its factors.

3.   Find whether the number entered by the user is a perfect square. Example: If number = 30, then factors are 2, 3, and 5

4.   Ask the user to enter two numbers and find the lowest common multiple. Example: If numbers are 30 and 20, then LCM is 60, as both 20 and 30 are factors of 60

5.   Ask the user to enter two numbers and find the highest common factor. Example: If numbers are 30 and 20, the HCF is 10

6.   Find the mean of numbers entered by the user.

$$\text{Mean} = \frac{x_1 + x_2 + x_3 + \dots + x_n}{n}$$

7.   Find the variance and standard deviation of the numbers entered by the user.

8.   Ask the user to enter the values of a and b and find a^{b^a}.

9.   Find the common factor of n numbers entered by a user.

10. Ask the user to enter three numbers and find all possible permutations of these numbers.

11. In the above question, what happens if we have four numbers in place of three?

12. Can the above logic be extended for n numbers?

13. Ask the user to enter n numbers and find the minimum of the numbers without using arrays.

14. Ask the user to enter n numbers and find the maximum of the numbers without using arrays.

15. Create a list of authors in which the record of each author is itself a list consisting of the name of the book, publisher, year of publication, ISSN, and the city. Now process the list using `for` loop.

CHAPTER **5**

FUNCTIONS

After reading this chapter, the reader will be able to

- Appreciate the importance of modular programming
- Define and classify functions
- Understand the concept of the scope of a variable
- Understand and use recursion

5.1 INTRODUCTION

If you have to perform a bigger task, then it is advisable to divide it into smaller, more manageable tasks. This division has many advantages, which are discussed in the following sections. The units of programs, which can be called on as its basis, take some input, process it and may generate some output which i referred to as functions.

> Functions are units which perform a particular task, may take some input, and which may give some output.

This concept is the soul of procedural programming. The readers familiar with C (or for that matter C++, Java, C#, etc.) will be familiar with the idea and use of functions. However, a brief discussion on the futures and advantages of functions follows in the next section.

This chapter introduces the concept of functions. The chapter has been organized as follows. The next section briefly explains the features of a function; the third section explains the basic terminology, and the following section discusses the definition and use of a function. The fifth section presents a brief discussion on the scope of a variable. The sixth section presents recursion and the last section of the chapter concludes.

5.2   FEATURES OF A FUNCTION

As discussed earlier, functions form the basis of procedural programming. One of the most obvious advantages is the division of a program into smaller parts. This section briefly discusses the advantages of dividing the program into functions.

5.2.1   Modular Programming

If a program is divided into small parts in such a way that different parts each perform some specific task, then each part can be called as per the requirement.

5.2.2   Reusability of Code

A function can be called many times. This spares the programmer from the horror of rewriting the same code again, which in turn can reduce the length of the program.

5.2.3   Manageability

Dividing a bigger task into smaller functions makes the program manageable. It becomes easy to locate bugs and therefore make the program reliable. It also becomes easy to carry out local optimization in a function. To summarize, manageability leads to the following:

5.2.3.1   *Easy Debugging*

In order to understand why creating functions will make debugging easy, let us consider White Box Testing. This type of testing, which uses code for testing, requires elicitation of paths and crafting test cases catering to them. In this case it becomes easy to effectively analyze smaller functions rather than the whole task.

5.2.3.2 *Efficient*

It is essential to make code efficient both in terms of time and memory. As a matter of fact, even in "C's" compiler most of the code optimization is attributed to the developer rather than the compiler.

The above factors point to the fact that dividing the task into functions is good practice. It may be noted here that even object-oriented programming, described in Section 2 of this book, relies on functions for implementing the behavior of a class.

5.3   BASIC TERMINOLOGY

The importance of functions in procedural programming has already been discussed in the previous section. This section briefly introduces the terminology of functions and presents the syntax which will form the foundation stone of the discussion that follows.

5.3.1   Name of a Function

A function can have any legal literal name. For example, sum1 is a valid function name as it satisfies all the requisite constraints. It may be stated here that in a class we can have more than one function with the same name and different parameters. This is referred to as overloading. The concept has been discussed in Section 2 of this book.

5.3.2   Arguments

The arguments of a function denote the input given to a function. A function can have any number of arguments. As a matter of fact, it is possible that a function may not have any argument.

5.3.3   Return Value

A function may or may not return a value. The beauty of Python lies in not specifying the return type and therefore using the same functions for various data types.

In Python a function can be made in the command prompt. This implies that unlike C (or for that matter C++, Java, or C#) a function need not be a part of a program. Moreover, the return type as described in this section need not be mentioned. This inculcates flexibility in the procedures.

5.4 DEFINITION AND INVOCATION

This section discusses how to define a function and call a function that has been defined. The definition of a function depicts the behavior of the function. The task to be performed by the function is contained in the definition. In the discussion that follows, the components of a definition have been explained in detail.

The invocation of a function refers to calling a function. As explained in Section 5.6, a function can also be called within itself. This is referred to as recursion. It may also be noted that a function is defined only once. However, it can be called any number of times.

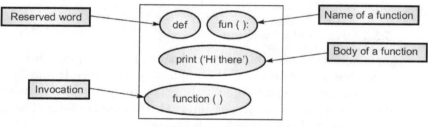

FIGURE 5.1 Example of a function

The definition of a function contains the following:

Name of a function: The name of a function is any valid identifier. It should be noted though that the name of a function should be meaningful and, if possible, convey the task to be performed by the function.

Parameter: The list of parameters (separated by commas) is given in the parentheses following the name of the function. The parameters are basically the input to the function. A function may have any parameters.

Body of the function: The body of the function contains the code that implements the task to be performed by the function.

Figure 5.1 shows the name of the function (fun), the list of parameters in the parentheses following the name of the function (in this case there are no parameters) and the body of the function.

It may also be noted that the closing parentheses containing the parameters is followed by a colon. The body of a function starts with a proper indentation.

The invocation of a function can be at any place after the definition. However, exceptions to this premise are found in the case of recursion.

The syntax of a function is depicted in Figure 5.2.

Syntax

def < name of the function>(list of parameters):

<body>

FIGURE 5.2 Syntax of a function

5.4.1 Working

Consider a function which multiplies two numbers passed as parameters.

```
def product(num1, num2):
    prod= num1*num2
    print('The product of the numbers is \t:'+str(prod))
```

The name of this function is product. It takes two arguments as input (num1 and num2), calculates the product and displays the results.

The function can be invoked as follows:

```
num1=int(input('Enter the first number\t:'))
num2=int(input('Enter the second number\t:'))
print('Calling the function...')
product(num1, num2)
print('Back to the calling function');
```

Here calling product shifts the control to the function, inside which the product is calculated and the result is displayed. The control then comes back to the calling function (Figure 5.3).

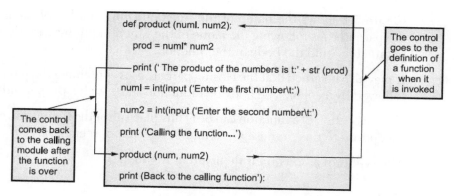

FIGURE 5.3 Calling a function

A function can be called any number of times. The following example shows a function which does not take any input and does not return anything. The function called just prints the lines of Ecclesiastes. The following listing shows the function, and the output of the program follows.

Illustration 5.1: Basic Function

Listing

```
def Ecclesiastes_3():
 print('To everything there is a season\nA time for every
                              purpose under Heaven')
  print('A time to be born\nand a time to die\nA time to
                        plant\nand a time to reap')
  print('A time to kill\nand a time to heal\nA time to
                   break down\nand a time to build up')
  print('A time to cast away stones\nand a time to gather
         stones\nA time to embrace\nand a time to refrain')
  print('A time to gain\nand a time to lose\nA time to
                   keep\nand a time to cast away')
  print('A time of love\nand a time of hate\nA time of war\
                          nand a time of peace')
print('Calling function\n')
Ecclesiastes_3()
print('Calling function again\n')
Ecclesiastes_3()
>>>
```

Output

```
Calling function

To everything there is a season
A time for every purpose under Heaven
A time to be born
and a time to die
A time to plant
and a time to reap
A time to kill
and a time to heal
A time to break down
and a time to build up
A time to cast away stones
and a time to gather stones
A time to embrace
and a time to refrain
A time to gain
and a time to lose
A time to keep
and a time to cast away
A time of love
and a time of hate
A time of war
and a time of peace
```

5.5   TYPES OF FUNCTION

Based on the parameters and the return type, functions can be divided into the following categories. The first type of function does not take any parameter or return anything. The program given in Illustration 5.1 shows one such function.

The second type of function takes parameters but does not return anything. Illustration 5.2 is an example of a function. The third type of function takes parameters and returns an output. The example that follows adds two numbers using functions. The task has been accomplished in three different ways – in the first function (sum1) the input is taken inside the function and the result is displayed in a print statement, which is also present inside the function.

The second function takes the two numbers as input (via parameters), adds them and prints the result inside the function itself. The third function (`sum3`) takes two parameters and returns the sum.

Illustration 5.2: Write a program to add two numbers using functions. Craft three functions, one of which does not take any parameters and does not return anything. The second function should take parameters and not return anything. The third function should take two numbers as parameters and should return the sum.

Program

```
>>>
def sum1():
    num1=int(input('Enter the first number\t:'))
    num2=int(input('Enter the second number\t:'))
    sum= num1+num2
    print('The sum of the numbers is \t:'+str(sum))

def sum2(num1, num2):
    sum= num1+num2
    print('The sum of the numbers is \t:'+str(sum))

def sum3(num1, num2):
    sum= num1+num2
    return(sum)

print('Calling the first function...')
sum1()
num1=int(input('Enter the first number\t:'))
num2=int(input('Enter the second number\t:'))
print('Calling the second function...')
sum2(num1, num2)
print('Calling the third function...')
result=sum3(num1, num2)
print(result)
>>>
```

Output

```
RUN C:/Users/ACER ASPIRE/AppData/Local/Programs/Python/
            Python35-32/Tools/scripts/sum_of_numbers.py
Calling the first function...
Enter the first number      3
Enter the second number     4
```

```
The sum of the numbers is    7
Enter the first number       2
Enter the second number      1
Calling the second function...
The sum of the numbers is    3
Calling the third function...
3
>>>
```

5.5.1   Advantage of Arguments

In Python, unlike "C" while defining a function the types of arguments are not specified. This has the advantage of giving different types of arguments in the same function. For example in the function that follows, the first invocation passes an integer value in the function. The function multiplies the number by two. In the case of the second invocation the multiply operator repeats the string, passed as a parameter, n number of times.

Illustration 5.3: Types of functions.

Listing 1

```
def sum1(num1, num2):
    return (num1+num2)
```

Output

```
>>> sum1(3,2)
5
>>> sum1('hi', 'there')
'hithere'
>>>
```

Listing 2

```
>>>
def sum1(num1, num2):
    return (num1+num2)
print('Calling function with integer arguments\t: Result:
                            '+str(sum1(2,3)))
print('Calling the function with string arguments\t:
                    Result: '+sum1('this',' world'))
```

Output

```
Calling function with integer arguments   : Result: 5
Calling the function with string arguments : Result: this
                                                    world
>>>
```

5.6 IMPLEMENTING SEARCH

This section demonstrates one of the most important uses of the topics studied so far: **Searching**. In the search problem if the element is present in a given list then its position should be printed, otherwise a message "Not Found" should be displayed. There are two major strategies used to accomplish the task. They are linear search and binary search. In linear search, the elements are iterated one by one. If the required element is found, the position of the element is printed. The absence of an element can be judged using a flag. The algorithm has been implemented in Illustration 5.4.

Illustration 5.4: Write a program to implement a linear search.

Solution:

```python
def search(L, item):
    flag=0
    for i in L:
        if i==item:
            flag=1
            print('Position ',i)
        if flag==0:
            print('Not found')
L =[1, 2, 5, 9, 10]
search(L, 5)
search(L, 3)
```

Output

```
Position     5
Not found
>>>
```

The above search strategy works well. However, there is another strategy of search called binary search. In binary search, the input list must be sorted.

The algorithm checks whether the item to be searched is present at the first position, at the last position or at the middle position. If the requisite element is not present at any of these positions and it is less than the middle element, then the left part of the list becomes the input of the procedure; else the right part of the element becomes the input to the procedure. The reader is advised to implement binary search.

The complexity of the binary search is O(logn).

5.7   SCOPE

The scope of a variable in Python is the part of the program wherein its value is legal or valid. It may be seated here that although Python allows a global variable, the value of a local variable must be assigned before being referenced. Illustration 5.5 exemplifies this concept. The illustration has three listings. In the first listing the value of 'a' has been assigned outside the function as well as inside the function. This leads to a problem as a variable cannot be referenced before being assigned.

In the second case this contention is resolved. Finally, the last listing shows that global variables are very much allowed in Python for some strange reason. As an active programmer, I firmly believe that should not have been allowed and there are multiple reasons for not allowing global variables in a programming language.

Illustration 5.5: Listings to scope of a variable.

Listing 1

```
# Note that a = 1does not hold when function is called
a = 1
def fun1():
    print(a)
    a=7
    print(a)

def fun2():
    print(a)
    a=3
    print(a)
```

```
    fun1()
    fun2()
    >>>
```

Output

```
============ RUN C:/Python/Functions/scope.py ===========
Traceback (most recent call last):
 File "C:/Python/Functions/scope.py", line 12, in <module>
   fun1()
 File "C:/Python/Functions/scope.py", line 3, in fun1
   print(a)
UnboundLocalError: local variable 'a' referenced before
                                       assignment
>>>
```

Listing 2

```
a = 1
def fun1():
    a=1
    print(a)
    a=7
    print(a)

def fun2():
    a=1
    print(a)
    a=3
    print(a)

fun1()
fun2()
```

Output

```
>>>
=========== RUN C:/Python/Functions/scope.py ===========
1
7
1
3
>>>
```

Also, note that had "a" been not assigned in the functions, the global value would have sufficed.

Listing 3

```
a = 1
def fun1():
        print(a)
def fun2():
        print(a)
fun1()
fun2()
```

Output

```
>>>
=========== RUN C:/Python/Functions/scope.py ============
1
1
>>>
```

5.8   RECURSION

At times a function needs to be called within itself. Calling a function in itself is referred to as recursion. The concept is used to accomplish many tasks easily and intuitively. For example, consider the following series:

```
1, 1, 2, 3, 5, 8, 13, ...
```

Note that each term is the sum of the previous two terms; the first and the second term being 1 and 1 respectively. This series is referred to as the Fibonacci series. The series is due to a famous rabbit problem which has been described as follows in mathematics.

5.8.1   Rabbit Problem

A pair of rabbits does not breed for the first two months together, after which they generate a pair of rabbits each month. This way there is a single pair of rabbit for the first two months, after which the growth follows a fascinating sequence (Table 5.1).

Table 5.1 Fibonacci series

Month	Pair of Rabbits	Number of Pairs
1	R0	1
2	R0	1
3	R0 → R01	2
4	R0 → R01, R02	3
5	R0 → R01 (→R010), R02, R03	5
6	R0 → R01 (→R010, R011), R02 (→R020), R03, R04	8

Note that in the above series, each term is the sum of the two preceding terms. The series can be represented as follows:

$$fib\ (n) = \begin{cases} 1, for\ n = 1 \\ 1, for\ n = 2 \\ fib\ (n-1) + fib\ (n-2) \end{cases}$$

Illustration 5.6 depicts the implementation of the Fibonacci series using recursion.

Illustration 5.6: Ask the user to enter the value of n and find the nth Fibonacci term.

Solution:

```
def fib(n):
    if n==1:
            return 1
    elif n==2:
            return 1
    else
            return (fib(n-1) + fib(n-2))
n=input('Enter the number\t:')
f=fib(n)
print('The nth fib term is ',str(f))
```

Output

```
========== RUN C:/Python/Functions/factoorial.py ==========
Enter the number:5
The nth fib term is 5
```

Note that the calculation of Fibonacci uses the Fibonacci term calculated earlier. For example, the calculation of the 5th Fibonacci term requires the following calculations: fib(5) requires fib(4) and fib(3), fib(4) requires fib(3) and fib(2) and fib(3) requires fib(2) and fib(1) (Figure 5.4).

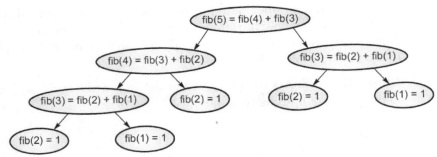

FIGURE 5.4 Calculation of the 5th Fibonacci term

The next example calculates the factorial of a number using recursion. The factorial of a number n (positive, integer) is the product of all the integers from 1 to n. That is:

$$n! = 1 \times 2 \times 3 \times ... \times n$$

Note that since $\quad (n-1)! = 1 \times 2 \times 3 ... \times (n-1)$

Therefore, $\quad\quad\quad n! = n \times (n-1)!$

Also the factorial of 1 is 1, that is, $1! = 1$ which can be used as the base case while implementing factorial using recursion. The program has been depicted in Illustration 5.7.

Illustration 5.7: Ask the user to enter the value of n and calculate the factorial of n using recursion.

Solution:

```
def fac(n):
    if n==1:
        return 1;
    else:
        return(n*fac(n-1))
n = int(input('Enter the number\t:'))
factorial = fac(n)
print('Factorial of ',n, ' is ', factorial)
```

Output

```
>>>
========== RUN C:/Python/Functions/factoorial.py ==========
```

```
Enter the number        5
Factorial of  5  is   120
>>>
```

The power of a number raised to the power of another can also be calculated using recursion. Since that is power (a, b) = a*power (a, b - 1).
Also, a^1, that is power (a, 1) = 1. The above logic has been implemented
in the illustration that follows.

Illustration 5.8: Ask the user to enter the values of *a* and *b* and calculate *a*
to the power of *b*, using recursion.

Program

```
def power(a , b):
    if b==1:
    return a
    else:
    return (a*power(a, b-1))
a = int(input('Enter the first number\t:'))
b = int(input('Enter the second number\t:'))
p = power(a,b)
print(a, ' to the power of ',b,' is ', p)
```

Output

```
>>>
========== RUN C:/Python/Functions/power.py ==========
Enter the first number        3
Enter the second number        4
3  to the power of  4  is   81
>>>
>>>
```

5.8.2 Disadvantages of Using Recursion

In spite of the fact that recursion makes things easy and helps to accomplish
some of the tasks intuitively, there is a flip side. Consider the first illustration. Though the program calculates the nth Fibonacci term easily, the
complexity of the procedure is too high $(O(\emptyset^n)))$ where Φ is gold number.
The same task can be accomplished in linear time using a paradigm called
dynamic programming.

Similarly, the recursive procedures in divide and conquer also require a huge
amount of time. In addition to the above problem, there is another flip side.

Recursion requires a lot of memory. Though a portion of the memory is reserved for stacks, a recursive procedure may eat up all the available memory. However, recursion is fun so let's enjoy recursion.

5.9   CONCLUSION

The chapter introduces the concept of functions. The idea of dividing the given program into various parts is central to manageability. The chapter forms the foundation stone of the chapters that follow. It may also be stated that function implements the behavior of a class; therefore before moving to the object-oriented paradigms, one must be familiar with functions and procedures.

The concept of recursion is also central to the implementations which involve the ideas of divide and conquer and that of dynamic programming. So, one must also be equipped with the power of recursion and should be able to use the concept to solve problems if possible.

The discussion continues in the next chapter where the ideas of iterators, generators, and comprehensions have been introduced. As a matter of fact, all of them are functions but with special purposes.

GLOSSARY

- **Function:** Functions accomplish a particular task. They help with making a program manageable.
- **Argument:** Arguments are the values passed in a function.
- **Recursion:** A function may call itself. This is referred to as recursion.

POINTS TO REMEMBER

- A function can have any number of arguments.
- A function may return a maximum of one value.
- A function may not even return a value.
- A function may call itself.
- A function can be called any number of times.
- A function needs to be called in order to be able to accomplish a particular task.

EXERCISES

MULTIPLE CHOICE QUESTIONS

1. Which of the following keywords is used to define a function?
   (a) Def
   (b) Define
   (c) Definition
   (d) None of the above

2. The values passed in a function are called
   (a) Arguments
   (b) Return values
   (c) Yield
   (d) None of the above

3. A recursive function is one that calls
   (a) Itself
   (b) Other function
   (c) The main function
   (d) None of the above

4. Which of the following should be present in a recursive function?
   (a) Initial values
   (b) Final values
   (c) Both
   (d) None of the above

5. Which of the following can be accomplished using recursion?
   (a) Binary search
   (b) Fibonacci series
   (c) Power
   (d) All of the above

6. Which of the following control structures is allowed in a function?
   (a) If
   (b) For
   (c) While
   (d) All of the above

7. Which types of functions are supported in Python?
   (a) Build in
   (b) User defined
   (c) Both
   (d) None of the above

8. Which of the following is true?
   (a) A function helps in dividing a program in small parts
   (b) A function can be called any number of times
   (c) Both
   (d) None of the above

9. Which of the following is true?
   (*a*) One can have a function that can be called any number of times
   (*b*) Only a limited number of functions can be called from a function
   (*c*) Nested functions are not allowed in Python
   (*d*) Nested functions are allowed only in certain conditions

10. Nested functions incorporates the concept of
    (*a*) Stack
    (*b*) Queue
    (*c*) Linked List
    (*d*) None of the above

PROGRAMMING EXERCISE

1. Write a function that calculates the mean of numbers entered by the user.

2. Write a function that calculates the mode of numbers entered by the user.

3. Write a function that calculates the median of numbers entered by the user.

4. Write a function that calculates the standard deviation of the numbers entered by a user.

5. Write a function that finds the maximum of the numbers from a given list.

6. Write a function that finds the minimum of the numbers from a given list.

7. Write a function that finds the second maximum of the numbers from a given list.

8. Write a function that finds the maximum of three numbers entered by the user.

9. Write a function that converts the temperature in Celsius to that in Fahrenheit.

10. Write a function that searches for an element from a given list.

11. Write a function that sorts a given list.

12. White a function that takes two lists as input and returns the merged list.

13. Write a function that finds all the factors of a given number.

14. Write a function that finds common factors of two given numbers.

15. Write a function that returns a number obtained by reversing the order of digits of a given number.

QUESTIONS BASED ON RECURSION

Use recursion to solve the following problems

1. Find the sum of two given numbers.

2. Find the product of two given numbers.

3. Given two numbers, find the first number to the power of the second.

4. Given two numbers, find the greatest common divisor of the numbers.

5. Given two numbers, find the least common multiples of the numbers.

6. Generate n Fibonacci terms.

- In a series the first three terms are 1, 1 and 1; the ith term is obtained using the following formula
$$f(i) = 2 \times f(i-1) + 3 \times f(i-2)$$
- Write a function to generate n terms of the sequence.
- Find the element in a given sorted list.
- Find the maximum from a given list.
- Reverse the order of digits of a given number.

THEORY

1. What are the advantages of using functions in a program?

2. What is a function? What are the components of a function?

3. What is the importance of parameter and return type in a function? Can a function have more than one return value?

4. What is recursion? Which data structure is used internally while implementing recursion?

5. What are the disadvantages of recursion?

EXTRA QUESTIONS

1. What will be the output of the following program?
```
def fun1(n):
 if n==1:
    return 1
 else:
    return (3*fun1(n-1)+2*fun1(n))
fun1(2)
```
(a) 1

(b) 5

(c) 3

(d) Maximum iteration depth reached

2. What will be the output of the following?
```
def fun1(n):
 if n==1:
    return 1
 elif n==2:
    return 2
 else:
    return (3*fun1(n-1)+2*fun1(n))
fun1(5)
```
(a) 5

(b) 27

(c) Maximum iteration depth reached

(d) None of the above

3. What will be the output of the following?
```
def fun1(n):
 if n==1:
    return 1
 elif n==2:
    return 2
 else:
    return (3*fun1(n-1)+2*fun1(n-2))
print(fun1(5))
```
(a) 5

(b) 100

(c) 25

(d) Maximum iteration depth reached

4. What will be the output of the following?

```
def fun1(n):
 if n==1:
    return 1
 elif n==2:
    return 2
 else:
    return (3*fun1(n-1)+2*fun1(n-2))
for i in range(10):
 print(fun1(i), end=' ')
```

(a) 1 2 8 28 100 356 1268 4516 16084

(b) 1 3 5 7 9 11 13 15

(c) Maximum iteration depth reached

(d) None of the above

5. What will be the output of the following?

```
def fun1(n):
 if n==1:
    return 1
 elif n==2:
    return 2
 else:
    return (3*fun1(n-1)+2*fun1(n-2))
for i in range(1, 10, 1):
 print(fun1(i), end=' ')
```

(a) 1 2 8 28 100 356 1268 4516 16084

(b) 1 3 5 7 9 11 13 15

(c) Maximum iteration depth reached

(d) None of the above

6. What will be the output of the following?

```
def _main_():
  print('I am in main')
  fun1()
  print('I am back in main')

def fun1():
  print('I am in fun1')
  fun2()
  print('I am back in fun1')
```

```
def fun2():
  print('I am in fun 2')

  _main_()am in fun 2')
>>>
```

(a) I am in main
    I am in fun 1
    I am in fun 2
    I am back in fun 1
    I am back in main

(b) Reverse of the above

(c) None of the above

(d) The program does not execute

7. Conceptually which data structure is implemented in the above program?

  (a) Stack

  (b) Queue

  (c) Graph

  (d) Tree

8. Which technique is implemented in the following code?

```
def search(L, item):
    flag=0
    for i in L:
        if i==item:
        flag=1
        print('Position ',i)
        if flag==0:
        print('Not found')
L =[1, 2, 5, 9, 10]
search(L, 5)
search(L, 3)
```

  (a) Linear search

  (b) Binary search

  (c) None of the above

  (d) The code does not execute

9. What is the complexity of the above?

  (a) $O(n)$

  (b) $O(n^2)$

  (c) $O(\log n)$

  (d) None of the above

10. Which is better - linear search or binary search?

  (a) Linear

  (b) Binary

  (c) Both are equally good

  (d) Depends on the input list.

CHAPTER **6**

ITERATIONS, GENERATORS, AND COMPREHENSIONS

After reading this chapter, the reader will be able to

- Understand the use and application of iterators
- Use iterators to produce sequences
- Use generators to generate sequences
- Understand and use list comprehensions

6.1   INTRODUCTION

So far basic data types, operators and control structures have been covered. These are essential part of any procedural language. Python also provides the programmers with lists, strings, tuples, dictionary, and files, which makes it a powerful language. However, one should be able to efficiently access and manipulate these elements to accomplish the given task. For example if the formula of the ith element of a list is known, then the whole list can be generated/accessed in one go. To accomplish this task, `for` loop comes to our rescue. However, Python also comes with better options like iterators, which help us to do the said task easily. One can also define iterable objects in Python. There is another marvel in Python that facilitates the generation of lists and sequences, which is **generator**. This chapter also introduces **comprehension**.

The chapter has been organized as follows. The second section of this chapter revisits `for`. The iterators have been introduced in the third section of this chapter. The fourth section explains so as to how to define your own iterable objects. The generators are introduced and explained in section five of this chapter. The sixth section of this chapter deals with comprehensions, which makes the task of generating specific lists, etc., easy and the last section concludes the chapter.

The chapter assumes importance as it forms the foundation stone of many of the difficult tasks presented in the following chapters. Also, the knowledge of these will make the day to day tasks easy and spare the programmer from the horror of writing long codes.

6.2 THE POWER OF "FOR"

A `for` loop can be used to iterate through a list, tuple, string, or a dictionary. This section briefly explains how to use the loop for the above iterable objects. Let us start with the syntax of `for`.

Syntax

```
for i in L:
    #do something
```

L is list, string, tuple or dictionary

When one writes " `i in L`", where `L` is a list, `i` becomes the first element of the list and as the iteration progresses, `i` becomes the second element, the third element and so on. These elements can be then independently manipulated. The concept has been exemplified in Illustration 6.1. The illustration shows the manipulation of a list using the `for` loop. In the illustration the given list contains a set of numbers, some of them positive and some negative. The negative numbers are appended to a list called N, where the positive numbers are appended in a list called P.

Illustration 6.1: From a given list, put all the positive numbers in one list and negative numbers in the other list.

Solution: Create two lists, P and N. Initialize both of them to []. Now check each number in the list. If the number is positive put it in P and if the number is negative put it in N.

Program

```
L= [1, 2, 5, 7, -1, 3, -6, 7]
P=[]
N=[]
for num in L:
 if(num >0):
    P.append(num)
 elif (num<0):
    N.append(num)
print('The list of positive numbers \t:',P)
print('The list of negative numbers \t:',N)
>>>
```

Output

```
========== RUN C:/Python/Iterations/for list.py ==========
The list of positive numbers  : [1, 2, 5, 7, 3, 7]
The list of negative numbers  : [-1, -6]
>>>
```

A `for` loop can also be used to manipulate strings. When one writes " `i in str`", where `str` is a string, `i` becomes the first character of the string and as the iteration progresses, `i` becomes the second character, the third character and so on. These characters can be then independently manipulated. The concept has been exemplified in Illustration 6.2, in which the vowels and consonants of a given string are put in two strings.

Illustration 6.2: Ask the user to enter a string and put all the vowels of the string in one string and the consonants in the other string.

Solution: Create two strings: `str1` and `str2`. Initialize both to `""`. Now, check each character in the given string. If it is a vowel, concatenate it with `str1` otherwise concatenate it with `str2`.

Program

```
string =input('Enter a string\t:')
str1=""
str2=""
for i in string:
    if((i =='a')|(i=='e')|(i=='i')|(i=='o')|(i=='u')):
        str1=str1+str(i)
    else :
        str2=str2+str(i)
```

```
print('The string containing the vowels is '+str1)
print('The string containing consonants '+str2)
>>
```

Similarly, a *for* loop can be used to iterate through a tuple and keys of a dictionary as shown in Illustrations 6.3 and 6.4.

Illustration 6.3: This illustration demonstrates the use of `for` for iterating through a tuple.

Solution:

```
T=(1, 2, 3)
for i in T:
 print(i)
print(T)
>>>
```

Output

```
========== RUN C:/Python/Iterations/forTuple.py ==========
1
2
3
(1, 2, 3)
>>>
```

Illustration 6.4: This illustration demonstrates the use of `for` for iterating through a dictionary.

Solution:

```
Dictionary={'Programming in C#': 499, 'Algorithms
                            Analysis and Design':599}
print(Dictionary)
for i in Dictionary:
 print(i)
>>>
```

Output

```
========== RUN C:/Python/Iterations/for dic.py ==========
{'Programming in C#': 499, 'Algorithms Analysis and
                            Design': 599}
Programming in C#
Algorithms Analysis and Design
>>>
```

6.3 ITERATORS

The above tasks (Illustrations 6.1-6.4) can also be accomplished using iterators. The "iter" function returns the iterator of the object passed as an argument. The iterator can be used to manipulate lists, strings, tuples, files, and dictionary, in the same way as a for loop. However, the use of an iterator ensures flexibility and additional power to a programmer. This will be established in the following sections.

An iterator can be set on a list using the following:

```
<name of the iterator> = iter(<name of the List>
```

The iterator can move to the next element, using the _next_() method. An iterator, as stated earlier, can iterate through any iterable object including lists, tuples, strings or a directory. When there are no more elements then a StopIteration exception is raised.

The following illustration shows the manipulation of a list using iterators. In the illustration, the given list contains a set of numbers, some of them positive and some negative. The negative numbers are appended to a list called N, whereas the positive numbers are appended in a list called P. The same problem was solved using the for loop in Illustration 6.1.

Illustration 6.5: Using iterators the program puts the positive and negative numbers of a list into two separate lists and raises an error at the end of the program.

Solution:

```
L = [ 1,2,3,-4,-5,-6]
P = []
N = []
t = iter(L)
try:
    while True:
            x = t. next ()
            if x >= 0:
                    P.append(x)
            else:
                    N.append(x)
except StopIteration:
    print( 'original List- ' , L , '\nList containing the
            positive numbers- ', P , '\nList containing the
                                    negative numbers- ', N )

    raise StopIteration
```

The next example deals with a string. The iterator is set to the first element of the string and is then set to the second element, third element and so on. If the character is a vowel it is appended to `vow`, otherwise it is appended to `cons`. The following illustration uses the same problem as that stated in Illustration 6.2.

Illustration 6.6: Write a program that uses iterators to separate the vowels and consonants of a given string and raises an error at the end of the program.

Solution: The `vow` and `cons` strings are initialized to `""` and each character of the given list is checked. If the character is a consonant it is concatenated to `cons`, otherwise it is concatenated to vow.

```
s = 'color'
t = iter(s)
vow = ''
cons = ''
try:
    while True:
            x = t._next_()
            if x in ['a','e','i','o','u']:
                        vow += x
            else:
                        cons += x
except StopIteration:
    print( 'String - ' + s + '\nVowels - ' + vow + '\
                        nConsonents - ' + cons )
    raise StopIteration
```

A slightly more complex application of iterators has been shown in the following illustration.

Illustration 6.7: Write a program to add the corresponding elements of two given lists and sort the final list.

Solution:

```
#The program concatenates two lists into one by iterating
    over individual elements of the lists using the list
        function and then sorts the concatenated list.
l1 = [ 3, 6, 1, 8, 5]
l2 = [ 7, 4, 6, 2, 9]
i1 = iter(l1)
```

```
i2 = iter(l2)
l3 = sorted( list(i1) + list(i2) )
print( 'List1 - ', l1 , '\nList2 - ', l2 , '\nSortedCombn
                                      - ', l3 )
```

6.4   DEFINING AN ITERABLE OBJECT

One can define a class, in which _init_, _iter_, and _next_ can be
defined as per the requirement. The init function initializes the variables of the class, the iter defines the mechanism of iterations and the next
method implements the jump to the next item.

Illustration 6.8: Generate the terms of an arithmetic progression using an
iterator by creating an iterable object.

Solution:

```
class yrange:
    def _init_(self, n):
        self.a = int(input('Enter the first term\t:'))
        self.d=int(input('Enter the common differnce\t:'))
        self.i=self.a
        self.n=n

def _iter_(self):
    return self
def _next_(self):
    if self.i <self.n:
        i=self.i
        self.i = self.i + self.d
        return i
    else:
        raise StopIteration()
y=yrange
y._init_(y, 8)
print(y)
print(y._next_(y))
print(y._next_(y))
print(y._next_(y))

>>>
```

Output

```
=========== RUN C:/Python/Iterations/Class.py ===========
Enter the first term     :1
Enter the common differnce     :2
<class ' main .yrange'>
1
3
5
>>>
```

6.5   GENERATORS

Generators are functions that generate the requisite sequences. However, there is an inherent difference between a normal function and a generator. In a generator, the values are generated as and when we proceed. So, if one comes back to the function once a particular value is generated, then instead of starting from the beginning the function starts from the point where we left off.

The task seems difficult but has an advantage. The concept can help the programmer to generate lists containing the desired sequences. For example if one wants to generate a list containing the terms of an arithmetic progression in which each term is "d" more than the first term, `generators` come to the rescue. Similarly, the sequences like geometric progression, Fibonacci series, etc., can be easily generated using generator.

Python comes with `'yield'`, which helps to start from the point where we left off. This is markedly different from `'return'` used in normal functions which does not save the state where we left off. If the function having `'return'` is called again, it starts all over again.

The following illustration exemplifies the use of generators to produce simple sequences like arithmetic progression, geometric progression, Fibonacci series, etc.

Illustration 6.9: Write a generator to produce arithmetic progression where in the first term, the common difference and the number of terms is entered by the user.

Solution:

```
def arithmetic_progression(a, d, n):
  i=1
```

```
  while i<=n:
    yield (a+(i-1)*d)
    i+=1
a=int(input('Enter the first term of the arithmetic
                                   progression\t:'))
d=int(input('Enter the common differnce of the arithmetic
                                   progression\t:'))
n=int(input('Enter the number of terms of the arithmetic
                                   progression\t:'))
ap = arithmetic_progression(a, d, n)
print(ap)
for i in ap:
  print(i)
>>>
```

Output

```
========= RUN C:/Python/Iterations/generator 1.py =========
Enter the first term of the arithmetic progression :3
Enter the common difference of the arithmetic progression :5
Enter the number of terms of the arithmetic progression :8
<generator object arithmetic_progression at 0x031C2DE0>
3
8
13
18
23
28
33
38
>>>
```

Illustration 6.10: Write a generator to produce geometric progression, where in the first term the common ratio and the number of terms is entered by the user.

Solution:

```
def geometric_progression(a, r, n):
  i=1
  while i<=n:
    yield(a*pow(a, i-1))
    i+=1
a=int(input('Enter the first term of the geometric
                                   progression\t:'))
```

```
r=int(input('Enter the common ratio of the geometric
                                    progression\t:'))
n=int(input('Enter the number o0f terms of the geometric
                                    progression\t:'))
gp=geometric_progression(a, r, n)
for i in gp:
  print(i)
>>>
```

Output

```
======== RUN C:/Python/Iterations/generators gp.py ========
Enter the first term of the geometric progression :3
Enter the common ratio of the geometric progression :4
Enter the number o0f terms of the geometric progession :7
3
9
27
81
243
729
2187
>>>
```

Illustration 6.11: Write a generator to produce a Fibonacci series.

Solution:

```
def fib(n):
  a=[]
  if n==1:
    a[0]=1
    yield 1
  elif n==2:
    a[1]=1
    yield 1
  else:
    a[0]=1
    a[1]=1
    i=2
    while i<=n:
      a[i]=a[i-1]+a[i-2]
    yield (a[i])
n=int(input('Enter the number of terms\t:'))
fibList=fib(n)
```

```
for i in fibList:
  print(i)
  >>>
```

In order to understand the concept, let us go through the following illustration.

Illustration 6.12: This illustration demonstrates the effect of yield on the value of the counter.

Solution: The reader is expected to note the change in the value after and before yield.

Program

```
def demo():
    print ('Start')
    for i in range(20):
      print('Value of i before yield\t:',i)
      yield i
      print('Value of i after yield\t:',i)
    print('End')
a=demo()
for i in a:
    print (i)
```

Output

```
========== RUN C:/Python/Iterations/generator. py ==========
Start
Value of i before yield   : 0
0
Value of i after yield    : 0
Value of i before yield   : 1
1
Value of i after yield    : 1
Value of i before yield   : 2
2
Value of i after yield    : 2
Value of i before yield   : 3
3
Value of i after yield    : 3
Value of i before yield   : 4
4
Value of i after yield    : 4
Value of i before yield   : 5
5
```

```
Value of i after yield    : 5
Value of i before yield   : 6
6
Value of i after yield    : 6
Value of i before yield   : 7
7
Value of i after yield    : 7
Value of i before yield   : 8
8
Value of i after yield    : 8
Value of i before yield   : 9
9
Value of i after yield    : 9
Value of i before yield   : 10
10
Value of i after yield    : 10
Value of i before yield   : 11
11
Value of i after yield    : 11
Value of i before yield   : 12
12
Value of i after yield    : 12
Value of i before yield   : 13
13
Value of i after yield    : 13
Value of i before yield   : 14
14
Value of i after yield    : 14
Value of i before yield   : 15
15
Value of i after yield    : 15
Value of i before yield   : 16
16
Value of i after yield    : 16
Value of i before yield   : 17
17
Value of i after yield    : 17
Value of i before yield   : 18
18
Value of i after yield    : 18
Value of i before yield   : 19
19
Value of i after yield    : 19
End
>>>
```

6.6   COMPREHENSIONS

The aim of a programming language should be to make things easy for a programmer. A task can be performed in many ways but one which requires the least coding is the most appealing to a coder. Python has many features which facilitate programming. Comprehensions are one of them. Comprehensions allow sequences to be built from other sequences. Comprehensions can be used for lists, dictionary and set comprehension. In the earlier version of Python (Python 2.0) only list comprehensions were allowed. However, in the newer versions comprehensions can be used with dictionary and sets also.

The following illustration explains the use of comprehensions to generate lists in various cases:

- The range (n) function generates numbers up to n. The first comprehension generates the list of numbers which are cubes of all the numbers generated by the range function.
- The second comprehension works in the same way but generates 3 to the power of x.
- The third comprehension generates a list having numbers generated by the range (n) function, which are multiples of 5.

In the fourth comprehension the comprehension takes the words of the sentence "Winter is coming" and generates a list containing the word in caps, in running and the length of the word.

Illustration 6.13: Generate the following lists using comprehensions

- x^3, i from 0 to 9
- 3^x, i from 2 to 10
- All the multiples of 5 from the previous list
- The caps, running version and the length of each word in the sentence "Winter is coming"

Solution:

```
L1 = [x**3 for x in range(10)]
print(L1)
L2 = [3**x for x in range(2, 10, 1)]
print(L2)
L3 = [x for x in L2 if x%5==0]
print(L3)
String = "Winter is comming".split()
print(String)
```

```
String_cases=[[w.upper(), w.lower(), len(w)] for w in String]
for i in String_cases:
    print(i)
list1 = [1, '4', 9, 'a', 0, 4]
square_int = [ x**2 for x in list1 if type(x)==int]
print(square_int)
>>>
```

Output

```
>>>
====== RUN C:/Python/Iterations/Comprehensions 1.py ======
[0, 1, 8, 27, 64, 125, 216, 343, 512, 729]
[9, 27, 81, 243, 729, 2187, 6561, 19683]
[]
['Winter', 'is', 'comming']
['WINTER', 'winter', 6]
['IS', 'is', 2]
['COMMING', 'comming', 7]
[1, 81, 0, 16]
>>>
```

A comprehension contains the input sequence along with the expression that represents the members. A comprehension may also have an optional predicate expression.

In order to understand the concept let us consider one more illustration. The list of temperatures in Celsius is given and the corresponding list containing the temperatures in Kelvin is to be generated. It may be stated here that the temperatures in Celsius and Kelvin are related as follows.

$$\text{Kelvin (T)} = \text{Celsius(T)} + 273.16$$

Illustration 6.14: Given a list containing temperatures in Celsius, generate a list containing temperatures in Kelvin.

Solution: The list L_kelvin, is a list where in each element is 273.16 more than the corresponding element in L_cel. Note that the task has been accomplished in the definition of the list L_Kelvin itself.

Program

```
L_Cel = [21.2, 56.6, 89.2, 90,1, 78.1]
L_Kelvin = [x +273.16 for x in L_Cel]
print('The output list')
for i in L_Kelvin:
    print(i)
```

Output

```
>>>
====== RUN C:/Python/Iterations/comprehension_cel.py ======
The output list
294.36
329.76000000000005
362.36
363.16
274.16
351.26
>>>
```

Another important application of comprehension is to generate the Cartesian product of two sets. The cross product of two sets, A and B, is a set containing tuples of the form (x, y), where x belongs to the set A and y belongs to the set B. Illustration 6.15 implements the program.

Illustration 6.15: Find the Cartesian product of two given sets.

Solution:

```
A= ['a', 'b', 'c']
B= [1, 2, 3, 4]
AXB = [(x, y) for x in A for y in B]
for i in AXB:
  print(i)
  >>>
```

Output

```
======== RUN C:/Python/Iterations/cross_product.py ========
('a', 1)
('a', 2)
('a', 3)
('a', 4)
('b', 1)
('b', 2)
('b', 3)
('b', 4)
('c', 1)
('c', 2)
('c', 3)
('c', 4)
>>>
```

The above program is important because the concept of relations and therefore functions in mathematics originates from the cross product. As a matter of fact any subset of A × B is a relation from A to B. There are four types of relations in mathematics: one to one, one to many, many to one, and many to many. Out of these relations, one to one and many to one are referred to as functions.

6.7 CONCLUSION

The chapter explains the use of `for` for iterating over a list, string, tuple, or a dictionary. It may be stated here that in C or C++, *for* is generally used for the same purpose as `while`. However in Python, `for` can be used to visit each element individually. Note that this can also be done in Java or C#. In order to define an iterable object, `_iter` and `_next` need to be defined for the requisite class. The reader is also expected to take note of the fact that `yield` and `return` perform different tasks in Python. The use of these two has been demonstrated in the illustrations presented in this chapter. Finally, while defining a list each element can be crafted as per the need of the question. This can be done with the help of comprehensions. The chapter, though easy, becomes important in the light of excessive use of these techniques in machine learning and pattern recognition tasks which are introduced in the last section of this book.

GLOSSARY

- Iterator takes an iterable object and helps to traverse the object.
- `_next_()`: The next function helps in iterating over the value of the iterable object.
- `_iter_()`: It helps in creating a user defined iterable object.
- `yield()`: It does not return anything.

POINTS TO REMEMBER

- `for` statement can be used for looping over a list, string, tuple, file, and dictionary
- `iter` takes an object and returns the corresponding iterator
- The `_next_` gives us the next element
- Built in functions, lists, etc., accept iterator as arguments
- A generator produces a sequence of results
- Yield is used when many values are to be produced from a function/generator

EXERCISES

MULTIPLE CHOICE QUESTIONS

1. Which of the following can be an argument in `_iter()_`?
   (a) String
   (b) Tuple
   (c) List
   (d) Dictionary
   (e) All of the above

2. The `iter` takes which type of object?
   (a) Iterable
   (b) Any object
   (c) Comprehension
   (d) Generator

3. What is the function of `_next()_`?
   (a) To iterate over the items of an iterable object.
   (b) To produce a new iteration
   (c) To iterate through a generator
   (d) None of the above

4. Which of the following transfers the control to the calling function?
   (a) `return`
   (b) `yield`
   (c) Both
   (d) None of the above

5. Which of the following does not transfer the control to the calling function?
    (*a*) `return`   (*b*) `yield`
    (*c*) Both   (*d*) None of the above

6. Which of the following is essentially used in generators?
    (*a*) `yield`   (*b*) `return`
    (*c*) Both   (*d*) None of the above

7. Which of the following is true?
    (*a*) One can use iterators with generators
    (*b*) One can use iterators with list
    (*c*) One can use iterators with comprehensions
    (*d*) All of the above

8. Which of the following can be iterated using a `for` loop
    (*a*) String   (*b*) List
    (*c*) Tuple   (*d*) All of the above

9. Which of the following can be iterated using a `for` loop
    (*a*) String   (*b*) Comprehension
    (*c*) File   (*d*) All of the above

10. Which of the following behaves in the same manner as the combination of `_iter()_` and `_next()_`?
    (*a*) `for`   (*b*) `if`
    (*c*) Both   (*d*) None of the above

THEORY

1. Explain how a `for` can be used to iterate over an iterable object.

2. Explain the iteration protocol in Python.

3. What is the function of a generator?

4. What is the difference between `yield` and `return`?

5. What are list comprehensions? Explain how comprehensions help in generating a sequence.

6. Explore some iteration tools in Python.

7. Do you believe that `iter` improves the time complexity vis-a-vis `for`?

PROGRAMMING EXERCISE

1. Write a generator that produces the terms of arithmetic progression.

2. For the above question write the corresponding iterator class.

3. Write a generator that produces the terms of a geometrical progression.

4. For the above question write the corresponding iterator class.

5. Write a generator that produces the terms of a harmonic progression.

6. For the above question write the corresponding iterator class.

7. Write a generator that produces all the prime numbers up to a given number.

8. For the above question write the corresponding iterator class.

9. Write a generator that produces all the Fibonacci numbers up to n.

10. For the above question write the corresponding iterator class.

11. Write a generator that produces all the Armstrong numbers up to n.

12. For the above question write the corresponding iterator class.

13. Write a generator that produces Pythagoras triples in the range $(1, 20)$.

14. For the above question write the corresponding iterator class.

15. Write a generator that produces all the multiples of 6 up to the given number.

16. For the above question write the corresponding iterator class.

17. Write a list comprehension that produces all the numbers that are multiple of 2 or 5.

18. Write a list comprehension that converts a list containing the temperature in degrees Celsius to that in Fahrenheit.

19. Write a list comprehension that produces all the prime numbers.

20. Write a list comprehension that produces all the numbers which leave remainder 1 when divided by 5.

21. Write a list comprehension that produces all the vowels of a given string.

22. Write a list comprehension that produces the fourth power of numbers of a given list.

23. Write a list comprehension that produces the absolute values of numbers in a given list.

FILE HANDLING

After reading this chapter, the reader will be able to

- Understand the importance of file handling
- Appreciate the mechanisms of file handling in Python
- Learn various file access modes and the open function
- Understand various functions for file handling in Python
- Implement the concepts studied in the chapter

7.1 INTRODUCTION

The data types and control structures discussed so far will help us to accomplish many simple tasks. The problem so far is that we have not been able to store the data or the results obtained for future use. Moreover, at times the results produced by a program are voluminous. In such cases it becomes difficult to store data in the memory or even to read the data. In such cases file handling comes to our rescue.

The reader will also appreciate the fact that the main memory is volatile. The data produced by a program cannot be used for future endeavors. Many times it is required to store the data for use in future. For example, if one develops a student management system, the user should be able to retrieve the data as and when required.

As we understand, the data is stored in the binary format in a disk. Therefore, while storing data the format of the data should be taken care of. At the programmer's level, however, the data can be stored in files or in databases. Databases store and manage related data. The ease of retrieval, the security and the flexibility make databases one of the most important topics in computer science. The concept of databases, their usage, and related issues constitute a dedicated subject. This chapter only concentrates on file handling. A file can be perceived as set of records where each record has some fields. The fields, in turn, have certain bytes. Files, as discussed later, can have many formats. This chapter concentrates on binary and text files. The two formats differ in the representation of the end of the file and in the storage of standard data types. A file may have certain permissions associated with it. For example, one may not have write permissions for a file which is to be used by the operating system. For that matter, a user may not even have read permissions for such files. Such constraints need to be kept in mind while writing programs for file handling.

Python provides many functions to carry out operations related to file handling. The creation of a file, writing data to a file, reading the data, appending something to the file and standard directory operations are discussed in this chapter. Moreover, to make things interesting the use of the above operations in encryption has also been discussed.

The chapter has been organized as follows. The second section discusses the general file handling mechanism. The third section discusses the `open()` function and the various modes in which a file can be opened. The fourth section discusses the functions for reading and writing to the file. This section also introduces the functions to get and set the position of a cursor in a file. The fourth section also discusses some important factions to carry out various tasks and the fifth section briefly discusses the command line arguments. The last section of this chapter concludes.

7.2   THE FILE HANDLING MECHANISM

In Python, files are accessed using the file objects. As a matter of fact, the file objects help us to access not just normal disk files but can help us to accomplish many other tasks involving other kinds of files, which are explained later in this chapter.

The file handling mechanism in Python is simple. The file needs to be opened first. As in, the file is hooked to an Object [1]. This is done with the help of the `open()` function. The function takes the name of the file and the mode as its arguments. In fact, the function can have three arguments. The third is discussed in the next section. The `open` function returns an object of the file. The object then uses the library functions to read the file, write into it or append it. Finally, the memory space occupied by the object is freed using the `close()` function. The mechanism has been depicted in the following figure (Figure 7.1).

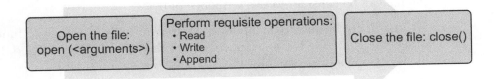

FIGURE 7.1 File handling in Python

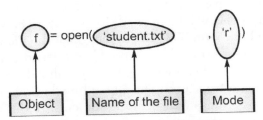

FIGURE 7.2(a) The open function

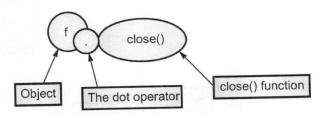

FIGURE 7.2(b) The close function

Having discussed the mechanism of handling a file, now let us move on to the file access modes and the open function in Python.

7.3 THE OPEN FUNCTION AND FILE ACCESS MODES

The files are accessed using the object created with the help of `open()` function. In fact, there are many more functions used to create an object of the file type. Note that the said functions return a file object or a file like object. This abstraction is helpful for considering files as interfaces for communication. This communication can be perceived as a transfer of bytes and the file can be considered as a sequence of bytes.

So, in order to be able to do input/output to/from a file, the `open()` function is needed. If the file is opened successfully, the file object is returned. If the file is not opened successfully, the `IOERROR` exception is raised.

The `open` function takes three arguments. The first argument is the name of the file, the second the mode in which the file is opened and the third indicates the buffer string. As a matter of fact, the third will rarely be used. The first argument is a string of characters, which is either a valid filename or a path. The path can be relative or absolute. The access mode is the mode in which the file will be opened (Figure 7.2). The various modes have been presented in Figure 7.3. The modes open the file in read, write or append mode. In the read mode ("*r*") the file is opened, if it exists. The write mode ("*w*") opens the file for writing. If the file already exists, the existing contents of the file are truncated. The append mode ("*a*") opens the file for writing but does not truncate the existing contents. In this mode if the file does not exist, it will be created.

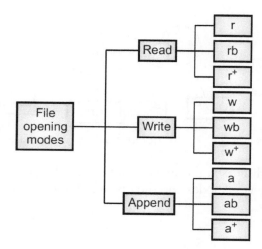

FIGURE 7.3 File opening modes in Python

The modes can be suffixed with a letter "*b*" indicating binary access. The "+" suffix can be used to grant read and write access to the file. Table 7.1 presents the various modes and the corresponding operations that can be performed.

Table 7.1 Access modes for File

File Mode	Operations
r	reading from a file
w	write to a file; creates the file if it does not exist; truncate the file if it already exists.
a	append to the file; if the file does not exist this creates the file
r+	open for read and write
w+	w for both read and write
a+	a for both read and write
rb	read a binary file
wb	write mode for a binary file
ab	append mode for a binary file
rb+	r+ for a binary file
wb+	w+ for a binary file
ab+	a+ for a binary file

7.4   PYTHON FUNCTIONS FOR FILE HANDLING

Python provides various library functions to carry out the standard tasks. The functions help us, say, to read from a file, write to a file and to append something in the existing file. Moreover, Python also provides the programmer with functions to take the cursor to a particular location, or to read from a given location.

7.4.1   The Essential Ones

This section briefly introduces the various functions. The use of these functions has been explained in the following sections. The reader is expected to experiment with the functions in order to get a clear insight into them.

The `read()` function

The function reads bytes in a string. It may take an integer argument indicating the number of bytes to read. If the argument is -1, the files must be read to the end. Also if no argument is given, the default is taken as -1.

Tip

`read()` is same as `read(-1)`

If the content of the file is larger than the memory then only the content which can fit into the memory will be read. Moreover, when the read operation ends a " "(an empty string) is returned.

`readline()` and `readlines()`

The `readline()` method is used to read a line until the newline character is read. It may be stated here that the newline character is retained in the string that is returned. The `readlines()` method reads all the lines from a given file and returns a list of strings.

`write()` and `writelines()`

The `write()` method writes the string in a given file. The method is complementary to the `read()` method. The `writelines()` method writes a list of strings to the file.

Tip

There is no `writeline()` method in Python 3.x

`seek()`

The `seek()` method takes the cursor to the starting position in the given file. The position is decided with respect to the offset given. The offset can be 0, 1, or 2. "0" indicates the beginning of the file. The value "1" indicates the current position and the value "2" indicates the "end of the file."

`tell()`

`tell()` is complementary to the `seek()` function. The function returns the position of the cursor.

close()

The close() function closes the file. The object should be assigned to another file after it is closed. Though Python closes a file after a program finishes (see garbage collection in the following chapters), it is advisable to close the file when the required task is accomplished. The repercussions of not closing the file can be observed at the most unexpected times.

fileno()

The fileno() function returns a descriptor for the file. For example, the descriptor of the file named "Textfile.txt," in the following snippet is 3.

```
>>> f=open('Textfile.txt')
>>> f.fileno()
3
>>>
```

7.4.2   The OS Methods

The methods that deal with the issues related to operating systems help the programmer to create a generic program. The methods also spare the programmer from the horror of dealing with uncanny formatting details. For example, the end of a line is represented by different character sets in different operating systems. In Unix, a newline is indicated by "\n," In MAC the newline character is, "\r" and in DOS it is "\r\n." Similarly, file separator Unix is "/,", whereas that in Windows is "\" and that in MAC is ":." Their inconsistencies make the life of a programmer miserable. This is the reason why a consistent approach is needed to handle such situations. Table 7.2 presents the names and functions of OS methods.

Table 7.2 OS methods

os method	Function
linesep	string used to separate lines in a file
sep	used to separate file pathname components
pathsep	delimit a set of file pathnames
curdir	current directory
pardir	parent directory

7.4.3 Miscellaneous Functions and File Attributes

As well as the functions stated above, flush and isatty are also used to make a program more robust.

flush(): The flush function flushes the internal buffer.

isatty(): The function returns a "1," if the file is a tty-like device.

For more such functions, the reader may refer to the Appendix of this book.

File attributes

It may also be stated here that the file attributes help the programmer to see the state of a file and its features like the name, mode, and the softspace. Table 7.3 presents some of the most important file attributes.

Table 7.3 File attributes

File Attribute	Importance
file.closed	1 if file is closed, 0 otherwise
file.mode	access mode
file.name	name of the file

The following illustration demonstrates the use of the above attributes.

Illustration 7.1: Open a file called "Textfile.txt" in the read mode. Check the name of the file, its mode, and find whether it is closed using the file attributes.

Solution:

```
f=open('Textfile.txt','r')
print('Name of the file\t:',f.name)
print('Mode\t:',f.mode)
print('File closed?\t:',f.closed)
f.close()
print('Mode\t:',f.mode)
print('File cloased?\t:',f.closed)
```

Output

```
>>>
========= RUN C:/Python/file handling/fileattar.py =========
Name of the file  : Textfile.txt
```

```
Mode  : r
File closed?      : False
Mode  : r
File closed?      : True
>>>
```

7.5 COMMAND LINE ARGUMENTS

If the compiler knows the name of the script, then the name of the script along with the additional arguments that may be given along are stored in a list called `argv`. The `argv` variable is in the `sys` module. The arguments, along with the name of the script, are called the command line arguments. It may be noted here that even the name of the script is part of the list. As a matter of fact, the name of the script is the first element of the list. The rest of the arguments are stored in the succeeding locations of the list. The `argv` can be accessed by importing the sys module. The following illustration demonstrates the use of the `argv` variable.

Illustration 7.2: Display the number of command line arguments and the individual arguments.

Solution:

```
import sys
print('The number of arguments',len(sys.argv))
print('Arguments\n')
for x in sys.argv:
    print('Argument\t:',x)
```

Output

```
>>>
======= RUN C:/Python/file handling/commandLine.py =======
The number of arguments 1
Arguments
Argument : C:/Python/file handling/commandLine.py
>>>
```

The following example presents the bubble sort which takes the numbers entered at the command line as the input.

Illustration 7.3: Sort the numbers (using bubble sort) entered as the command line arguments.

Solution:

```python
import sys
def sort(L):
    i=0;
    while(i<(len(L)-1)):
        print('\nIteration\t:',i,'\n');
        j=0
        flag=0
        while(j<(len(L)-i-1)):
        if(L[j]<L[j+1]):
          flag=1
          temp=L[j]
          L[j]=L[j+1]
          L[j+1]=temp
        #print(L[j],end=' ')
        j=j+1
      print(L)
      if(flag==0): break
      i=i+1
    return(L)
L=[]
for x in sys.argv:
    L.append(x)
print('Before sorting\t:',L)
print(sort(L))
```

7.6 IMPLEMENTATION AND ILLUSTRATIONS

Having seen the mechanism of file handling, the functions and the attributes, let us now have a look at the usage of the above functions. We will begin with the most basic tasks and then use the functions to write something to a file (say "TextFile.txt"), and open the file in the write mode. The open function, in this case, will have two parameters: name of the file ("TextFile.txt") and the mode ("w"). Also, the file needs to be closed. Note that the write function returns the number of bytes written in the file.

```python
>>> f = open('TextFile.txt','w')
>>> f.write('Hi there\nHow are you?')
21
>>> f.close()
```

The read function reads the bytes of the given file. The open function, as stated earlier, may not take any argument. This implies reading a file until the end. The read text can be stored in a string ("text").

```
>>> text=f.read()
>>> text
'Hi there\nHow are you?'
>>> f.close()
>>>
```

A file can be renamed using the rename function of OS. The rename function takes two arguments: the first being the name of the original file and the second being the new name of the file. In the following snippet, a file called "TextFile.txt" is renamed to "TextFile1.txt" and read into "str" using the open function.

```
>>> import os
>>> os.rename('TextFile.txt','TextFile1.txt')
>>> f=open('TextFile1.txt','r')
>>> str=f.read()
>>> str
'Hi thereHow are you'
>>>
```

Writing a list of strings in a file

As stated earlier, a list of strings can be written into a file using the write-lines() function. The use of the function has been illustrated as follows. In the following snippet, the lines entered by the user are put into a list, L, and this list is then written into the file f.

Illustration 7.4: Write a program to ask the user to enter lines of text. The user should be able to enter any number of lines. In order to stop, he must enter "\e." The lines should be appended to an empty list (say L). This list should then be written to a file called lines.txt. The program should then read the lines of lines.txt.

Solution:

```
print('Enter text, press \'\\e\' to exit')
L=[]
i=1
in1=input('Line number'+str(i)+'\t:')
while(in1 !='\e'):
    L.append(in1)
    i=i+1
    in1=input('Line number'+str(i)+'\t:')
```

```
print(L)
f=open('Lines.txt','w')
f.writelines(L)
f.close()
f=open('lines.txt','r')
for l in f.readline():
    print(l, end=' ')
f.close()>>>
```

Output

```
========== RUN C:/Python/file handling/Write.py ==========
Enter text, press '\e' to exit
Line number1      :Hi there
Line number2      :How are you
Line number3      :I am good
Line number4      :\e
['Hi there', 'How are you', 'I am good']
Hi      there How are      youI am good
>>>
```

Reading *n* characters and the seek() function

The use of the `read(n)` function, which reads the first "n" characters of the file has been demonstrated in the following illustration (Illustration 7.5). Note that the tell function tells the position of the cursor, which is why the value of `pos` changes as and when we move forward. The `seek()` function takes two parameters, the first being the offset and the second the position. Note that `seek(0, 0)` positions the cursor at the first position from the beginning.

Illustration 7.5: Open a file TextFile.txt and write a few lines in it. Now open the file in the read mode and read the first 15 characters from the file. Then read the next five characters. In each step show the position of the cursor in the file. Now, go back to the first position in the file and read 20 characters from the file.

Solution:

```
f=open('TextFile.txt','w')
f.writelines(['Hi there', 'How are you'])
f.close()
f = open('TextFile.txt', 'r+')
str =  f.read(15)
```

```
print('String str\t: ', str)
pos = f.tell()
print('Current position\t:', pos)
str1=f.read(5)
print('Str1\t:',str1)
pos = f.seek(0, 0)
print('Current position\t:',pos)
str = f.read(20);
print('Again read String is : ', str)
f.close()
```

Output

```
>>>
========= RUN C:\Python\file handling\Position.py =========
String str  : Hi thereHow are
Current position  : 15
Str1  : you
Current position  : 0
Again read String is : Hi thereHow are you
>>>
```

Creating directories and navigating between them

One can also create directories in Python using the `mkdir()` function. The function takes the name of the directory as one of the essential arguments. The reader is advised go through the appendix of this book for a detailed description. The `chdir()` function changes the current directory and the `getpwd()` function prints the name (along with the path) of the current working directory. The use of these functions has been demonstrated as follows:

```
'>>> import os
>>> os.mkdir('PythonDirectory')
>>> os.chdir('PythonDirectory')
>>> os.getcwd()
'C:\\Python\\file handling\\PythonDirectory'
>>>
```

An example of encryption

The following illustration uses the `ord(c)` function which prints the ASCII value of the character "*c*," and that of the `chr(n)` function which returns a character corresponding to the ASCII value *n*.

Illustration 7.6: Write "Hi there how are you" in a file called "TextFile. txt." Now, read characters from the file, one by one and write the character obtained by adding *k* (entered by the user) to the ASCII value of the character. Also, decrypt the string in the second file by subtracting "k" from the ASCII values of the characters in the second file.

Solution:

```
f=open('TextFile.txt','w')
f.write('Hi there how are you')
f.close()
k=int(input('Enter a number'))
f =open('TextFile.txt','r')
f1=open('TextFile1.txt','w')
for s in f.read():
    for c in s:
        print('Character ',c,' Ascii value\t:',ord(c))
        f1.write(str(chr(ord(c)+k)))

f1.close()
print((open('TextFile1.txt').read()))
f1 =open('TextFile1.txt','r')
f2=open('TextFile2.txt','w')
for s in f1.read():
    for c in s:
        print('Character ',c,' Ascii value\t:',ord(c))
        f2.write(str(chr(ord(c)-k)))
f2.close()
print((open('TextFile2.txt').read()))
```

Output

```
Enter a number4
Character H Ascii value     : 72
Character i Ascii value     : 105
Character   Ascii value     : 32
Character t Ascii value     : 116
Character h Ascii value     : 104
Character e Ascii value     : 101
Character r Ascii value     : 114
Character e Ascii value     : 101
Character   Ascii value     : 32
Character h Ascii value     : 104
Character o Ascii value     : 111
Character w Ascii value     : 119
```

```
Character   Ascii value   : 32
Character a Ascii value   : 97
Character r Ascii value   : 114
Character e Ascii value   : 101
Character   Ascii value   : 32
Character y Ascii value   : 121
Character o Ascii value   : 111
Character u Ascii value   : 117
Lm$xlivi$ls{$evi$}sy
Character L Ascii value   : 76
Character m Ascii value   : 109
Character $ Ascii value   : 36
Character x Ascii value   : 120
Character l Ascii value   : 108
Character i Ascii value   : 105
Character v Ascii value   : 118
Character i Ascii value   : 105
Character $ Ascii value   : 36
Character l Ascii value   : 108
Character s Ascii value   : 115
Character { Ascii value   : 123
Character $ Ascii value   : 36
Character e Ascii value   : 101
Character v Ascii value   : 118
Character i Ascii value   : 105
Character $ Ascii value   : 36
Character } Ascii value   : 125
Character s Ascii value   : 115
Character y Ascii value   : 121
Hi there how are you
>>>
```

7.7 CONCLUSION

File handing provides the user with the power of persistence. The user must be equipped with the knowhow of the file access modes, the `open()`, `close()` functions and the functions which help in reading a file and writing to it. The chapter briefly explains the most essential functions used for file handling in Python. The chapter also introduces the user to OS methods and the essential file attributes to help the user achieve the task at hand. The chapter includes ample illustrations and explanations to make the concept clear in the simplest manner. The reader is advised to go through the appendix for a detailed explanation of the different types of files in Python and a detailed write up on command line arguments.

POINTS TO REMEMBER

- The open function takes three arguments.
- The mode of opening file decides the tasks that can be accomplished.
- The file should be closed after the required task has been completed.
- The `seek` method helps to move the cursor within a file.
- The `file name` attribute prints the name of the file.
- The `file mode` attribute gives the file access mode.
- The `os.getpwd` function returns the present working directory.
- The `os.chdir` function changes the directory.

EXERCISES

MULTIPLE CHOICE QUESTIONS

1. Which of the following is a solid argument for using file handling?
   (*a*) It is not possible to store all data produced by the program in the main memory
   (*b*) It is used for persistent storage
   (*c*) Both
   (*d*) None of the above

2. In which of the formats is the end of the line denoted by "\n" and "\r"?
   (*a*) Text   (*b*) Binary
   (*c*) Both   (*d*) None of the above

3. To be able to use a file it must be opened. The reason for doing so is
   (*a*) To allocate memory to the object formed
   (*b*) To specify the access mode
   (*c*) To specify the offset (optional)
   (*d*) All of the above

4. In f = open("*abc*.txt", "*r*"), the offset is
    (*a*) 0 from the beginning   (*b*) 0 from the end
    (*c*) Random   (*d*) None of the above

5. How many arguments does the open function take?
    (*a*) 1   (*b*) 2
    (*c*) 3   (*d*) None of the above

6. The file must be closed if it is opened in which of the following modes?
    (*a*) *r*   (*b*) *w*
    (*c*) Both   (*d*) None of the above

7. If the file is not opened successfully, which of the following exceptions is raised?
    (*a*) File not found   (*b*) IOERROR
    (*c*) IO   (*d*) None of the above

8. In f = open("*abc*.txt", "*w*"), if the file "*abc*.txt" does not exist, then
    (*a*) IOERROR is raised   (*b*) The program does not compile
    (*c*) A new file is created   (*d*) None of the above

9. Which suffix is used for opening a binary file
    (*a*) *b*   (*b*) bin
    (*c*) *ab*   (*d*) None of the above

10. The + suffix allows
    (*a*) Read   (*b*) Read and write
    (*c*) Read or write   (*d*) None of the above

11. How many file access modes are there in Python?
    (*a*) 3   (*b*) 6
    (*c*) 9   (*d*) 12

12. The integer argument in the read() function denotes the number of bytes to be read; if no argument is given, which of the following is the default argument?
    (*a*) –1   (*b*) 0
    (*c*) len(file)   (*d*) None of the above

13. To read all the lines in a file, which of the following functions can be used?
    (a) readline ()   (b) readlines ()
    (c) Both   (d) None of the above

14. Which of the following methods can be used to write a list of strings in a file?
    (a) writeline ()   (b) writelines ()
    (c) write ()   (d) None of the above

15. Which of the following arguments in the seek() function denotes the end of the file?
    (a) 1   (b) 2
    (c) 0   (d) None of the above

16. Which function returns the descriptor of the file?
    (a) fileno ()   (b) filedisp()
    (c) descriptor ()   (d) None of the above

17. The `linesep` function is used to find which of the following?
    (a) The new line   (b) The end of the file
    (c) The current directory   (d) None of the above

18. Which of the following is not a file attribute?
    (a) Closed   (b) Opened
    (c) Name   (d) Softspace

19. In which of the following variables is the command line argument saved?
    (a) argv   (b) argc
    (c) Both   (d) None of the above

20. Which of the following functions helps to create a directory?
    (a) os.mkdir()   (b) os.chdir()
    (c) os.getpwd()   (d) None of the above

21. Which of the following functions helps to change the current directory?
    (*a*) os.mkdir() (*b*) os.chdir()
    (*c*) os.getpwd() (*d*) None of the above

22. Which of the following functions helps to print the name of the current directory?
    (*a*) os.mkdir() (*b*) os.chdir()
    (*c*) os.getpwd() (*d*) None of the above

23. Which function is used to find the ASCII value of a character?
    (*a*) ascii (*b*) ord
    (*c*) chord (*d*) None of the above

24. Which of the following is not a file access mode in Python?
    (*a*) a (*b*) ab
    (*c*) ab+ (*d*) abc

25. Which of the following is incorrect?
    (*a*) *f* = open ('file.txt') (*b*) *f* = open('file.txt','*r*')
    (*c*) *f* = open ('file.txt','*r*',0) (*d*) None of the above is incorrect

THEORY

1. What is the importance of file handling? Explain the mechanism of file handling in Python.

2. Explain various file access modes.

3. Explain the signature and usage of the following functions
    (*a*) open (*b*) close
    (*c*) read (*d*) write
    (*e*) readline (*f*) readlines
    (*g*) writeline (*h*) seek

4. What are file attributes? Explain the file attributes provided by Python.

5. Briefly explain the usage of the following os functions in Python
   (*a*) mkdir   (*b*) chdir
   (*c*) getpwds

PROGRAMMING

1. Write a program to copy the contents of one file to another.

2. Write a program to capitalize the first character of each word in a file.

3. Write a program to find the ASCII value of each character in a file.

4. Write a program to find the frequency of each character in a file.

5. Write a program to find all occurrences of a word, entered by the user, in a given file.

6. Write a program to replace a given character with another in a file.

7. Write a program to replace a given word with another, in a given file.

8. Write a program to find the frequency of a given word in a file.

9. Write a program to find the word used the minimum number of times in a given file.

10. Write a program to change the name of a file to the name entered by the user.

11. Write a program to create a directory and then create a new file in it.

12. Write a program to print the name, number of characters, and number of spaces in a file.

13. Write a program to convert the characters of a given file to binary format.

14. Write a program to find the words starting with a vowel from a given file.

15. Write a program to implement any substitution cipher on the text of a given file.

CHAPTER **8**

STRINGS

After reading this chapter, the reader will be able to

- Understand the concept and importance of strings
- Understand various string operators
- Learn about the built in functions to manipulate strings
- Learn how to solve problems using strings

8.1 INTRODUCTION

Strings are a sequence of characters. These data structures are used to store text. For example if one wants to store the name of a person, or for that matter his address, then string is the most appropriate data structure. As a matter of fact, the knowledge of strings is essential in the development of many applications like word processor and parser.

Strings in Python can be enclosed in single quotes or double quotes, or even in triple quotes. However, there is no difference between a string enclosed in single quotes or double quotes. That is "harsh" is same as "harsh." Triple quotes are generally used in special cases discussed later in the chapter. Strings in Python come with a wide variety of operators and built-in functions.

The chapter examines various aspects of strings like non-mutability, traversal, operators, and built-in functions. One of the most prominent differences between a string and a list is non-mutability. Once a value is given to a string, one cannot change the value of a character present at a particular position. For the users familiar with C, C++, C#, or Java, the operators discussed in the chapter - notably the * operator - will be a pleasant surprise. Moreover, Python provides many built in functions to help the programmers to handle strings.

This chapter examines the above issues and provides examples of them. The chapter has been organized as follows. The second section of the chapter explores the use of standard 'for' and 'while' loops in strings. The third section deals with the operators that can be used with strings. The built-in functions used for accomplishing various tasks have been dealt with in the fourth section and the last section concludes the chapter.

8.2   THE USE OF "FOR" AND "WHILE"

The traversal of a string has already been discussed in Chapter 4 of this book. This section revisits the 'for' and 'while' and their applications in strings.

As stated in the second and the fourth chapter, strings are iterable objects. The standard loops (read 'for' and 'while') can be used to iterate over a string. The 'for' loop helps to iterate through each character by storing the character in some variable. The following illustration depicts the use of a for loop to iterate the string.

The examples that follow use the for loop to carry out some basic and some intricate tasks. Basic tasks like calculating the length of a given string have been exemplified in Illustration 8.2. Illustrations 8.3, 8.4, and 8.5 implement transposition and substitution.

Illustration 8.1: Write a program to traverse a string.

Solution: Writing for i in <string> helps us to access one character at a time from a given string. The variable 'str1' stores the string entered by the user and it is iterated using the for loop.

Listing

```
str1= input('Enter a string\t:')
for i in str1:
    print('Character \t:',i)>>>
```

Output

```
=============== RUN C:/Python/String/str2.py ===============
Enter a string    :harsh
Character         :h
Character         :a
Character         :r
Character         :s
Character         :h
```

The above methodology can also help us to find the length of string. Note that there is a built-in function to accomplish the said task. However, the purpose here is to be able to use the `'for'` loop in order to imitate the `len` function. In the following illustration, a variable called length is initialized to 0 and is incremented as we proceed.

Illustration 8.2: Write a program to find the length of the string entered by the user.

Solution: The concept has already been explained in the above discussion. The code follows.

Listing

```
name=input('Enter your name\t');
length=0
for i in name:
    length=length +1
print('The length of ',name,' is ',length)
```

Output

```
=============== RUN C:/Python/String/str1.py ===============
Enter your name    harsh
The length of      harsh    is    5
>>>
```

The ability to handle each character individually in a string gives the power to manipulate a given string. One of the exciting tasks can be to implement basic cryptography techniques. The example that follows displaces the characters two positions to the right. This is referred to as transposition. The next example shifts the characters by "k" positions, "k" being entered by the user.

Illustration 8.3: Ask the user to enter a string and displace two characters to the right.

Solution: Note that in each iteration, the position of the characters is shifted by two positions. The code follows:

```
str1=input('Enter the string\t:')
i=0
str2=""
while i<len(str1):
    str2[i]=str1[(i+2)%len(str1)]
print(str2)
```

Illustration 8.4: Ask the user to enter a string and displace k characters to the right.

Solution: Note that in each iteration, the position of the characters is shifted by k positions. The code follows:

```
str1=input('Enter the string\t:')
k=int(input('Enter the value of k\t:'))
i=0
str2=""
while i<len(str1):
    str2+=str1[(i+k)%len(str1)]
    print(str2)
    i+=1
print(str2)
    >>>
```

Output

```
========== RUN C:/Python/String/transposition.py ==========
Enter the string  :harsh
Enter the value of k    4
h
hh
hha
hhar
hhars
hhars
>>>
```

Another method of encryption is substitution. The replacement of a symbol by some other symbol is referred to as substitution. The example that follows implements one of the most basic types of substitutions. Here, each character is replaced by a character obtained by adding two to the ASCII value of the character, and finding the requisite character.

Illustration 8.5: Ask the user to enter a string. Replace each character by that obtained by adding two to the ASCII value of that character.

Solution:

```
str1=input('Enter the string\t:')
k=int(input('Enter the value of k\t:'))
i=0
str2=""
while i<len(str1):
    str2+=str((ascii(str1[i])+k))
    print(str2)
    i+=1
print(str2)
```

8.3   STRING OPERATORS

Python provides the programmer with a wide variety of extremely useful operators to manipulate strings. These operators help a user perform involved tasks with ease and efficiency. Here, it may be stated that the replication and membership operators make Python stand apart from its counterparts. This section briefly introduces and exemplifies these operators.

8.3.1   The Concatenation Operator (+)

The concatenation operator takes two strings and produces a concatenated string. The operator acts on values as well as variables. In the examples that follow, the concatenation operator's result has been stored in variables called result1 and str2.

```
name=input('Enter your name\t:')
result1 = 'Hi'+' there'
print(result1)
str1='Hello'
str2=str1 +' '+name
print(str2)
```

Output

```
>>>
============= RUN C:/Python/String/operator1.py =============
Enter your name    :Harsh
```

```
Hi there
Hello Harsh
>>>
```

Note that the same operator is used for adding two integers.

8.3.2 The Replication Operator

The replication operator in Python replicates the strings as many times as the first operand. The operator operates on two operands: the first being a number and the second being a string. The result is a string in which the input string is repeated as many times as the first argument. In the example that follows, the result has been stored in a variable called `result1`.

```
name=input('Enter your name\t:')
print('Hi', ' ', name)
str1=input('Enter a string\t:')
num=int(input('Enter a number\t:'))
result1=num*str1
print(result1)
```

Output

```
>>>
============= RUN C:/Python/String/operato2.py =============
Enter your name   :harsh
Hi harsh
Enter a string    :abc
Enter a number    4
abcabcabcabc
>>>
```

8.3.3 The Membership Operator

The membership operator checks whether a given string is present in a given list or not. The operator returns a True if the first string is a part of the given list, otherwise it returns a False.

```
>>> 'Hari' in ['Har', 'Hari', 'Hai']
True
>>>
>>> 'Hari' in ['Har', 'hari', 'Hai']
False
>>>
```

It may be noted here that this operator is also used for manipulating iterations. The reader is advised to go through Chapter 4 of this book for a detailed discussion regarding the use of "in" in for. It may also be noted that the operator can also be used in tuples. In the listing that follows, the string "Hari" is present in the given tuple and hence True is returned.

```
>>> 'Hari' in ('Hari', 'Har')
True
>>>
```

The reader may also note that corresponding to the "in" operator, there is a "not in" operator which works in the exactly opposite manner vis-a-vis "in."

A string in Python can span over many lines. This can be accomplished by putting a "\" at the end of the line. For example, str2 is "Harsh Bhasin Author Delhi". However, it has been written in three lines using the "\" character.

```
>>> str2="'Harsh Bhasin\
Author\
Delhi'"
>>> str2
"'Harsh BhasinAuthorDelhi'"
```

8.4 FUNCTIONS FOR STRING HANDLING

This section presents some of the most common functions used to manipulate strings in Python. It may be stated here that, although all the following tasks can be done without the predefined functions with varying degree of ease, the presence of these functions help the programmer to do the task easily and efficiently. Moreover when one crafts and implements one's version of a function, the implementation may not be efficient in terms of time or space or both. However, while crafting these predefined functions in Python the issues related to memory and time should be handled. Let us now have a look at the names, meanings, and usage of the pre-defined functions in Python.

8.4.1 len

Usage:

```
>>> len()
```

Explanation:

The function returns the number of characters in a string. For example if a variable called `str1` stores `'Harsh Bhasin'`, then the length of the string can be calculated by writing `len(str1)`. Note that the space between `'Harsh'` and `'Bhasin'` has also been taken into account while calculating the length of the string. The function takes a string argument and returns an integer, which is the length of the string.

Example (s):

```
>>> str1 ='Harsh Bhasin'
>>> len(str1)
12
>>>
>>> len('Harsh Bhasin')
12
>>>
>>> len('')
0
```

8.4.2 Capitalize

Usage:

```
>>> capitalize()
```

Explanation:

The function capitalizes the first character of the string. Note that only the first character will be capitalized. If one wants to capitalize the first characters of all the words in the string the `title()` function can be used.

Example (s):

```
>>> str2='harsh bhasin'
>>> str2
'harsh bhasin'
>>> str2.capitalize()
'Harsh bhasin'
```

8.4.3 find

Usage:

```
>>><name of the string>.find(<parameter(s)>)
```

Explanation:

The location of a given sub-string in a given string can be found by using the function find. Also, if the location of a sub-string after a particular position (and before a particular index) is to be determined, then three arguments can be passed to the function: the sub-string, initial index, and the final index. The following examples show the usage of the function.

Example(s):

```
>>> str2.find('ha')
0
>>>
>>> str2.find('ha',3,len(str2))
7
```

8.4.4 count

Usage:

```
>>><name of the string>.count(<parameter(s)>)
```

Explanation:

The number of occurrences of a particular substring can be found with the count function. The function takes three arguments: the sub-string, the initial index, and the final index. The following examples show the usage of the function.

Example(s):

```
>>> str3.count('ha',0,len(str3))
1
>>> str3.count('ka',0,len(str3))
0
```

8.4.5 Endswith

```
Usage: <name of the string>.endswith(<parameter(s)>)
```

Explanation:

One can determine if a string ends with a particular sub-string. This can be done using the endswith() function. The function returns a 'True' if the given string ends with the given sub-string, otherwise it returns a 'False'.

Example(s):

```
>>> str3.endswith('n')
True
```

8.4.6 Encode

```
Usage: <name of the string>.encode(<parameter(s)>)
>>>
```

Explanation:

Python provides a function to encode a given string in various formats. The function is `encode`. It takes two arguments: encoding=<value> and errors=<value>. The encoding can be one of the many encodings given in Appendix B of this book. The following examples demonstrate the use of this function.

Example(s):

```
>>> str3.encode(encoding='utf32',errors='strict')
b'\xff\xfe\x00\x00H\x00\x00\x00A\x00\x00\x00R\x00\x00\
    x00S\x00\x00\x00H\x00\x00\x00 \x00\x00\x00b\x00\x00\
    x00h\x00\x00\x00a\x00\x00\x00s\x00\x00\x00i\x00\x00\
                                x00n\x00\x00\x00'
```

8.4.7 Decode

Usage:

```
>>><name of the string>.decode(<parameter(s)>)
```

Explanation:

The function returns the decoded string.

8.4.8 Miscellaneous Functions

Though the purpose, usage and examples of the most important functions have been explained, the following functions are also important. A list of some more functions follows. The list is followed by a brief explanation.

List:

1. isanum()
2. isalpha()
3. isdecimal()

```
 4.  isdigit()
 5.  isidentifier()
 6.  islower()
 7.  isupper()
 8.  swapcase()
 9.  isspace()
10.  lstrip()
11.  rstrip()
12.  replace()
13.  join()
14.  strip() removes the leading and leaning spaces
```

Explanation:

The contents of a given string can be checked using the following functions. The isalnum() function if the given string is alphanumeric. The other functions like isalpha() and isdecimal() also check the type of contents in a given string.

Whether a given string contains only digits can be checked using the isdigit() function. Similarly, whether a given string is an identifier can be checked using the isidentifier() function. The islower() function checks if the given string contains only lower case characters and the isupper() function checks if the given string contains only upper case characters. The swapcase() function swaps the case of the given string, as in converts the upper case to lower and lower to upper. The presence of spaces (only) can be checked using the isspace() function. Extra spaces can be removed from the left and the right hand sides by using the lstrip() and rstrip() functions. The replace() function replaces the instances of the first argument by the string in the second argument. The split function splits the given strings into tokens. Illustration 8.6 depicts the use of this function for splitting the string into constituent words. The function of join() is exactly the opposite as that of split.

Example(s):

```
>>> str3.isalnum()
False
>>> str3.isalpha()
False
>>>
>>> str3.isdecimal()
False
>>>
>>> str3.isdigit()
```

```
False
>>>
>>> str3.isidentifier()
False
>>>
>>> str3.islower()
False
>>>
>>> str3.isnumeric()
False
>>>
>>> str3.replace('h','p')
'HARSH bpasin'
>>>
```

Illustration 8.6: A string str4 contains a sentence "I am a good boy." Split the string and also display each token using a for loop.

Solution:

```
>>> str4='I am a good boy'
>>> str4.split()
['I', 'am', 'a', 'good', 'boy']
>>>
>>> for i in str4.split():
          print('Token\t:',i)
```

Output

```
Token : I
Token : am
Token : a
Token : good
Token : boy
```

8.5   CONCLUSION

In C and C++, strings used to be character arrays. They were a special type of arrays with a "\0" character at the end. Strings in "C" came with a set of built-in functions. However, there were two problems. Firstly string was not an independent data type, and secondly an individual character could be changed. In Python, the importance of strings has been duly recognized by creating an object type. Moreover strings, in Python, are non-mutable. Strings come with a wide range of built-in functions. Also there are useful operators to help the programmer accomplish a given task easily and efficiently. This chapter introduces the concept, operators and functions of strings. However, the reader is expected to complete the end-chapter exercise to be able to understand and use strings.

GLOSSARY

String: Strings are a sequence of characters. These data structures are used to store text.

IMPORTANT POINTS

- Strings in Python are non-mutable.
- The negative index denotes the characters from the right hand.
- Strings are iterable objects.

EXERCISES

MULTIPLE CHOICE QUESTIONS

1. Which of the following is true?
   (*a*) A string in Python is iterable
   (*b*) A string in Python is not iterable
   (*c*) Iterablity of a string depends upon the situation
   (*d*) None of the above

2. Is a string in Python mutable?
   (*a*) No   (*b*) Yes
   (*c*) Depends on the situation   (*d*) None of the above

3. If `str1='Hari'`, what is the output of `print(str1[4])`
   (*a*) i   (*b*) \0
   (*c*) Exception is raised   (*d*) None of the above

4. If `str1='Hari'`, what is the output of `print(str1[-3])`
   (*a*) "a"   (*b*) "H"
   (*c*) Exception is raised   (*d*) None of the above

5. What is the output of `"Hari"=="hari"`
   (*a*) True   (*b*) False
   (*c*) An exception is raised   (*d*) None of the above

6. What is the output of `'a'!='A'`
   (*a*) True   (*b*) False
   (*c*) Exception is raised   (*d*) None of the above

7. What is the output of `'567'>'989'`
   (*a*) True   (*b*) False
   (*c*) An exception is raised   (*d*) None of the above

8. Which of the following helps to find the ASCII value of "C"?
   (*a*) `ord('C')`   (*b*) `chr('C')`
   (*c*) both   (*d*) None of the above

9. Which of the following helps to find the character represented by ASCII value 67?
   (*a*) `ord(67)`   (*b*) `chr(67)`
   (*c*) Both   (*d*) None of the above

10. What are `'in'` and `'not in'`, in Python?
    (*a*) Relational operators   (*b*) Membership operators
    (*c*) Concatenation operators   (*d*) None of the above

11. What is the output of `'A' + 'B'`
    (*a*) `'A+B'`   (*b*) `'AB'`
    (*c*) 131   (*d*) None of the above

12. What is the output of `3*'A'`
    (*a*) `'3A'`
    (*b*) Character corresponding to the ascii value 65 × 3?
    (*c*) `'AAA'`
    (*d*) None of the above

13. Which function capitalizes the first character of a given string?
    (*a*) `capitilize()`   (*b*) `titlecase()`
    (*c*) `toupper()`   (*d*) None of the above

14. The `find()` function in Python takes
    (*a*) 1 argument   (*b*) 3 arguments
    (*c*) Both   (*d*) None of the above

15. If `str1='hari'`, then what would be the output of `isalnum()`?
    (*a*) True   (*b*) False
    (*c*) Exception is raised (*d*) None of the above

16. If `str1='hari3'`, then what would be the output of `str1.asalnum()`?
    (*a*) True   (*b*) False
    (*c*) Exception is raised (*d*) None of the above

17. If `str1='hari feb'`, then what would be the output of `str1.asalnum()`?
    (*a*) True   (*b*) False
    (*c*) Exception is raised (*d*) None of the above

18. If `str1='123h'`, then what would be the output of `str1.isdigit()`?
    (*a*) True   (*b*) False
    (*c*) Exception is raised (*d*) None of the above

19. Which function checks whether all the characters in a given string are in lower case?
    (*a*) `lower()`   (*b*) `islower()`
    (*c*) `istitle()`   (*d*) None of the above

20. Which function checks whether all the characters in a given string are in upper case?

(a) upper() (b) isupper()

(c) istitle() (d) None of the above

21. Which function removes the whitespaces from the right hand of a given string?

(a) rstrip() (b) strip()

(c) lstrip() (d) None of the above

22. Which of the following functions convert a given string into a list of words?

(a) split() (b) break()

(c) breakup() (d) None of the above

23. Which of the following helps in breaking a string into two substrings of desirable length?

(a) Slicing (b) Splitting

(c) Both (d) None of the above

24. Which of the following functions combines the strings given as the argument?

(a) Split (b) Join

(c) Slice (d) None of the above

25. Which of the following is illegal in Python (assume that str1 is a string, having initial value 'hari')?

(a) str1= 'Harsh' (b) str1[0]= 't'

(c) str1[0]=str[2] (d) None of the above

THEORY

1. What is a string? Explain non-mutability. Is there any difference between a string in double quotes and that in triple quotes?

2. Explain the following functions vis-vis strings.

- +
- *
- in
- not-in

3. Explain the following string operators by giving an example.

- `capitalize()`
- `title()`
- `len()`
- `find()`
- `count()`
- `endswith()`
- `encode()`
- `decode()`

4. What is the difference between a string in Python and a string in "C"?

5. What is the difference between a list and a string?

PROGRAMMING PROBLEMS

1. Write a program to reverse a string.

2. Write a program to encode a string in UTF format.

3. Write a program to find the sum of ASCII values of the characters of a given string.

4. Write a program to find a particular substring in a given string.

5. Write a program to split a given text into tokens.

6. Write a program to check which of the tokens obtained in the above question are keywords.

7. Write a program to check how many alphanumeric strings there are in the tokens obtained in question 5.

8. Write a program to check how many alpha strings there are in the tokens obtained in question 5.

9. Write a program to check how many numeric strings there are in the tokens obtained in question 5.

10. Write a program to convert a string entered by a user to that obtained by adding "k" to each character's ASCII value.

11. Implement the first phase of compiler design (for "C"). Please refer to the following link for a brief overview of compiler design.

12. In the above question design deterministic finite acceptors for the keywords.

USEFUL LINKS

Strings and regular expressions are extensively used in developing the first phase of a compiler. The following links will be helpful to understand the topic:

- *https://www.cs.cmu.edu/~fp/courses/15411-f13/lectures/07-lex.pdf*
- *http://www.iith.ac.in/~ramakrishna/Compilers-Aug15/slides/02-lexical-analysis- part-1.pdf*
- *https://www.cs.utexas.edu/users/novak/cs375contents.html*

## CHAPTER 9

INTRODUCTION TO OBJECT ORIENTED PARADIGM

After reading this chapter, the reader will be able to

- Understand procedural, modular and object oriented paradigm
- Understand the concept of class
- Design a class
- Understand the elements of object oriented programming

9.1 INTRODUCTION

In the preceding chapters, the control structures of Python were discussed. The first section discussed loops, conditional statements, etc. However, these constructs were an integral part of C as well, which is a procedural language. The procedural programming is one that uses procedures. Each procedure is a set of instructions where each instruction directs the computer what is to be done. Python also supports object-oriented programming (OOP). This chapter introduces the principles of OOP and explains the need and importance of classes and objects. The chapter also discusses the difference between OOP and procedural programming to give an insight of why OOP is needed.

It may be stated here that the topics discussed in this chapter will be discussed in detail in the following chapters. Some of the readers not familiar with C++ (or for that matter C# or Java) may find the discussion abstract, but things will become clear as we proceed.

As stated earlier, in procedural programming each statement tells the program what to do. For example the following code asks the user for the input, calculates the square root and displays the result.

Code

```
>>> a = float(input("Enter a number\t:"))
Enter a number: 67
>>> b = math.sqrt(a)
>>> b
8.18535277187245
>>>
```

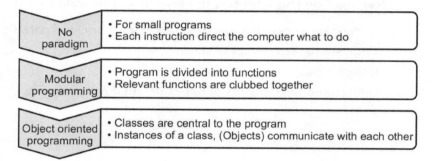

FIGURE 9.1 Programming paradigms

This strategy is good if the program is very small. Often telling the computer what to do, step by step, works if the task to be accomplished is not very complex. In such cases no other paradigm is needed.

In case of a moderately large program, division into functions makes the task easier. The division of a larger program into functions makes the program manageable and helps to achieve reusability of code. The functions generally accomplish a clearly defined task and become handy whenever that particular task is to be accomplished. The reader is advised to go through the chapter on functions in order to understand the advantages of functions. The clubbing together of functions on some basis give rise to what are commonly referred to as modules. The programming paradigm is called `modular programming`.

The problem with this paradigm is that the accidental clubbing together of unrelated functions, far from the real world situations, become a source of problems at some point in time. Moreover, the approach does not restrict the access of data in any module and may jeopardize the sanctity of the data.

It may be noted that the data should not be accessible to all the modules. The accessibility of data must be managed with utmost care otherwise a module, which should not have alerted the data as per the program logic, might change the data.

In order to understand the gravity of the problem, let us take an example of C. In C, a variable can be global or local. If it is global, then any module can change it. If it is local, then other modules cannot access it. So there is nothing in between. That is, we cannot make a variable which can be accessed only by designated methods not data.

The solution to the above problem is to model the software in such a way that the design is conceptually as close to the real world as possible. This modelling of real world situations requires the creation of entities having both attributes and behavior. The clubbing together of data and the functions that manipulate the data are be helpful in crafting the above entities. These entities will henceforth be referred to as `classes`. The instances of classes are `objects` and the paradigm is called `object oriented paradigm`. Various programming paradigms and their disadvantages have been summarized in Figure 9.1.

9.2 CREATING NEW TYPES

Though types are not explicitly declared in Python, the types were important in other languages (well most of them). For example, when one says that a "number" is of integer type, then he not only states the type of information but also its maximum and minimum value. Assume that an integer takes two bytes; the maximum value of "number" would be 32, 767 and the minimum value would be –32, 768. Moreover, saying that "number" is of integer type also specifies the operations that can be performed on the number.

Integer is a pre-defined type. Most of the languages also allow the user to create custom types and hence extend the power of built-in types. This is essential as the ability to create new data types will help us to create programs which are near to the real world. For example if one has to design an inventory management system then a type called "item" would make the matters uncomplicated. This item can have variables which are of predefined types, like integers and strings.

A new type can be created by declaring a class. A class has many components, most important of which are attributes and functions. This clubbing together of functions and data forms the basis of OOP. The functions, as we will see later, generally manipulate the data members of a class. Before proceeding any further let us have an overview of attributes and functions.

9.3 ATTRIBUTES AND FUNCTIONS

One can perceive a class as a prototype and an object as an instance of a class. For example, "movie" is a class and "The Fault in Our Stars", "Love Actually" and "Sarat" are objects (Figure 2). A class has attributes and behavior. The attributes generally store data and the behavior is implemented using functions. A class can be depicted using a class diagram. A class diagram has, generally, three parts; the first part contains the name, the second part has attributes, and the third part shows the functions of a class. The basics of attributes and behavior are discussed in the following section. In Figure 9.2, the class diagram (movie) has only the name.

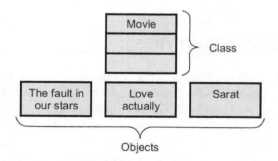

FIGURE 9.2 Example of a class and objects

9.3.1 Attributes

The attributes here depict the characteristics of the entity that we are concerned with. For example, when creating a website that gives the details of movies, a class `'movie'` will be needed. Say after detailed deliberations it was decided that this class would have attributes like name, year, genre, director, producer, actors, music director, and story writer.

Note that for the said purpose, only the above details are needed. Storing unnecessary details will not only make data management difficult, but will also violate one of the core principles - that of including only the details pertaining to the problem at hand. These attributes are generally shown in the second section of the class diagram. In Figure 9.3, the attributes of "movie" class have been shown.

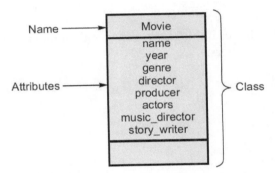

FIGURE 9.3 Name and attributes of a movie class

9.3.2 Functions

The next step will be to include functions in the above class. In our example there are two functions - `getdata()` and `putdata()`. The `getdata()` function asks for the values of the variables from the user and the `putdata()` function will display the data. Functions implement the behavior of a class. The functions, as stated earlier, accomplish a particular task. In a class there can be any number of functions, each accomplishing a particular task. As a matter of fact we have special functions for initializing the data members of a class as well. The functions of a class will henceforth be referred to as member functions. The functions (or behavior) are shown in the third section of a class diagram. In Figure 9.4, the functions of the "movie" class (`getdata()` and `putdata()`) have been shown in the third box.

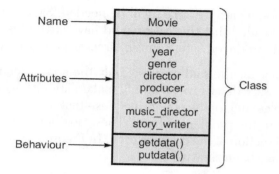

FIGURE 9.4 Name, attributes, and functions of a movie class

The following example shows a class called movies. The class has the following data members:

- Name
- Year
- Genre
- Director
- Producer
- Actors
- Music_Director
- Story_writer

The class has two functions - `getdata()`, which asks the user to enter the values of the data members and `putdata()`, which displays the values of the variables. In order to call the functions `getdata()` and `putdata()`, an instance of the employee class is created (`'m'`). As we will see later, the functions are called using the dot operator. The details regarding the syntax will be explained in the following chapter.

The following code implements the above class. Though the syntax etic.. has not been discussed as of yet, the code has been given to give an idea of how things actually work.

Code

```
class movie:
  def getdata(self):
    self.name=input('Enter name\t:')
    self.year=int(input('Enter year\t:'))
    self.genre=input('Enter genre\t:')
    self.director=input('Enter the name of the director\t:')
```

```
        self.producer=input('Enter the producer\t:')
        L=[]
        item=input('Enter the name of the actor\t:')
        L.append(item)
        choice=input('Press \'y\' for more \'n\' to quit')
        while(choice == "y"):
          item=input('Enter the name of the actor\t:')
          L.append(item)
         choice=input('Enter \'y\' for more \'n\' to quit')

        self.actors=L
        self.music_director=input('Enter the name of the
                                         music director\t:')
        def putdata(self):
        print('Name\t:',self.name)
        print('Year\t',self.year)
        print('Genre\t:',self.genre)
        print('Director\t:',self.director)
        print('Producer\t:',self.producer)
        print('Music_director\t:',self.music_director)
        print('Actors\t:',self.actors)
m=movie()
m.getdata()
m.putdata()
```

Output

```
============ RUN C:/Python/Class/class_basic2.py============
Enter name   :Kapoor
Enter year   :2016
Enter genre :Drama
Enter the name of the director       :ABC
Enter the producer       :Karan
Enter the name of the actor    :Siddarth
Press 'y' for more 'n' to quity
Enter the name of the actor    :Fawad
Enter 'y' for more 'n' to quitn
Enter the name of the music director       :XYZ
Name   :Kapoor
Year   2016
Genre :Drama
Director       :ABC
Producer       :Karan
Music_director       :XYZ
Actors         :['Siddarth', 'Fawad']
>>>
```

In object-oriented languages, a special function initializes the value of the data members. This function generally has the same name as that of the class. The function is called **constructor**.

One can create a **default constructor** in a class, which does not take any parameters. The **parameterized constructor**, on the other hand, takes arguments and initializes the data members using those arguments. The implementation of constructors and their uses will be dealt with in the next chapter.

When the lifetime of an object ends, a destructor is called. A **destructor** can be called using `'del'` in Python. The concept has been explained in the next chapter of this book.

Tip

A constructor acts when an object is created and a destructor is called when the lifetime of an object ends.

9.4   ELEMENTS OF OBJECT-ORIENTED PROGRAMMING

The following discussion briefly outlines the principles of object-oriented programming. The concepts encapsulation, data hiding, and polymorphism are all discussed in this section.

9.4.1   Class

A class is a real or a virtual entity, which has relevance to the problem at hand and has sharp physical boundaries. A class can be a real entity. For example, when one develops software for a car wash company, then `'Car'`, is central to the software and therefore there will be a class called `'Car'`. A class can also be a virtual entity. Another example is that when developing a student management system, a `'student'` class is crafted which is a virtual entity. In both the examples, the entity was crafted as it was important to the problem at hand.

The example of the `'student'` class can be taken further. The class will have attributes, which are needed in the program. The selection of attributes will decide on the physical boundaries of the class. The fact of the matter is we will not be needing unnecessary details like the number of cars a student has or where he went last evening in an educational institute for which we are making the student management system, so there is no point storing those details.

Examples of some of the classes that are central to the stated software are as follows (Table 9.1).

Table 9.1 Examples of classes central in various systems

System	class central to the software
Student Management System	Student
Employee Management System	Employee
Inventory Control	Item
Library Management	Book
Movie Review	Movie
Airline Management	Flight
Examination	Test

9.4.2 Object

Consider a student management system that stores the data of each student of a school. Note that while entering data the operator would deal with an individual student, not the idea of a student. The idea of a student is a class, whereas each student is an instance of class or an object.

An object is an instance of a class. The objects interact with each other and get the work done. Generally, a class can have any number of objects. One can even form an array of objects. The example of `movie` had `m` as an object. As a matter of fact, we make an object and call the methods of a class (those which can be called).

In object-oriented paradigm, the program revolves around an object and therefore the type of programming is termed as an object-oriented program. Calling a method of an object is equivalent to sending message to an object.

9.4.3 Encapsulation

The class is an entity, which has both data and functions. The clubbing together of the data and the functions that operate on the data is called encapsulation. Encapsulation is one of the core principles of object-oriented paradigm. Encapsulation not only makes it easier to handle objects but also improves the manageability of the software.

Moreover, the functions in a class can be used in variety of ways. Their accessibility of data members and member functions can also be managed using access specifiers, as explained in the following sub-section.

9.4.4   Data Hiding

Data hiding is another important principle of object-oriented programming. As stated in the above discussion, the accessibility of data can be governed in a class. The data, in the case of procedural programming, is accessible to all throughout the program. This is referred to as global data. The data private to a class is one which can be accessed only by the members of the class. There are other access specifiers as well, explained in the following sections.

In C++, for example, the data in a class is generally kept private. That is, only the member functions of the class can access the data. This ensures that the data is not accidently changed. The functions, on the other hand, are public in C++. The public functions can be accessed anywhere in the program (Figure 9.5). In C++, Java, C#, etc., there is another access specifier, which is protected. If a member is to be accessed in the class and the derived class, then a protected specifier is used. C# and Java also have some other specifiers like internal.

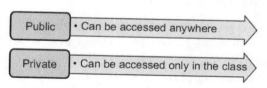

FIGURE 9.5 Access specifiers, public and private

Having discussed the data access, it must be clarified that deciding what is private and what is public is up to the discretion of the design and development team of the project. There is no hard and fast rule as to what should be private and what should be public. The designers must decide on the accessibility of a member based on their needs.

This protection of data is not related to the security of data but to accidental change. This is needed so that the data can be changed only via the functions which have the authority to change data.

9.4.5 Inheritance

Classes are made so that they can be sub-classed. This art of dividing the class into subclass(es) is inheritance. For example, the movie class can be sub-classed into various classes like `art_movie`, `commercial_movie`, etc. Likewise, the `student` class can be sub classed into `'regular stu-dent'` and `'part_time_student'`. In both the examples the subclass has many things which are there in the base class (the class from which the subclass has been derived) in common. In addition, each subclass can have functions and data that belongs to the sub-class only.

For example, the student class can have attributes namely `name, date_of_birth, address` etc. The subclass regular student will use all the above data members and can also have attributes like attendance associated with it. The class from which classes will be sub-classed is referred to as the base class and the subclasses would be called derived classes.

For example in Figure 9.6, `movie` is the base class and `commercial_movie` and `art_movie` are the sub-classes.

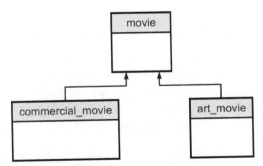

FIGURE 9.6 Deriving classes from other classes is inheritance. There are many types of inheritance. The above figure shows hierarchical inheritance

9.4.6 Polymorphism

Poly means many and morphism is forms, so polymorphism means many forms. Polymorphism can be implemented in many ways. One of the simplest examples of polymorphism is operator overloading. Operator overloading means using the same operator in more than one way. For example "+" is used between integers to add, with strings for concatenation and even can be used in user defined data types as explained in Chapter 12 of this book.

Likewise function overloading means having more than one function with the same name in a class with different arguments. Various forms of polymorphism are explained in Chapters 10 and 11 of this book.

9.4.7 Reusability

The procedural programming came with almost no reusability. Modular programming allowed reusability but only to certain extend. The functions could be used on an "as is basis" in modular programming. In object-oriented programming, the concept of reusability can be used in its full force. The concept of inheritance, introduced above and explained in Chapter 10 of this book, helps the programmer to reuse a code as per their requirements. a matter of fact, reusability is one of the USPs of the object-oriented paradigm.

However, there is a catch. Lately, some researchers have cast doubts on the ability of OOP vis-a-vis reusability.

9.5 CONCLUSION

While designing software, one must keep in mind the entities he is going to work on. The nitty-gritty can be decided at a later stage. As a matter of fact, popular literature does not consider the details of the operation as a matter of concern for the object-oriented programming. Hiding unnecessary details are, therefore, an important part of object-oriented programming.

For example, while developing a website for movies, the entity central to the problem is "Movie." So, one starts with an empty class called `"movie"`. The designer must then decide on the attributes needed to implement the functions. The attributes constitute the data members of the said class. The behavior of the entity is then deliberated upon. The member function determines the behavior of a class. The functions are then designed. The things like inheritance and polymorphism, discussed later in this section, come into play. And finally the system is created.

This journey of the formation of a class has been depicted in the following figure (Figure 9.7).

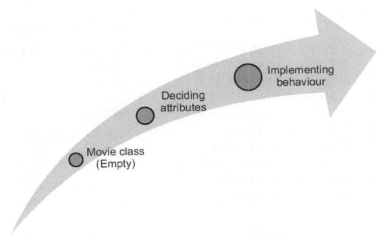

FIGURE 9.7 The design of a movie class

Programming is an art. A good programmer should be well-versed in the syntax of the language, the data structures and the concepts of algorithm analysis. In addition to the above, a programmer needs to decide the programming paradigm that he is going to use. The chapter briefly introduces various programming paradigms and the advantages and disadvantages of them. The chapter introduces the concept of object-oriented programming. The definitions of class, object, etc., have been discussed in the chapter. The chapter also introduces the features of OOP. The concepts introduced in this chapter will form the foundation of the rest of the chapter of this section. As already stated some of the concepts may appear abstract at this stage, but the following chapters will revisit the concepts and will demonstrate the implementation of the ideas dealt with in this chapter. In order to be able to make a program that uses OOP, one must get out of the mindset of doing things in procedural way and start thinking about the program that is centered on real world entities having attributes and behaviors.

It may also be stated that the designing of an object-oriented program is generally preceded by the design of class diagrams and sequence diagrams etc. These are part of Unified Modelling Language. The concept of class diagrams has been introduced in this chapter and UML has been introduced in the references at the end of the chapter. The reader is advised to go through the references at the end of the chapter before proceeding any further.

GLOSSARY

- **Class:** A class is a real or a virtual entity that has relevance to the problem at hand and has sharp physical boundaries.
- **Object:** An object is an instance of a class.
- **Encapsulation:** The clubbing together of the data and the functions that operate on the data is called encapsulation.
- **Inheritance:** The art of dividing the class into subclass(es) is inheritance.
- **Operator overloading:** Operator overloading, in general, means using the same operator in more than one way.
- **Function overloading:** This means having more than one function with the same name in a class with different arguments.

POINTS TO REMEMBER

- Telling the computer what to do, step by step, works if the task to be accomplished is not very complex. In such cases no other paradigm is needed.
- In the case of a moderately large program, division into functions makes the task easier.
- The division of a larger program into modules makes the program manageable and helps to achieve reusability of code.
- The clubbing together of functions, on some basis, gives rise to what is commonly referred to as modules. The programming paradigm is called modular programming.
- A class has two important components: attributes and behavior.
- A constructor initializes the members of a class.
- The destructor frees the memory occupied by an object.

EXERCISES

MULTIPLE CHOICE QUESTIONS

1. Which of the following is not object-oriented language?
   (a) C
   (b) C++
   (c) Python
   (d) C#

2. Which of the following is object-oriented language?
   (*a*) Python
   (*b*) C#
   (*c*) Java
   (*d*) All of the above

3. A student is a conceptual entity, which acts as a blueprint for each student. The mapping is similar to which of the following?
   (*a*) Class and object
   (*b*) Method and modular programming
   (*c*) Both
   (*d*) None of the above

4. Which of the following are the two most important components of a class?
   (*a*) Methods and attributes
   (*b*) List and tuple
   (*c*) Arrays and functions
   (*d*) None of the following

5. In object-oriented paradigm, a variable of a class is called
   (*a*) Data member
   (*b*) Member function
   (*c*) Global data
   (*d*) None of the above

6. In object-oriented paradigm, the functions of a class are
   (*a*) Member functions
   (*b*) Data members
   (*c*) Global functions
   (*d*) None of the above

7. An instance of a class is called
   (*a*) Object
   (*b*) Subject
   (*c*) Inject
   (*d*) None of the above

8. The clubbing together of data and the functions that operate on the data is called
   (*a*) Abstraction
   (*b*) Encapsulation
   (*c*) Overloading
   (*d*) None of the above

9. Allowing the selective access of data members in a class is the same as
   (*a*) Data Hiding
   (*b*) Encapsulation
   (*c*) Abstraction
   (*d*) None of the above

10. If we have the same name functions in a class, then it is called
    (a) Function overloading   (b) Overriding
    (c) Encapsulation   (d) None of the above

11. "+" can be used for adding two number types. However, a programmer can use "+" for the addition of two user defined data types (for example, complex numbers).
    This is
    (a) Method overloading   (b) Operator overloading
    (c) Encapsulation   (d) None of the above

12. Inheritance is helpful in handling
    (a) Reusability   (b) Redundancy
    (c) Overhead   (d) None of the above

13. If a function in the base class is extended in the derived class, then it is
    (a) Overloading   (b) Abstraction
    (c) Encapsulation   (d) None of the above

14. Which of the following is not a type of inheritance?
    (a) Simple   (b) Multiple
    (c) Hierarchical   (d) All of them are types of
                                          inheritance

15. Which of the following initializes the members of a class?
    (a) Constructor   (b) Destructor
    (c) Both   (d) None of the above

16. Which of the following is true for a well-defined class?
    (a) It has importance to a problem at hand
    (b) It has sharp physical boundaries
    (c) It is a real or a physical entity
    (d) All of the above

17. A language in which one can define a new data type is
    (*a*) Comprehensive   (*b*) Extensible
    (*c*) Both   (*d*) None of the above

18. In object-oriented paradigm, the focus is on
    (*a*) Data   (*b*) Way a work is done
    (*c*) Data Types   (*d*) None of the above

19. UML is
    (*a*) Ultra-Modern Language   (*b*) Unified Modelling Language
    (*c*) United Model League   (*d*) None of the above

20. Which of the following is not a principle of object-oriented paradigm?
    (*a*) Inheritance   (*b*) Data hiding
    (*c*) Encapsulation   (*d*) Divide and conquer

THEORY

1. Briefly explain the various paradigms of programming.

2. What is the difference between object-oriented paradigm and procedural programming?

3. What is a class? What are the essential components of a class? Define attributes and functions of a class.

4. What is the relation between an object and a class?

5. What is a class diagram? Give an example of a class diagram.

6. Explain the importance of encapsulation.

7. Explain the importance of data hiding. Is it related to the security of the data?

8. What is polymorphism? Explain the concept of operator overloading and function overloading.

9. What is the advantage of reusability? Explain the concept of reusability vis-a-vis object-oriented paradigm.

10. Explore some of the problems in object-oriented programming?

EXPLORE AND DESIGN

The reader is expected to go through material on the subject: Database Management System. The chapters on entity relationship diagrams have details of entities involved therein. Create class diagrams of the classes mentioned in Table 9.1, based on your research.

10

CLASSES AND OBJECTS

After reading this chapter, the reader will be able to

- Understand how to create a class in Python
- Instantiate a class
- Use objects
- Create member functions
- Differentiate between instance and class variables
- Use constructors and destructors
- Understand the type of constructors

10.1 INTRODUCTION TO CLASSES

Classes are real or virtual entities which have an importance to the problem at hand and sharp physical boundaries. The concept of classes has been discussed in the previous chapter. This chapter takes these discussions forward. It is easier to make a class in Python than in any other programming languages. A class in Python can hold any kind and any amount of data. Those with a C++ background might find the syntax and use of variables odd. As a matter of fact the mechanism of classes in Python is inspired not just by C++ but also by Modula-3.

A class in Python can be **sub-classed**. All types of inheritance, including multiple inheritances, are supported in Python. **Method overriding** is also allowed in Python. The **dynamic nature** of classes makes Python stand apart from other languages. Classes can be created at runtime and can even be changed as and when the program runs.

In a class all **data members are public** in nature; that is they can be accessed anywhere in the program. The **member functions in a class are all virtual**. In a class all the member functions must have the first argument as the object representing that class, from now on referred to as `'self'`. Interestingly, all the built in types are themselves classes in Python and they can be extended by the programmer.

The reader is advised to revisit the chapter on lists. Note that multiple names can be associated with the same object. Using pointers, for example, an object can be passed to a function using just one argument and in addition to that, the change done by the function is visible to the calling function also. In the case of Python, aliasing (having multiple names for the same object) can be used to accomplish the above task.

This chapter has been organized as follows. Section 10.2 presents the definition of a class. Section 10.3 presents the concept of objects and discusses the instantiation of a class. Section 10.4 discusses the scope of data members. Section 10.6 discusses constructor overloading. Section 10.7 discusses destructors and the last section concludes the chapter.

10.2   DEFINING A CLASS

In Python, a class can be defined using the `class` keyword. The `class` keyword is followed by the name of the class. The body of the class follows. It must have proper indentations.

Syntax

```
class <name of the class>:
      def <function name>(<arguments>):
            . . .
      <members>
```

For example the `employee` class having data members `name` and `age` and member functions `getdata()` and `putdata()` can be defined as follows (testing). It was stated earlier that every function in the class must have at least one argument, `self`. The functions of this class have been defined in the traditional way. The `getdata()` function here asks for the values of name and age from the user. The data members are accessed via the self object as they belong to the class and not just the function. Likewise the putdata() function displays the values of the data members. Note that the members of a class are accessed via self.

Tip

- *A class definition has functions but can also have other members.*
- *The attribute of an object is data attribute, and the function that belongs to an object is method.*

10.3   CREATING AN OBJECT

An object is created by associating a name with an instance of the class, initialized using the default constructor. For example, in creating an object of the employee class the following statements are used.

e1=employee()

Here, e1 is the name of the object and employee() is the constructor of the class. An object can also be created using a parameterized constructor, as explained in the following sections. The creation of an object is referred to as **instantiation**.

The function of a class can be called using the dot operator with a given class. For example, to call the getdata() function of the employee class the following statements are used.

e1.getdata()

Likewise, the other methods of a class can be called using the dot operator.

Code

```
class employee:
  def getdata(self):
    self.name=input('Enter name\t:')
    self.age=input('Enter age\t:')
  def putdata(self):
    print('Name\t:',self.name)
    print('Age\t:',self.age)
e1=employee()
e1.getdata()
e1.putdata()
```

```
>>>
============== RUN C:/Python/Class/employee.py ==============
Enter name  :Harsh
Enter age   :28
Name  : Harsh
Age   : 28
>>>
```

Tip

An object support the following operations
- *Instantiation*
- *Attribute references*

10.4 SCOPE OF DATA MEMBERS

The **scope** of a namespace is the region where it is directly accessible. In fact, in Python scopes are used dynamically. In determining the scope of a namespace, the following rules are followed:

- First of all, the innermost scope is searched
- Then the scope of enclosing functions are searched
- Then the global namespaces are searched
- Then the built-in names are seen

The nonlocal statements rebind the variables in the global scope. In order to understand the above concept, consider the following code. The following points concerning the code are worth noting:

- The value of a for all instances of the class is 5, until a function that changes the value of a is called.
- In putdata() a does not exist, a is local to getdata()
- b can be accessed in both the functions as b is a data member of the class (note that every time b is called, 'self.b' is used)
- On the basis of the above discussion the reader is expected to decode the following program.

Code

```
class demo_class:
  a=5
  def getdata(self,b):
    a=7;
    self.b=b
```

```
   def putdata(self):
     print('The value of\'a\'is''a'and that of\'b\'is',self.b)
d=demo_class()
d.getdata(9)
d.putdata()
>>>
========= RUN C:/Python/Class/variable_visibility.py =========
Traceback(most recent call last):
File "C:/Python/Class/variable_visibility.py", line 11,
                                        in <module>
    d.putdata()
File "C:/Python/Class/variable_visibility.py", line 7, in
                                        putdata
    print('The value of \'a\' is',a,'and that of \'b\'
                                        is',self.b)
NameError: name 'a' is not defined
```

In the following code, 'a' is common for all the classes. 'b' is a member of the class. Here,'self.b=b' means the data member 'b' of the class (self.b) is assigned value 'b', which is the second argument of the function getdata(). 'c' is local to getdata(), so 'c' of getdata() is not same as that of putdata().

Definition: Instance variable and class variable

An instance variable is one which is unique to each instance and a class variable is one which is shared by all instances. For example, in the following code b can be assigned a different value in each instance but c remains the same.

Code

```
class demo_class:
    a=5
  def getdata(self,b):
    c=7;
    self.b=b
    print('\'c\' is ',c,' and \'b\' is ',self.b)
  def other_function(self):
    c=3
    print('Value',c)
    def putdata(self):
    print('\'b\' is',self.b)
 d=demo_class()
 d.getdata(9)
 print(d.a)
 d.other_function()
```

```
d.putdata()
e=demo_class()
print(e.a)
>>>
======== RUN C:/Python/Class/variable_visibility2.py ========
'c' is 7 and 'b' is 9
5
Value 3
'b' is 9
5
```

In addition to the above a global data member can be made outside the class, which is accessible to all the methods (until the scope of the data member is changed). In the following code `'a'` is common for all instances of the class, `'b'` is the data member of the class and `'c'` is a local variable.

Code

```
global f
f=7
class demo_class:
    a=5
  def getdata(self,b):
    c=7;
    self.b=b
    print('\'c\' is ',c,' and \'b\' is ',self.b,'\'f\'',f)
  def other_function(self):
    c=3
    print('Value',c)
  def putdata(self):
    print('\'b\' is',self.b)
d=demo_class()
d.getdata(9)
print(d.a)
d.other_function()
d.putdata()
e=demo_class()
print(e.a)
>>>
======== RUN C:/Python/Class/variable_visibility2.py ========
'c' is 7 and 'b' is 9 'f' 7
5
Value 3
'b' is 9
5
```

10.5   NESTING

The designing of a class requires conceptualization of an entity, which has attributes and behavior. The object of a class can be made in another class also. That is, a class can also have the objects of another class as its members. This is called nesting. Note that the attributes of a class can themselves be entities. For example, in the following code an instance of the date class is created in the `student` class. This makes sense, as `student` is an entity made up of other entities (like `date`).

Code

```
class date:
  def getdata(self):
    self.dd=input('Enter date (dd)\t:')
    self.mm=input('Enter month (mm)\t:')
    self.yy=input('Enter year (yy)\t:')
  def display(self):
    print(self.dd,':',self.mm,':',self.yy)
class student:
  def getdata(self):
    self.name=input('Enter name\t:')
    self.dob= date()
    self.dob.getdata()
    def putdata(self):
    print('Name \t:',self.name)
    self.dob.display()

s= student()
s.getdata()
s.putdata()
>>>
========== RUN C:/Python/OOP/Nesting of classes.py ==========
Enter name          :Harsh
Enter date (dd)     :03
Enter month (mm)    :12
Enter year (yy)     :1981
Name  : Harsh
03 : 12 : 1981
>>>
```

10.6   CONSTRUCTOR

Note that each time a class is instantiated, a constructor (for example, e1= employee()) is used. In C++ terminology, a constructor is a function which has the same name as that of the class and initializes the data members. The above examples used default constructors, which were not made by the programmer. One can initialize the objects as per the need, by crafting constructors. The following discussion focuses on two types of constructors: default and parameterized. A **default constructor** does not take any argument (for example the employee() constructor). In Python, the constructors are called using the functions having the same name as that of the class. However, they are implemented by making the _init_() function inside the class.

In the following code, the object e1 behaves as expected. The values entered by the user in the getdata() function are displayed when putdata() is called. In the case of e2 the function getdata() is not called, therefore the values assigned in _init_() are displayed.

Code

```
class employee:
  def getdata(self):
    self.name=input('Enter name\t:')
    self.age=input('Enter age\t:')
  def putdata(self):
    print('Name\t:',self.name)
    print('Age\t:',self.age)
  def_init_(self):
    self.name='ABC'
    self.age=20
e1= employee()
e1.getdata()
e1.putdata()
e2=employee()
e2.putdata()
>>>
============ RUN C:/Python/Class/Constructor1.py ============
Enter name  :Harsh
Enter age   :28
Name   : Harsh
Age    : 28
```

```
Name    : ABC
Age     : 20
>>>
```

A **parameterized constructor** is one which takes arguments - for example in the following code, the parameterized constructor which takes two parameters name and age has been created. In order to assign the values to the object, the instantiation must be of the form:

```
e2=employee('Naved', 32)
```

Note that while defining the parameterized __init__, the first parameter is always 'self' and the rest of the parameters are the values to be assigned to different data members of the class. In the case of employee class, three parameters 'self', 'name', and 'age' are given.

Code

```
>>>
class employee:
  def getdata(self):
    self.name=input('Enter name\t:')
    self.age=input('Enter age\t:')
  def putdata(self):
    print('Name\t:',self.name)
    print('Age\t:',self.age)
  def_init_(self, name, age):
    self.name=name
    self.age=age
  def_del__():
    print('Done')
#e1=employee()
#e1.getdata()
#e1.putdata()
e2=employee('Naved', 32)
e2.putdata()

>>>
============ RUN C:/Python/Class/Constructor2.py ============
Name    : Naved
Age     : 32
>>>
```

10.7   CONSTRUCTOR OVERLOADING

Having the same name function in a class with a different number of parameters, or different type of parameters, is called function **overloading**. In C++, Java, C#, etc., the constructors can also be overloaded - that is one can have more than one constructors with each having different parameters. In Python, however, we cannot have more than one _init_ in a class. For example, if we try executing the following code an error crops up.

The reason is that is one makes a parameterized _init_. Python looks for the rest of the parameters in the instantiation.

Code

```
class employee:
  def getdata(self):
    self.name=input('Enter name\t:')
    self.age=input('Enter age\t:')
  def putdata(self):
    print('Name\t:',self.name)
    print('Age\t:',self.age)
  def_init_(self, name, age):
    self.name=name
    self.age=age
e1= employee()
e1.getdata()
e1.putdata()
e2=employee('Naved', 32)
e2.putdata()
>>>
============ RUN C:/Python/Class/Constructor2.py ============
Traceback (most recent call last):
  File "C:/Python/Class/Constructor2.py", line 11, in <module>
    e1=employee()
TypeError:_init_() missing 2 required positional arguments:
'name' and 'age'
>>>
```

Having studied the importance and implementation of constructors, let us now implement a constructor and let's consider the "movie" class, discussed here. The following code has a movie class, which contains a getdata() and putdata() function and init (self) for initializing the variables. Note that the object 'm' does not call the getdata() function but just putdata(). The values assigned in the constructor are displayed.

Code

```
class movie:
  def getdata(self):
    self.name=input('Enter name\t:')
    self.year=int(input('Enter year\t:'))
    self.genre=input('Enter genre\t:')
    self.director=input('Enter the name of the director\t:')
    self.producer=input('Enter the producer\t:')
    L=[]
    item=input('Enter the name of the actor\t:')
    L.append(item)
    choice=input('Press \'y\' for more \'n\' to quit')
    while(choice == "y"):
      item=input('Enter the name of the actor\t:')
      L.append(item)
      choice=input('Enter \'y\' for more \'n\' to quit')
    self.actors=L
    self.music_director=input('Enter the name of the music
                                           director\t:')

  def putdata(self):
    print('Name\t:',self.name)
    print('Year\t',self.year)
    print('Genre\t:',self.genre)
    print('Director\t:',self.director)
    print('Producer\t:',self.producer)
    print('Music_director\t:',self.music_director)
    print('Actors\t:',self.actors)

  def init (self):
    self.name='Fault'
    self.year=2015
    self.genre='Drama'
    self.director='XYZ'
    self.producer='ABC'
    self.music_director='LMN'
    self.actors=['A1', 'A2', 'A3', 'A4']

m=movie()
#m.getdata()
m.putdata()
>>>
============ RUN C:\Python\Class\class_basic2.py ============
Name    : Fault
Year    2015
```

```
Genre : Drama
Director     : XYZ
Producer     : ABC
Music_director    : LMN
Actors      : ['A1', 'A2', 'A3', 'A4']
>>>
```

10.8 DESTRUCTORS

A constructor initializes the data members of a class and a destructor frees
the memory. The destructor is created using _del_ and called by writing the
keyword del and the name of the object. The following code exemplifies a
destructor in the employee class described in the previous sections.

Code

```
class employee:
  def getdata(self):
    self.name=input('Enter name\t:')
    self.age=input('Enter age\t:')
  def putdata(self):
    print('Name\t:',self.name)
    print('Age\t:',self.age)
  def_init_(self, name, age):
    self.name=name
    self.age=age
  def_del_(self):
    print('Done')

#e1=employee()
#e1.getdata()
#e1.putdata()
e2=employee('Naved', 32)
e2.putdata()
del e2
============= RUN C:/Python/Class/Constructor2.py =============
Name  : Naved
Age   : 32
Done
>>>
```

The next example is the same as the previous one. However, the following
code also demonstrates the use of _class_. _name_, which displays the

name of the object that calls the function. This is useful as the name of the object whose destructor (or for that matter any method) is being called.

Code

```
class employee:
  def getdata(self):
    self.name=input('Enter name\t:')
    self.age=input('Enter age\t:')
  def putdata(self):
    print('Name\t:',self.name)
    print('Age\t:',self.age)
  def_init_(self, name, age):
    self.name=name
    self.age=age
  def_del__(self):
    print(_class_._name__,'Done')

#e1=employee()
#e1.getdata()
#e1.putdata()
e2=employee('Naved', 32)
e2.putdata()
del e2
>>>
============= RUN C:/Python/Class/Constructor2.py =============
Name  : Naved
Age   : 32
employee Done
>>>
```

- The reader is advised to go through the references for if name = "__main__":
- The docstring associated with the class can be mentioned in the definition of the class within three double quotes ("""" ...""").
- The docstring associated with the class can be accessed through doc , as shown in the following example.

Code

```
class employee:
  """The employee class"""
  def getdata(self):
    self.name=input('Enter name\t:')
    self.age=input('Enter age\t:')
  def putdata(self):
    print('Name\t:',self.name)
```

```
    print('Age\t:',self.age)
  def_init_(self):
    self.name='ABC'
    self.age=20
e1 = employee()
e1.getdata()
e1.putdata()
print(e1._doc_)
>>>
========= RUN C:/Python/Class/employeedocstring.py =========
Enter name  :Sakib
Enter age   :17
Name  : Sakib
Age   : 17
The employee class
>>>
```

The above chapter discusses what is referred to as an instance method. However another type of method can be created in a class, which is referred to as a class method.

10.9   CONCLUSION

The last chapter introduced the concepts of object-oriented programming. This chapter takes the topic further. The chapter introduces the syntax of a class and the creation of objects. The concept of constructors, their creation, types and implementation have also been discussed in the chapter. The chapter also introduces the idea of destructors. Ample examples have been given in the chapter, which explain the implementation of the concepts introduced earlier. The following chapter will introduce the idea of inheritance and polymorphism, which are essential to object-oriented programming. However to be able to inherit a class or implement operator overloading, one must be versed with the creation of a class and its use.

GLOSSARY

- **Data attribute and method:** The attribute of an object is **data attribute** and the function that belongs to an object is **method**.

- **Instance variable and class variable:** An instance variable is one which is unique to each instance and a class variable is one which is shared by all instances.
- **Constructor:** A constructor initializes the data members.
- A **parameterized constructor** is one which takes arguments.

POINTS TO REMEMBER

- The classes in Python can be sub-classed.
- All types of inheritance including multiple inheritances are supported in Python.
- A class can be defined using the `class` keyword in Python.
- An object is created by associating a name with an instance of the class, initialized using the default constructor.
- The function of a class can be called using the dot operator with a given class.
- While defining the parameterized `init` the first parameter is always `'self'`, and the rest of the parameters are the values to be assigned to different data members of the class.
- A constructor initializes the data members of a class and a destructor frees the memory.
- The destructor is created using `del` and called by writing the keyword `del` and the name of the object.
- `__class__.__name__` displays the name of the object that calls the function.
- The docstring associated with the class can be accessed through `doc`.

EXERCISES

MULTIPLE CHOICE QUESTIONS

1. A class generally has
   (a) Function and data members
   (b) Function and lists
   (c) Lists and tuples
   (d) None of the above

2. A class can have
   (a) Any number of functions   (b) Any type of data members
   (c) A variable local to a function   (d) All of the above

3. 'self' is
   (a) Object of the same class   (b) Object of the base class
   (c) Object of a predefined class   (d) None of the above

4. Each function in Python must have at least one parameter, which is
   (a) Data   (b) List
   (c) self   (d) None of the above

5. The init function
   (a) Initializes the data members   (b) Is compulsory
   (c) Must be overloaded   (d) None of the above

6. The init function in a class
   (a) Must be overloaded   (b) Can be overloaded
   (c) Cannot be overloaded   (d) None of the above

7. The docstring of a class can be accessed using
   (a) __init__   (b) __doc__
   (c) __class__   (d) None of the above

8. A global variable
   (a) Can be accessed anywhere   (b) Can be accessed only in __init__
   (c) Both of the above   (d) None of the above

9. The nonlocal variable
   (a) Is generally associated and then used
   (b) Must not be associated
   (c) Does not exist
   (d) None of the above

10. A variable shared by all the instances of a class is
   (*a*) Class variable   (*b*) Instance variable
   (*c*) Both   (*d*) None of the above

11. A variable unique to an instance is
   (*a*) Instance variable   (*b*) Class variable
   (*c*) Both   (*d*) None of the above

12. Which of the following keywords is used to define a class?
   (*a*) class   (*b*) def
   (*c*) del   (*d*) None of the above

13. Which of the following is used to define a function that acts as a destructor?
   (*a*) del   (*b*) init
   (*c*) Both   (*d*) None of the above

14. Which of the following operations are supported by an object?
   (*a*) Instantiation   (*b*) Attribute reference
   (*c*) Both   (*d*) None of the above

15. Suppose e1 is an object, which of the following codes is used to call del?
   (*a*) del (e1)   (*b*) e1. del__
   (*c*) Both   (*d*) None of the above

16. If the name of the object is to be displayed in a function of a class, then which of the following can be used?
   (*a*) __class . name__   (*b*) object . name__
   (*c*) Both   (*d*) None of the above

17. In a class all variables are _ by default?
   (*a*) Public   (*b*) Private
   (*c*) Cannot say   (*d*) Depends on the type of variables

18. In Python, which of the following operators is used to access methods?
    (*a*) Dot   (*b*) Plus
    (*c*) []   (*d*) None of the above

19. Can a list of objects be created?
    (*a*) Yes, if the type of variables is public
    (*b*) Yes, in all cases
    (*c*) No, in all cases
    (*d*) Yes, if the type of variables is private

20. Data members of a class
    (*a*) Must be private   (*b*) Can be private
    (*c*) Must be public   (*d*) None of the above

THEORY

1. What is an object? How is an object created in Python?

2. Explain the scope of variables in a class. Give an example of data members of a class which are shared by all the objects and of those which are unique to an object.

3. What is a constructor? What are the different types of constructors in Python?

4. Can we overload a constructor in Python?

5. How can one access the name of the docstring in Python?

6. How can one access the name of an object in Python?

7. What is a destructor? How is a constructor created in Python?

8. Give an example of use of a destructor in Python.

9. Give an example of instantiation of a class.

10. Explain the concept of aliasing in Python.

PROGRAMMING EXERCISES

A start-up employs interns. The following details of interns are stored

first_name
last_name
address
mobile_number
e_mail

1. Create a class called Intern, which stores the above details. Craft two functions `getdata()` which asks the user to enter data and `putdata()` to display the data.

2. In the above program create `init` which takes only one parameter (self).

3. In question 1, create `init`, which takes 6 parameters - the first being "self" and the rest the values of variables stated in question 1.

4. In the above question, craft a destructor.

5. A library management system is to be created, in which the following details of a "Book" are to be stored.

Name
Publisher
Year
ISBN
Authors

The authors, above, is a list consisting of all the authors of that book. Create a class called Book, which stores the above details. Craft two functions - `getdata()` which asks the user to enter data and `putdata()` to display the data.

6. In the above program, create `init` which takes only one parameter (self).

7. In question 6, create `init`, which takes 6 parameters with the first being "self" and the rest the values of variables stated in question 5.

8. In the above question, craft a destructor and call it.

9. Create a class called complex, having `real_part` and `ima_part` as its two data members and `getdata()` and `putdata()` as its member functions.

10. In the above question, craft `init` and `del`.

11. Create a function called add, which takes two complex numbers as its parameters and returns the sum of the two complex numbers.

12. Create a function called `sub`, which takes two complex numbers as its parameters and returns the difference of the two complex numbers.

13. Create a function called multiply, which takes two complex numbers as its parameters and returns the product of the two complex numbers.

14. Create a function called div, which takes two complex numbers as its parameters and returns the result of division of the two complex numbers.

15. Create a class called date having day, month, and year as its data members and `getdata()` and `putdata()` as its member functions. Instantiate the class, ask user to enter data and display the data.

CHAPTER 11

INHERITANCE

After reading this chapter, the reader will be able to

- Understand the concept and importance of inheritance
- Differentiate between inheritance and composition
- Understand the types of inheritance
- Appreciate the role of 'self' in methods
- Understand the search in an inheritance tree
- Understand the concept and importance of super
- Appreciate the need of an abstract class

11.1 INTRODUCTION TO INHERITANCE AND COMPOSITION

Those of you from a C++ background will have studied the importance of inheritance and composition. Inheritance was projected as a path breaking concept, which promised to solve all the problems and bring about a change in the way programming is done. But you must have understood that those who make such tall claims generally create more problems than they claim to solve. Inheritance may also create problems; many more than you can imagine.

Many programmers believe that inheritance is a black hole which somehow attracts programmers, who falls in the trap of tall claims and end up landing themselves in a situation which tempts them to use multiple inheritance. Multiple inheritance is like Voldemort, and the object-oriented programming environment is Hogwart's. Therefore, it is better to avoid multiple inheritance as much as possible.

Object-oriented programming has its charms but also comes with its own problems, it is like demonetization. So, use inheritance only if required. Also remember never ever to use multiple inheritance. Remember that anything that can be done using inheritance can be done also in another way too. Composition, introduced later in the chapter, can be easily used to accomplish most of the tasks that can be done using inheritance.

In hindsight, inheritance means a class would get features (all or some) from the parent class. So, when one writes

```
class SoftwareDeveloper(Employee):
...
```

it implies that the class SoftwareDeveloper is a subclass of the class Employee. This relationship falls in the category of an "is a" type relationship. That is, 'SoftwareDeveloper' is-a 'Employee'.

The class from which class(es) are derived from is called a **base class** and those that inherit features from the base class are **derived classes**. In the above example, Employee is the base class and SoftwareEmpolyee is the derived class. Note that inheritance does not affect the base class. The derived class can use the modules of the base class in a variety of ways which are discussed as follows.

11.1.1 Inheritance and Methods

As far as modules are concerned, inheritance can help the programmer to derive the features by one of the following ways.

The method is not present in the child class, but only in the parent class: In such cases if an instance of the child class calls the said method, the parent class's method is called. For instance, in the following snippet the derived class does not have a method called show() so calling show using an instance of the derived class (consider, in this case) calls the method of the parent class.

Code

```
class ABC:
    def show(self):
        print("show of ABC")
```

```
class XYZ(ABC):
      def show1(self):
            print("show of XYZ")

A = ABC()
A.show()
B= XYZ()
B.show()
B.show1()
```

The method is present in both the parent class and in the derived class: In such cases, if this method is invoked using an instance of the derived class then the method of the derived class is called. If the method is called using an instance of the base class, the method of the base class is called. Note that in such cases, the derived class redefines the method. This **overriding** ensures that the search of the method in the inheritance tree ends up invoking this method only. For example, in the following snippet x.show() calls the show() method of the derived class, whereas y.show() calls the method of the base class.

Code

```
class ABC:
      def show(self):
            print("show of ABC")

class XYZ(ABC):
      def show(self):
            print("show of XYZ")

A = ABC()
A.show()
B= XYZ()
B.show()
```

The inherited class modifies the method of the base class and in this process invokes the method of the base class inside the method of the derived class also. Note that in the following snippet the show method of the derived class prints a message, then calls the method of the base class and finally prints another message. Note that in this case, the method of the base class can be called by qualifying the name of the method with the name of the base class. For example in the following snippet the show method of the base class can be called using ABC.show(self). The importance of the self argument has been explained in Section 11.3.

Code

```
class ABC:
      def show(self):
          print("show of ABC")
class XYZ(ABC):
      def show(self):
          print("Something before calling the base
                                class function")
ABC.show(self)
print("Something after calling the base class function")
A = ABC()
A.show()
B= XYZ()
B.show()
```

The first type of inheritance will henceforth be referred to as **implicit inheritance**. In this type the method of the base class can be called using an instance of the derived class.

The second type of inheritance will henceforth be referred to as **explicit overriding**. As stated earlier, the derived class will redefine the method of the base class and calling this method using an instance of the derived class will invoke the method of the derived class.

The third type of inheritance is the most important and practical form of overriding methods. This type of inheritance leaves the room of not making an instance of the base class, if not required, still using the function.

The following illustration combines the three types of inheritance:

Illustration 11.1: Create a class called Student having _init_ and show methods. The Student class should have a data member called name. The _ init_ should assign value to name and show should display the value. Create another class called RegularStudent, which will be the derived class of the Student class. The class should have two methods _init_ and show. The _init_ should assign values to age and should call the _init_ of the base class and pass the value of name to the base class. The show method must display the data of the RegularStudent. In addition to the above both classes should have methods called random, both of which should be independent of each other (Figure 11.1). Find what happens when the methods of the base class and the derived classes are called using the instances of the base and the derived classes.

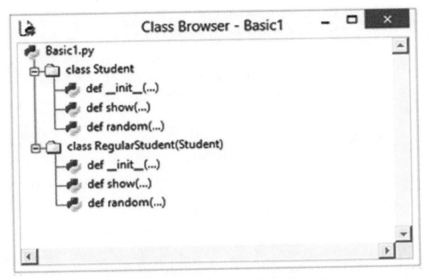

FIGURE 11.1 Class hierarchy for Illustration 11.1

Solution:

Code

```
class Student:
    def_init_(self,name):
        self.name=name
    def show(self):
        print("Name\t:"+self.name)
    def random(self):
        print("A random method in the base class")

class RegularStudent(Student):
    def_init_(self,name):##overrides the base class
                    method and calls the base class method
        self.age=22
        Student._init__(self,name)
    def show(self):##redefines the base class method
        print("Name (derived class)\t:"+self.name+" Age\
                                    t:"+str(self.age))

    def random(self):##nothing to do with the base class
                                                method
        print("Random method in the derived class")
```

```
naks = Student("Nakul")
hari = RegularStudent("Harsh")
naks.show()
hari.show()
##The variables can be seen outside the class also
print(naks.name)
print(hari.name)
```

Output

```
>>>
=========== RUN C:/Python/Inheritance/Basic1.py ===========
Name   :Nakul
Name (derived class)    :Harsh Age   :22
Nakul
Harsh
>>>
```

11.1.2 Composition

Making an instance of another class inside a class makes things easy and helps the programmer to accomplish many tasks. In order to understand the concept, let us consider an example. Consider that a `Student` and his `PhDguide` are subclasses of the `person` class. Also, the data of the `PhD guide` includes the list of students guided by him/her. This is where composition comes into play. The instantiation of the `students` in the `PhDGuide` class can be done as explained in the following illustration.

Illustration 11.2: Create a class called Student, having `name` and `email` as its data members and `_init_(self, name, email)` and `putdata(self)` as bound methods. The `_init_` function should assign the values passed as parameters to the requisite variables. The `putdata` function should display the data of the student. Create another class called `PhDguide` having `name`, `email`, and `students` as its data members. Here, the `students` variable is the list of students under the guide. The `PhDguide` class should have four bound methods: `_init_`, `putdata`, `add`, and `remove`. The `_init_` method should initialize the variables, the `putdata` should show the data of the guide, include the list of students, the `add` method should add a student to the list of students of the guide and the `remove` function should remove the student (if the student exists in the list of students of that guide) from the list of students.

Solution:

The details of the classes have been shown in Figure 11.2. It may be noted that since students is a list therefore a *for* loop is needed to display the list of students. Also, while adding the student to the list the data of the passed parameter has been stored in s (an instance of Student) and s has been added to the list of the students. The same procedure has been adopted to remove a student. The code is as follows:

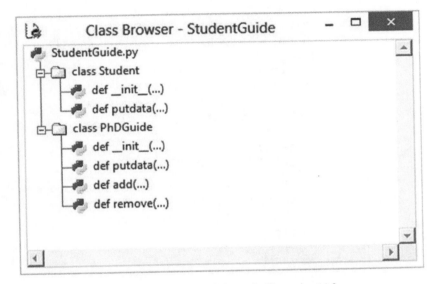

FIGURE 11.2 Details of classes for Illustration 11.2

Code

```
class Student:
    def _init_(self,name,email):
        self.name=name
        self.email=email

    def putdata(self):
        print("\nStudent's details\nName\t:",self.name,"\
                            nE-mail\t:",self.email)
class PhDGuide:
    def _init_(self, name, email,students):
        self.name=name
        self.email=email
        self.students=students
```

```
      def putdata(self):
            print("\nGuide Data\nName\t:",self.name,"\nE-mail\
                                      t:",self.email)
            print("\nList of students\n")
            for s in self.students:
            print("\t",s.name,"\t",s.email)
      def add(self, student):
            s=Student(student.name,student.email)
            if s not in self.students:
            self.students.append(s)
      def remove(self, student):
            s=Student(student.name,student.email)
            flag=0
            for s1 in self.students:
                  if(s1.email==s.email):
                              print(s, " removed")
                  self.students.remove (s1)
                  flag=1
            if flag==0:
                  print("Not found")
Harsh=Student("Harsh","i_harsh_bhasin@yahoo.com")
Nav=Student("Nav","i_nav@yahoo.com")
Naks=Student("Nakul","nakul@yahoo.com")
print("\nDetails of students\n")
Harsh.putdata()
Nav.putdata()
Naks.putdata()
KKA=PhDGuide("KKA","kka@gmail.com",[])
MU=PhDGuide("Moin Uddin","prof.moin@yahoo.com",[])
print("Details of Guides")
KKA.putdata()
MU.putdata()
MU.add(Harsh)
MU.add(Nav)
KKA.add(Naks)
print("Details of Guides (after addition of students")
KKA.putdata()
MU.putdata()
MU.remove(Harsh)
KKA.add(Harsh)
print("Details of Guides")
KKA.putdata()
MU.putdata()
```

Output

```
>>>
========= RUN C:/Python/Inheritance/StudentGuide.py =========
Details of students

Student's details
Name        : Harsh
E-mail      : i_harsh_bhasin@yahoo.com

Student's details
Name        : Nav
E-mail      : i_nav@yahoo.com

Student's details
Name        : Nakul
E-mail      : nakul@yahoo.com
Details of Guides

Guide Data
Name        : KKA
E-mail      : kka@gmail.com
List of students

Guide Data
Name        : Moin Uddin
E-mail      : prof.moin@yahoo.com

List of students

Details of Guides (after addition of students

Guide Data
Name        : KKA
E-mail      : kka@gmail.com

List of students
      Nakul nakul@yahoo.com

Guide Data
Name        : Moin Uddin
E-mail      : prof.moin@yahoo.com

List of students
      Harsh i_harsh_bhasin@yahoo.com
      Nav   i_nav@yahoo.com
<__main__.Student object at 0x03A49650>    removed
Details of Guides
```

```
Guide Data
Name : KKA
E-mail : kka@gmail.com

List of students
      Nakul nakul@yahoo.com
      Harsh i_harsh_bhasin@yahoo.com

Guide Data
Name : Moin Uddin
E-mail : prof.moin@yahoo.com

List of students
      Nav i_nav@yahoo.com
```

11.2   INHERITANCE: IMPORTANCE AND TYPES

The concept of classes was introduced in the previous chapter. It was mentioned   that classes are real or conceptual entities which have sharp physical boundaries and relevance to the problem at hand. A class has attributes (data members) and behavior (class methods). However, at times these classes must be extended to be able to solve some specific problem without having to meddle with the original class. To be able to do so, the language should support inheritance. As a matter of fact, the presence of classes in the language is primarily because it can be inherited. Inheritance is, as per most of the authors, one of the most essential features of object-oriented language.

Using inheritance one can create new classes (derived classes) from an existing class (base class(es)). Note that a derived class can have even more than one base class, referred to as **multiple inheritance**, which is one of the most undesirable forms of inheritance. Also a base class can itself be a derived class of some other class. The derived class will have all the allowed features of the base class plus some features of its own.

A class can be depicted using a class diagram. A class diagram is the diagrammatic representation of a class, which generally has three sections. In the representation used next, the first section has the name of the class. The second section has the attributes and the third section has the class methods. The following figure (Figure 11.3) shows the class diagram in which the Book class is the base class and the Text_Book class is the derived class. Note that the arrow is from the derived class to the base class. The arrow indicates "is derived from" or "is inherited from." The next figure (Figure 11.4) gives the details of the two classes. Note that the Book class has the following attributes:

- name
- authors
- publisher
- ISBN
- year

The class methods of this class are `getdata()` and `putdata()`. The `Text_Book` class has another attribute, `course`. Figure 11.5 shows the class browser showing the two classes and the relation between them. The corresponding program is presented in Illustration 11.3.

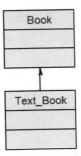

FIGURE 11.3 Text_book is the derived class of the Book class

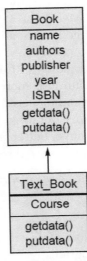

FIGURE 11.4 A class diagram generally has three components: the name of the class, the data members, and the methods of the class. The book class and the textbook class have attributes and methods as shown in the figure.

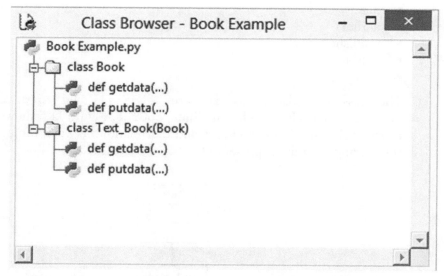

FIGURE 11.5 The book examples' class hierarchy in the class browser of Python

11.2.1 Need for Inheritance

In really large programs, it is difficult to code and debug a class. Once the programmer has crafted a class, there is little need to meddle with it. If one needs to craft classes having the same features as the class that has been developed (and add some more features to it), then it makes sense to derive classes from the existing class. So, inheritance helps to reuse a code. Reusing the code has its own advantages. It not only saves time but also money. The reliability of the program also increases by reusing a code. One can also develop his class by extending classes developed by others. That is, inheritance helps in distributing libraries. Inheritance also helps to implement a design that is more intuitive, better, and more practical. Inheritance also has some disadvantages, which were discussed in the previous section.

Inheritance is important because of the following factors:

- Reusability
- Increased reliability
- Distributing libraries
- Intuitive, better programs

11.2.2 Types of Inheritance

This section presents various types of inheritance and corresponding examples. Note that the reader is expected to execute the problem given in the illustrations and analyze the output. As explained earlier, inheritance means deriving new classes from the existing classes. The classes from which features have been derived are called the **base classes** and the class which derives features is called the **derived class**. There are five types of inheritance: simple, hierarchical, multilevel, multiple, and hybrid.

11.2.2.1 Simple Inheritance

The simple inheritance has a single base class and a single derived class. Illustration 11.3 exemplifies this type. The following illustration has two classes: `Book` and `Text_Book`. The Book class has two methods: `getdata` and `putdata`. The `getdata` method asks the user to enter the `name of the book, number of authors`, the `list of authors, publisher, ISBN`, and `year`. The derived class `Text_Book` has another attribute called `course`. The `getdata` and the `putdata` methods extend the base class methods (refer to the previous section).

Illustration 11.3: Implement the following hierarchy (Figure 11.6). The `Book` function has `name`, `n` (number of authors), `authors` (list of authors), `publisher`, `ISBN`, and `year` as its data members and the derived class has `course` as its data member. The derived class method overrides (extends) the methods of the base class.

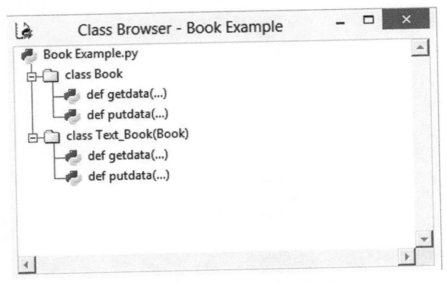

FIGURE 11.6 The class hierarchy for Illustration 11.3

Solution:

The following code implements the above hierarchy. The output of the program follows.

Code

```
class Book:
    def getdata(self):
        self.name=input("\nEnter the name of the book\t:")
       self.n=int(input("\nEnter the number of authors\t:"))
        self.authors=[]
        i=0
        while i<self.n:
        author=input(str("\nEnter the name of the "+str(i)
                           +"th author\t:"))
        self.authors.append(author)
        i+=1
        self.publisher=input("\nEnter the name of the
                                       publisher\t:")
        self.ISBN=input("\nEnter the ISBN\t:")
        self.year=input("\nEnter year of publication\t:")
    def putdata(self):
        print("\nName\t:",self.name,"\nAuthor(s)\t:",self.
                authors,"\nPublisher\t:",self.publisher,"\
                nYear\t:",self.year,"\nISBN\t:",self.ISBN)
class Text_Book(Book):
    def getdata(self):
        self.course=input("\nEnter the course\t:")
        Book.getdata(self)
    def putdata(self):
        Book.putdata(self)
        print("\nCourse\t:",self.course)
Book1=Book()
Book1.getdata()
Book1.putdata()
TextBook1=Text_Book()
TextBook1.getdata()
TextBook1.putdata()
```

Output

```
======== RUN C:/Python/Inheritance/Book Example.py ========
Enter the name of the book          : Programming in C#
Enter the number of authors           1
Enter the name of the 0th author    : Harsh Bhasin
Enter the name of the publisher     : Oxford
Enter the ISBN                      : 0-19-809740-9
Enter year of publication           : Oxford
Name                                : Programming in C#
Author(s)                           : ['Harsh Bhasin']
Publisher                           : Oxford
Year                                : Oxford
ISBN                                : 0-19-809740-9
Enter the course                    : Algorithms
Enter the name of the book          : Algorithms Analysis
                                      and Design
Enter the number of authors           1
Enter the name of the 0th author    : Harsh Bhasin
Enter the name of the publisher     : Oxford
Enter the ISBN                      : 0-19-945666-6
Enter year of publication           : Oxford
Name                                : Algorithms Analysis
                                      and Design
Author(s)                           : ['Harsh Bhasin']
Publisher                           : Oxford
Year                                : Oxford
ISBN                                : 0-19-945666-6
Course                              : Algorithms
```

11.2.2.2 Hierarchical Inheritance

In hierarchical inheritance, a single base class has at least two derived classes. Illustration 11.4 exemplifies this type. The following illustration has three classes: Staff, Teaching, and NonTeaching. Both Teaching and

NonTeaching are the derived classes of the Staff class. The Staff class has two methods: getdata and putdata. The getdata method asks the user to enter the name and the salary of the member of the staff. The derived class Teaching has another attribute called subject. The getdata and the putdata methods extend the base class methods. Similarly, the derived class NonTeaching has an attribute called department. The getdata and the putdata methods extend the base class methods.

Illustration 11.4: Implement the following hierarchy (Figure 11.7). The Staff function has name and salary as its data members, the derived class Teaching has subject as its data member and the class NonTeaching has department as its data member. The derived class method overrides (extends) the methods of the base class.

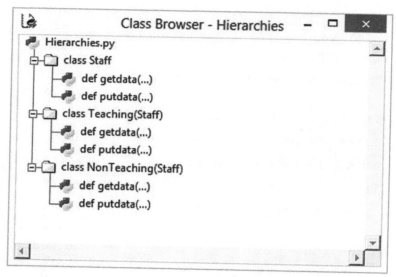

FIGURE 11.7 The class hierarchy for Illustration 11.4

Solution:

The following code implements the above hierarchy. The output of the program follows.

Code

```
>>>
##Hierarchies
```

```
class Staff:
    def getdata(self):
        self.name=input("\nEnter the name\t:")
        self.salary=float(input("\nEnter salary\t:"))
    def putdata(self):
        print("\nName\t:",self.name,"\nSalary\t:",self.
                                                    salary)

class Teaching(Staff):
    def getdata(self):
        self.subject=input("\nEnter subject\t:")
        Staff.getdata(self)
    def putdata(self):
        Staff.putdata(self)
        print("\nSubject\t:",self.subject)

class NonTeaching(Staff):
    def getdata(self):
        self.department=input("\nEnter department\t:")
        Staff.getdata(self)
    def putdata(self):
        Staff.putdata(self)
        print("\nDepartment\t:",self.department)

X=Staff()
X.getdata()
X.putdata()
##Teacher
Y=Teaching()
Y.getdata()
Y.putdata()
##Non Teaching Staff
Z=NonTeaching()
Z.getdata()
Z.putdata()
```

Output

```
>>>
========= RUN C:/Python/Inheritance/Hierarchies.py =========
Enter the name    :Hari

Enter salary      :50000

Name              : Hari
Salary            : 50000.0
```

```
Enter subject      :Algorithms
Enter the name     :Harsh
Enter salary       :70000
Name               :  Harsh
Salary             :  70000.0
Subject            :  Algorithms
Enter department   :HR
Enter the name     :Prasad
Enter salary       :52000
Name               :  Prasad
Salary : 52000.0
Department : HR
>>>
```

11.2.2.3 *Multilevel Inheritance*

In multilevel inheritance a base class has derived classes which themselves becomes a base class for some other class. Illustration 11.5 exemplifies this type. The following illustration has three classes: Person, Employee, and Programmer. The Person class is the base class. The Employee class has been derived from the Person class. The programmer class has been derived from the Employee class. The Person class has two attributes - name and age and two methods - getdata and putdata. The getdata method asks the user to enter the name and the age of the member of the staff. The derived class Employee has another attribute called emp_code. The getdata and the putdata methods extend the base class methods. Similarly, the class Programmer has another attribute called language. The getdata and the putdata methods extend its base class methods (Employee class).

Illustration 11.5: Implement the following hierarchy (Figure 11.8). The Staff class has name and salary as its data members, the derived class Teaching has subject as its data member and the class NonTeaching has department as its data member. The derived class method overrides (extends) the methods of the base class.

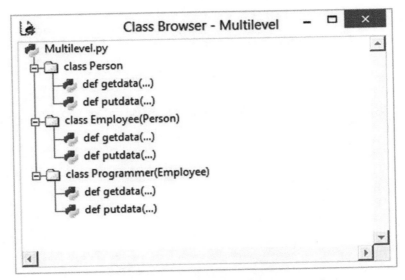

FIGURE 11.8 The class hierarchy for Illustration 11.5

Solution:

The following code implements the above hierarchy. The output of the program follows.

Code

```python
class Person:
    def getdata(self):
        self.name=input("\nEnter Name\t:")
        self.age=int(input("\nEnter age\t:"))
    def putdata(self):
        print("\nName\t:",self.name,"\nAge\t:",str(self.age))

class Employee(Person):
    def getdata(self):
        Person.getdata(self)
        self.emp_code=input("\nEnter employee code\t:")
    def putdata(self):
        Person.putdata(self)
        print("\nEmployee Code\t:",self.emp_code)

class Programmer(Employee):
    def getdata(self):
```

```
        Employee.getdata(self)
        self.language=input("\nEnter Language\t:")
    def putdata(self):
        Employee.putdata(self)
        print("\nLanguage\t:",self.language)
A=Person()
print("\nA is a person\nEnter data\n")
A.getdata()
A.putdata()
B=Employee()
print("\nB is an Empoyee and hence a person\nEnter data\n")
B.getdata()
B.putdata()
C=Programmer()
print("\nC is a programmer hence an employee and employee
                            is a person\nEnter data\n")
C.getdata()
C.putdata()
```

Output

```
>>>
========== RUN C:/Python/Inheritance/Multilevel.py ==========
A is a person
Enter data
Enter Name          :Har
Enter age           28
Name                : Har
Age                 : 28
B is an Empoyee and hence a person
Enter data
Enter Name          :Hari
Enter age           29
Enter employee code :E001
Name                : Hari
Age                 : 29
Employee Code       : E001
C is a programmer hence an employee and employee is a person
Enter data
Enter Name          :Harsh
Enter age           30
```

```
Enter employee code :E002
Enter Language      :Python
Name                : Harsh
Age                 : 30
Employee Code       : E002
Language            : Python
>>>
```

11.2.2.4 Multiple Inheritance and Hybrid Inheritance

In multiple inheritance a class can be derived from more than one base class. This type of inheritance can be problematic as it can lead to ambiguity. It is therefore advised to avoid this kind of inheritance as far as possible. However, the following sections throw some light on this type and the problems associated with this type.

A design may have a combination of more than one type of inheritance. In the following figure (Figure 11.9) two classes B and C have been derived from class A. However, for the class D, the classes B and C are the base classes. This is an example of combining hierarchical and multiple inheritance. Such a type is referred to as hybrid inheritance.

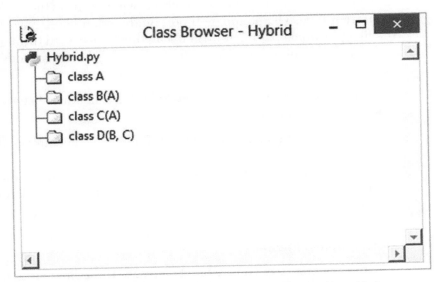

FIGURE 11.9 Classes B and C have been derived from A (hierarchical inheritance) and D is derived from B and C (multiple inheritance)

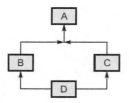

FIGURE 11.10 Classes B and C have been derived from A (hierarchical inheritance) and D is derived from B and C (multiple inheritance)

11.3   METHODS

The importance of functions and methods has already been stated in the first section of this book. Methods are, as stated earlier, just functions with a special positional parameter within a class. Methods, in fact, help the programmer to accomplish many tasks. Methods can be bound or unbound. The unbound methods do not have 'self' as a parameter. While calling such methods, the first argument must be the instance of the class itself. It is worth mentioning here that, in Python 3.X, the unbound methods are same as functions whereas in Python 2.X they are a different type. The bound methods, on the other hand, have 'self' as the first positional parameter when a method is accessed through qualifying an instance of a class. Here, the instance of the class needs not to be passed.

In spite of the above differences, the following similarities between the two types may not be missed:

- A method in Python is also an object. Both bound and unbound methods are objects.
- The same method can be invoked as a bound method and an unbound method. The discussion and illustrations that follow will clarify the second point.

11.3.1   Bound Methods

A method can be invoked in a variety of ways. If the first positional parameter of the method is "self", it is bound. In such cases, the instance of the class can call the method by passing the requisite parameters.

A variable which holds `<Object name>.<method name>` (`Hari.display`), in the following example, can also be used to invoke the method. Those of you from a C# background may find the concept similar to that of delegates.

A method can also be invoked by creating an unmanned instance of the class. The third call of the display method depicts this way of calling method.

Illustration 11.6: Calling a bound method

This illustration has a class called student. The `Student` class has a display method, which takes two arguments - the first being the positional parameter and the second being a string that is printed. Note that the display method is a bound method and hence is called through an instance of the class.

Code

```
class Student:
    def display(self, something):
        print("\n"+something)

##Invoking a bound method
Hari = Student()
Hari.display("Hi I am Hari")
##display() can also be invoked through an instance of
                                            the method

X= Hari.display
X("Hi I am through X")
##display called again
Student().display("Caling diaplay again")
```

Output

```
>>>
========= RUN C:\Python\Inheritance\BoundUnbound.py =========
Hi I am Hari
Hi I am through X
Caling diaplay again
>>>
```

11.3.2   Unbound Method

An unbound method does not have self. Therefore the positional parameter needs not to be passed in method. In such methods, the variables should not be qualified by 'self'. Calling such methods in the same way as before would result in an error, as shown in the output of Listing 1 of Illustration 11.7. The second listing calls the unbound method in an appropriate way. Such methods must be called by the name of the class and not the object. In Python 3.X, as stated earlier, such methods work in the same manner as functions. Also note that normal functions can be called using the class, of which they are members, as shown in the previous illustration.

Illustration 11.7: Calling an unbound method

This illustration extends the previous illustration and adds the getdata method, which does not take self as a parameter and therefore is called by the class itself. Note that this is similar to the static methods in C++.

Code

```
class Student:
    def display(self, something):
        print("\n"+something)
    def getdata(name,age):
        name=name
        age=age
        print("\nName\t:",name,"\nAge\t:",age)
##Creating a new student
Naved=Student()
name=input("\nEnter the name of the student\t:")
age=int(input("\nEnter the age of the student\t:"))
Naved.getdata(name,age)
```

Output

```
>>>
========= RUN C:/Python/Inheritance/BoundUnbound.py =========
Enter the name of the student :Naved

Enter the age of the student  :22
Traceback (most recent call last):
File "C:/Python/Inheritance/BoundUnbound.py", line 21, in
                                        <module>
Naved.getdata(name,age)
>>>
```

Snippet 2:

Code

```
class Student:
    def display(self, something):
        print("\n"+something)
    def getdata(name,age):
        print("\nName\t:",name,"\nAge\t:",str(age))

##Creating a new student
Naved=Student()
name=input("\nEnter the name of the student\t:")
age=int(input("\nEnter the age of the student\t:"))
Student.getdata(name,age)
```

Output

```
>>>
======== RUN C:/Python/Inheritance/BoundUnbound1.py ========
Enter the name of the student :Naved
Enter the age of the student  :22
Name  : Naved
Age   : 22
>>>
```

11.3.3   Methods are Callable Objects

Methods, like any other object in Python, can be stored in a list and called as per the requirement. In the illustration that follows the class operations has a constructor _init_(self, number), which assigns the value of the second parameter to the data member called number. The class has two methods square and cube. The first method calculates (and returns) the square of the number and the second calculates (and returns) the cube of the number. Two instances of the class operations have been created: X and Y. X is initialized to 5 and Y to 4. The list List stores the objects X.square, X.cube, Y.square, and Y.cube. The elements of the list are then called one by one and invoked.

Illustration 11.8: Methods as callable objects

Code

```
class operations:
    def_init_(self, number):
        self.number=number
```

```
        def square(self):
            return (self.number*self.number)
        def cube(self):
            return(self.number*self.number*self.number)
Num1=operations(5)
Num2=operations(4)
List= [Num1.square, Num1.cube, Num2.square, Num2.cube]
                                for callable_object in List:
print(callable_object())
```

Output

```
>>>
======= RUN C:/Python/Inheritance/CallableObjects.py =======
25
125
16
64
>>>
```

11.3.4   The Importance and Usage of Super

A class may have data members and member functions (method). A method is just a function in a class, defined using the keyword 'def'. As discussed in the earlier chapters, the methods depict the behavior of a class. Generally, the method's first argument is an instance of the class itself. The first argument, generally referred to as `self`, is similar to 'this' of C++. Using `self` with the variable name indicates that the reference is to the instance variable, not that in the global scope. For example in the following snippet, the _init_ method has two arguments: the first being `self` and the second being the `name`. Assigning name to self.name implies that the local variable name is given value "name" (the second argument of _init_). Similarly, the `putdata` method has a positional parameter indicating the data for the instance which invokes `putdata` must be shown. Note that the output reinforces the fact that self-binds the method call with the instances.

Code

```
class Student:
    def _init_(self,name):
        self.name=name
```

```
    def putdata(self):
        print("name\t:",self.name)
Hari=Student("Hari")
Hari.putdata()
Naks=Student("Nakul"
Naks.putdata()
>>>
```

Output

```
============ RUN C:/Python/Inheritance/Basic.py ============
name    : Hari
name    : Nakul
>>>
```

However, methods can also be crafted without the 'self' argument. These are unbound methods. The concept has been discussed in Section 11.3.2 of this chapter. A method of a class is an instance method by default. So, generally, the method of a class can be called by creating an instance of the class and using the dot operator to call the method. Note that this was the case in languages like C#, Java, etc. Note that there are other ways of invoking a method, as discussed in this chapter.

However, there are other types of methods as well. For example, the static methods do not require the instance of a class as their first argument.

11.3.5 Calling the Base Class Function Using Super

The functions of the base class can be called using super. In fact, super can be used to call any function of the base class and it clearly depicts the calling of the base class's function. In order to understand the usage of super, let us go through the following example. In the following example, BaseClass has two methods: _init_ and printData. _init_ has one positional parameter and one parameter that initializes "data" (the data member of the BaseClass.) The DerivedClass is the derived class of the BaseClass. This class has _init_, which takes a positional parameter (self), and two other parameters. The first initializes the data member of DerivedClass and the second is passed onto the init of the base class (BaseClass) using super. The super takes the name of the class (DerivedClass), the positional parameter (self) and calls the _init_ of the base class by passing all parameters except the positional parameter. Note that the second function also uses super in the same manner.

Code

```
class BaseClass:
    def _init_(self, data):
        self.data=data
    def printData(self):
        print("Data of the base class\t:",self.data)
class DerivedClass(BaseClass):
    def_init_(self,data1, data2):
        self.data1=data1
        super(DerivedClass, self)._init_(data2)
    def printData(self):
        super(DerivedClass,self).printData()
        print("Data of the derived class\t:",self.data1)
```

Output

```
>>>
========== RUN C:/Python/Inheritance/superDemo.py ==========
Data of the base class    : 4
Data of the base class    : 5
Data of the derived class     : 6
>>>
```

11.4   SEARCH IN INHERITANCE TREE

An object is searched for in the inheritance tree in a bottom up fashion. First of all, the class is searched for the given object. If it is found then the found object is used to accomplish the given task. If not, then its super class (base class) is searched for the object. In case of more than one base class, ambiguity can occur.

For example, in the following illustration the Derived1 class has been derived from BaseClass. The show() method of this class displays the values of 'data1' and 'data'. The former is in the class and therefore its value is displayed. However the former is not in the class, so the inheritance tree is searched for the object. Note that 'data' exists in the base class (BaseClass) and therefore its value will be displayed. This is true for methods also. Even if the derived class does not have a particular method, it can be invoked if it exists in the parent class or in any other class up the inheritance tree. It may also be stated here that the objects are generally searched from left to right in a particular level.

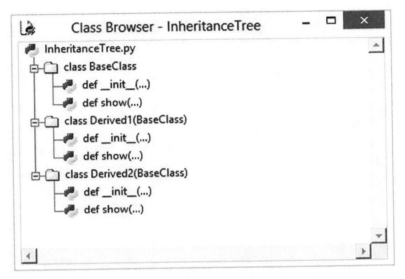

FIGURE 11.11 The class hierarchy for given illustration

Code

```
class BaseClass:
    def _init_(self,data):
        self.data=data
    def show(self):
        print("\nData\t:",self.data)

class Derived1(BaseClass):
    def _init_(self,data,data1):
        self.data1=data1
        BaseClass._init_(self,data)
    def show(self):
        print("\nData\t:",self.data1,"\nBase class data\
                                        t:",self.data)

class Derived2(BaseClass):
    def_init_(self,data,data2):
        self.data2=data2
        BaseClass._init_(self,data)
    def show(self):
        print("\nData\t:",self.data2,"\nBase class data\
                                        t:",self.data)

X=BaseClass(1)
X.show()
print(X.data)
```

```
Y=Derived1(2,3)
Y.show()
Z=Derived2(4,5)
Z.show()
Inheritance tree
>>>
```

Output

```
======= RUN C:/Python/Inheritance/InheritanceTree.py =======
Data    : 1
1
Data    : 3
Base class data    : 2
Data    : 5
Base class data    : 4
>>>
```

11.5   CLASS INTERFACE AND ABSTRACT CLASSES

At times the classes are crafted so that they can be sub classed. While designating, there is no intention of instantiating the class. The classes which will not be instantiated but will only be used to create base classes are called abstract classes. In order to understand the concept, let us consider an example. The following example has four classes: `BaseClass`, `Derived1`, `Derived2`, and `Derived3`.

The `BaseClass` has two methods: `method1` and `method2` . The first method has some task associated with it, whereas the second wants the derived class to implement it. The derived class should, to be able to call this method, have a method called action. The first derived class (`Derived1`), replaces `method1`. So if an instance of `Derived1` calls `method1`, the version defined in `Derived1` would be called. The second method extends `method1`, it adds something to `method1` and also calls the `BaseClass` version of `method1`. When `method1` is called from `Derived2`, the `BaseClass` version is called as the search in the inheritance tree invokes the base class version of the method. The third derived class (`Derived3`) also implements the action method defined in the base class. Note that when `method2` is called through an instance of `Derived3`, the base class version of `method2` is invoked. This version calls action and a new search is initiated, thus resulting in the invocation of action of `Derived3`. Illustration 11.9 presents the code.

Note that the above concept can be extended and a class may have methods that would be implemented by the derived classes. Interestingly, Python has provisions that such classes would not be instantiated until all such methods are not defined. Such base classes are called abstract classes. The implementation of abstract classes has been discussed in the appendix of this book.

Illustration 11.9: Implement the following hierarchy. `'method1'` of `Derived1` should replace `method1` of the base class, `method1` of `Derived2` should extend `method1` of the base class and `action` of `Derived3` should implement `method2` of the `BaseClass`.

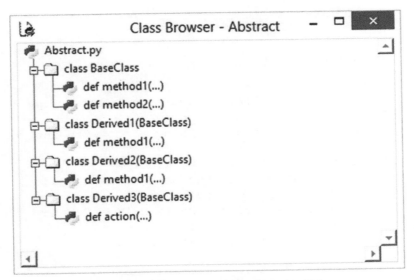

FIGURE 11.12 Class hierarchy for Illustration 11.9

Solution:

```
class BaseClass:
    def method1(self):
        print("In BaseClass from method1")
    def method2(self):
        self.action()
class Derived1(BaseClass):
    def method1(self):
```

```
            print("A new method, has got nothing to do with
                                that of the base class")
class Derived2(BaseClass):
    def method1(self):
        print("A method that extends the base class
                                           method")
        BaseClass.method1(self)
class Derived3(BaseClass):
    def action(self):
        print("\nImplementing the base class method")

for className in (Derived1, Derived2, Derived3):
print("\nClass\t:",className)
className().method1()
X=Derived3()
X.method2()
\
```

Output

```
>>>
============ RUN C:/Windows/System32/Abstract.py ============
Class : <class '_main__.Derived1'>
A new method, has got nothing to do with that of the base
                                                      class
Class : <class '_main__.Derived2'>
A method that extends the base class method
In BaseClass from method1
Class : <class '_main__.Derived3'>
In BaseClass from method1
Implementing the base class method
```

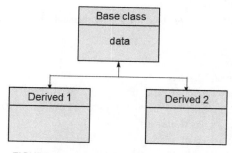

FIGURE 11.13 Searching in an inheritance tree

11.6   CONCLUSION

The chapter introduces the concept of inheritance, which is one of the most important ingredients of object-oriented programming. Inheritance, as explained in the chapter, helps the program in reusing the code and making the program more structured. However it should be used wisely, as in many cases it leads to problems like ambiguity. The reader must also appreciate that it is not always necessary to use inheritance. Most of the tasks can be accomplished using composition. However even if using inheritance becomes a necessity, be clear about the type of inheritance required, the type of method calls required and the use of bound methods. The discussion on object-oriented programming paradigms continues in the next chapter also, where the concept of operator overloading has been introduced. The last chapter, this chapter and the next one will help the reader to successfully develop a software using OOP.

GLOSSARY

Inheritance: Inheritance is the process of creating subclasses from existing classes.

Base class and derived class: The class from which other classes are derived is the base class and the classes that inherit from the base class are the derived classes.

Implicit inheritance: In this type, the method of the base class can be called using an instance of the derived class.

Explicit overriding: In this type of inheritance, the derived class will redefine the method of the base class and calling this method using an instance of the derived class would invoke the method of the derived class.

POINTS TO REMEMBER

- Inheritance provides reusability and increased reliability.
- Types of inheritance are simple inheritance, multiple inheritance, multilevel inheritance, hierarchical inheritance, and hybrid inheritance.

- Multiple inheritance may lead to ambiguity.
- A bound method has a "self" parameter whereas an unbound method does not have "self" parameter.
- A class can also be instantiated in another class.
- Super can be used to access the base class methods.
- The inheritance tree is searched to find the version of method to be invoked.

EXERCISES

MULTIPLE CHOICE QUESTIONS

1. A class that cannot be instantiated until all its methods have been defined by its subclass(es) is called
   (a) Abstract class
   (b) Meta class
   (c) Base class
   (d) None of the above

   A class called operation has an_init__, which takes a positional parameter and an integer as an argument. Two instances of operations Num1 and Num2 have been defined as follows. The class has two functions; the first calculates the square of a number and the second calculates the cube. A list called List1 is created which contains the names of the four methods (two of Num1 and two of Num2). A for loop is then used to call the methods as shown in the following snippet:

```
Num1=operations(5)
Num2=operations(4)
List= [Num1.square, Num1.cube, Num2.square, Num2.cube]
for callable_object in List:
     print(callable_object())
```

2. The program containing the above code (assume that the rest of the code is correct)
   (a) Has no syntax error but does not execute
   (b) Has syntax error
   (c) Has no syntax error and executes
   (d) Insufficient information

3. In the above question, what would the output be (if the code is correct)?

    (*a*) The code is not correct   (*b*) 25 125 16 64

    (*c*) 125 25 64 16   (*d*) None of the above

4. The names of the methods in the list (question 2) are similar to (in 'C#')

    (*a*) Meta classes   (*b*) Delegates

    (*c*) Both   (*d*) None of the above

5. `'self'` in Python is similar to

    (*a*) `'this'` is 'C#'   (*b*) `'me'` in 'C#'

    (*c*) Delegate in 'C#'   (*d*) None of the above

6.
```
class Student:
    def display(self, something):
        print("\n"+something)
    def getdata(name,age):
        name=name
        age=age
        print("\nName\t:",name,"\nAge\t:",age)
```

In the above snippet, how would you invoke `getdata`? (assume that Hari is an instance of `Student`).

    (*a*) `Student.getdata("Harsh", 22)`

    (*b*) `Hari.getdata("Harsh", 24)`

    (*c*) Both are correct

    (*d*) None of the above

7. Can a method also be invoked by creating an un-named instance of a class?

    (*a*) Yes   (*b*) No

    (*c*) Insufficient data

    (*d*) There in nothing called unnamed instance of a class in Python

8. Which of the following is used in searching an inheritance tree?

    (*a*) Breadth First search   (*b*) Depth First search

    (*c*) Both   (*d*) None of the above

9. In an inheritance tree at the same level, which policy is used to search an object?
   (a) Left to right   (b) Right to left
   (c) Any   (d) None of the above

10. 'super' can be used to call
    (a) The init of the base class
    (b) Any method of the base class
    (c) Cannot be used to call methods of the base class
    (d) None of the above. The usage of 'super' depends on the type of inheritance

11. Which type of inheritance leads to ambiguity?
    (a) Multiple   (b) Multilevel
    (c) Both   (d) None

12. Which type of inheritance has just one base class and a single derived class?
    (a) Simple   (b) Hierarchical
    (c) Multiple   (d) None of the above

13. Which type of inheritance has more than one base class(es) and a single derived class?
    (a) Simple   (b) Hierarchical
    (c) Multiple   (d) None of the above

14. Which type of inheritance has more than one derived class(es) and a single derived class?
    (a) Simple   (b) Hierarchical
    (c) Multiple   (d) None of the above

15. Can a derived class be a base class of some other class?
    (a) Yes   (b) No
    (c) Insufficient data   (d) None of the above

THEORY

1. What is inheritance? Explain the importance of inheritance.

2. What are the disadvantages of inheritance? Explain with reference to multiple inheritance.

3. What are the various types of inheritance? Give examples.

4. What are the problems in implementing multiple inheritance? How are they resolved?

5. What is composition? Is it a type of inheritance?

6. Is inheritance mandatory in object-oriented programming? Justify.

7. What is the difference between "is a" and "has a" relationships? Explain with the help of examples.

8. Which is better, inheritance or composition? Can all that can be achieved using inheritance be done using composition?

9. Explain the use of "super." How can it be used to call methods of the base class?

10. Are methods in Python objects? Justify your answer. What is meant by callable object?

11. What is an abstract class? How does an abstract class help in achieving the goals of OOPs?

12. What are bound methods? What are the various ways of invoking a bound method?

13. Differentiate between a bound and an unbound method. Give examples.

14. What is the importance of `'self'` in Python?

15. Explain the mechanism of search in an inheritance tree.

PROGRAMMING EXERCISE

1. A class called `Base1` has two methods: `method1(self, message)` and `method2(self)`. The first method prints the message passed as an argument to the method. The second invokes another method called

action1(self), which would be defined by the sub-class (Derived2) of Base1. Derived1, another derived class of Base1, redefines method1 and does nothing with method2. Derived2, on the other hand, does nothing with method1. Implement the hierarchy and find what happens in the following cases:

(*a*) An instance of Base1 calls method1

(*b*) An instance of Derived1 calls method1

(*c*) An instance of Derived2 calls method1

(*d*) An instance of Base1 calls method2

(*e*) An instance of Derived2 calls method2

(*f*) An instance of Derived1 calls method2

(*g*) An instance of Derived2 calls action

2. A class called operation has an _init_, which takes a positional parameter and an integer as an argument. The class has two functions; the first calculates the square root of a number and the second calculates the cube root. Two instances of operations, Num1 and Num2 are to be created. A list called List1 is to be created which contains the names of the four methods (two of Num1 and two of Num2). Implement the above and use a for loop to call all the callable objects from the list.

3. A class employee has two methods getdata(name, age) and getdata1(self, name, age). The getdata method stores the values in the local variables. Another method called putdata shows the data. Write a program to call the methods (the first is not bound but the second is) and display the data.

4. Create the following hierarchy and explain the search process of method called "show".

CHAPTER 12

OPERATOR OVERLOADING

After reading this chapter, the reader will be able to

- Understand the importance of operator overloading
- Implement constructor overloading
- Understand and be able to use various methods used for overloading operators
- Implement operator overloading for complex numbers and fractions
- Understand the importance of destructors

12.1   INTRODUCTION

Operators are defined for primary data structures in all the languages. For example, in Python the + operator adds two numbers or two floats or concatenates two strings. However, for user defined data types the programmer can't use these operators directly.

Operator overloading helps the programmer to define existing operators for user defined objects. This makes the language powerful and the work simple. This simplicity and intuitiveness in turn makes programming fun.

In Python, operator overloading is done by defining specific methods discussed in the sections that follow. Operator overloading can be used to intercept Python operators by classes and even to overload built-in operations, e.g. attribute access. The said methods which help in operator overloading have been specially named and Python calls these methods when instances of classes use the associated operator. Moreover, it's not always the case that operator overloading must be implemented.

This chapter discusses operator overloading. The chapter is organized as follows. Section 12.2 revisits _init_ and discusses how it can be overloaded. Section 12.3 presents some of the common operator overloading methods. Section 12.4 presents an example of overloading the binary operators. Section 12.5 discusses _iadd_. Section 12.6 discusses the comparison operators. Section 12.7 discusses bool and len and the next section presents the concept of destructors. The last section concludes the chapter.

12.2 _INIT_ REVISITED

The _init_ function has already been explained in Chapter 10 of this book. The function initializes the members of a class. Those of you from a C++ or Java background will find it hard to ignore the similarity between the constructors (which have the same name as that of the class in C++, etc.) and the _init_ function. Earlier it was stated that _init_ cannot be overloaded, which is partly true. Though one cannot have two _init_ functions in the same class, there is a way to implement constructor overloading as explained in the following discussion.

As stated earlier the purpose of _init_ is to initialize the members of the class. In the following example (Illustration 12.1), a class called complex has two members: real and imaginary, which are initialized by the parameters of the _init_ function. Note that the members of the class are denoted by self.real and self.imaginary and the parameters of the functions are initialized by real and imaginary. The example has a function called putData to display the values of the members. In the _main_() function, c1 is an instance of the class complex. The object c1 is initialized by 5 and 3 and the putData() of the class has been invoked to display the 'Complex Number'.

Illustration 12.1: Create a class called complex, having two members - real and imaginary. The class should have _init_, which takes two parameters to initialize the values of real and imaginary respectively and a function called putData to display the complex number. Create an instance of the complex number in the _main_() function, initialize it by (5, 3) and display the number by invoking the putData function.

Code

```
class Complex:
  def _init_(self, real, imaginary):
    self.real = real
    self.imaginary = imaginary
  def putData(self):
    print(self.real," + i ",self.imaginary)

def_ main_():
     c1=Complex(5, 3)
     c1.putData()

_main_()
```

Output

```
=== RUN C:\Python\Operator Overlaoding\_init_\Example1.py ===
5 + i 3
>>>
```

Let us consider another example of _init_. The example (Illustration 12.2) deals with the implementation of vectors. In the example, a class called Vector has two data members called args and length. Since arg can contain any number of items, the _init_ has *args as the parameter. The putData function displays the vector and the _len_ function calculates the length of the Vector (as in the number of arguments).

Illustration 12.2: Create a class called Vector, which can be instantiated with a vector of any length. Design the requisite _init_ function and a function to overload the len operator. The class should also have a putData function to display the vector. Instantiate the class with a vector having:

- no element
- one element
- two elements
- three elements

Display each vector and also display the length.

Code

```
class Vector:
  def _init_(self, * args):
    self.args=args
```

```
    def putData(self):
      print(self.args)
      print('Length',len(self))
    def _len_(self):
      self.length = len(self.args)
      return(self.length)
def _main_():
  v0= Vector()
  v0.putData()
  v1 = Vector(2)
  v1.putData()
  v2 = Vector(3, 4)
  v2.putData()
  v3 = Vector(7, 8, 9)
  v3.putData()

_main_()
```

Output

```
>>>
=== RUN C:\Python\Operator Overlaoding\_init_\Example2.py ===
()
Length        0
(2,)
Length        1
(3, 4)
Length        2
(7, 8, 9)
Length        3
>>>
```

Note that in the above example, _init_ has the same effect as having many constructors with different parameters. Although _init_ has not been overloaded in the literal sense, the program has the same effect as that of one having overloaded constructors.

12.2.1 Overloading _init_ (sort of)

Constructors can be overloaded by assigning None to the arguments (some or all, except for the positional argument). In order to understand the point, consider a class called Complex. The class must have two constructors; one which takes two arguments and one when no argument is given. In the first case the real and imaginary part of Complex should be initialized with the arguments of _init_ and in the second the real and imaginary should become zero. One of the simplest solutions is to check if the two arguments are None or not. If both of them are None, the data members should be made zero. In the second case they should contain the arguments, passed in _init_. Though the following program (Illustration 12.3) does not have two _init_, nevertheless the above task has been accomplished.

Illustration 12.3: Construct a class called Complex having real and ima as its data members. The class should have an _init_ for initializing the data members and putData for displaying the complex number.

Code

```
class Complex:
  def_init_(self, real=None, ima=None):
    if ((real == None)&(ima==None)):
      self.real=0
      self.ima=0
    else:
      self.real=real
      self.ima=ima
    def putData(self):
      print(str(self.real)," +i ",str(self.ima))
c1=Complex(5,3)
c1.putData()
c2=Complex()
c2.putData()
```

Output

```
>>>
== RUN C:/Python/Operator Overlaoding/_init_/Example 10.py ==
5 +i 3
0 +i 0
>>>
```

12.3 METHODS FOR OVERLOADING BINARY OPERATORS

The following methods (Table12.1) help in overloading the binary operators like +, −, *, and /. The operators operate on two operands: self and another instance of the requisite class. When an operator is used between objects, the corresponding methods are invoked. For example for objects c1 and c2 of a class called `Complex`, c1+c2 invokes the _add_ method. Similarly, the – operator would invoke the _sub_ method, the * would invoke the _mul_ method and so one. Table 12.1 shows the method and the operator due to which the method is invoked.

Table 12.1 Methods for overloading binary operators

Task	Method	Explanation
Addition	_add_	Helps in overloading the + operator. Generally, this takes two arguments: the positional parameter and the instance to be added.
Subtraction	_sub_	Helps in overloading the – operator. Generally, this takes two arguments: the positional parameter and the instance to be subtracted.
Multiplication	_mul_	Helps in overloading the ° operator. Generally, this takes two arguments: the positional parameter and the instance to be multiplied.
Division	_truediv_	Helps in overloading the / operator. Generally, this takes two arguments: the positional parameter and the instance to be divided.

The use of the above operators has been explained in the following section.

12.4 OVERLOADING BINARY OPERATORS: THE FRACTION EXAMPLE

The overloading of the operators shown in the above table can be easily understood by the example that follows. The following example overloads the addition (+), subtraction (-), multiplication (*), and division (/) operators for a class fraction. The fraction class depicts the standard fraction, having a numerator and a denominator. The details of the methods of the class are as follows:

1. _init_

The _init_ initializes the class by setting the numerator to 0 and the denominator to 1. The statement

```
x=fraction()
```

therefore, creates a fraction 0/1.

2. _add_

   The _add_ helps in overloading the + operator. The statement

   ```
   z=x+y
   ```

   calls the _add_ of *x* and takes *y* as the "other" argument. Therefore, it must have two arguments: a positional parameter (self) and a fraction (other). The addition of two fractions $\frac{a_1}{b_1}$ and $\frac{a_2}{b_2}$ is done as follows. The LCM of b_1 and b_2 becomes the denominator of the resultant fraction. The numerator is calculated using the following formula.

   $$numerator = \left(\frac{LCM}{b_1}\right) \times a_1 + \left(\frac{LCM}{b_2}\right) \times a_2$$

   Note that the resultant fraction is stored in another fraction (s). The method _add_ returns s.

3. _sub_

   The _sub_ helps in overloading the - operator. The statement

   ```
   t=x-y
   ```

   calls the _sub_ of x and takes y as the "other" argument. Therefore, it must have two arguments: a positional parameter (self) and a fraction (other). The difference of two fractions $\frac{a_2}{b_2}$ and $\frac{a_2}{b_2}$ is done as follows. The LCM of b_1 and b_2 becomes the denominator of the resultant fraction. The numerator is calculated using the following formula.

   $$numerator = \left(\frac{LCM}{b_1}\right) \times a_1 - \left(\frac{LCM}{b_2}\right) \times a_2$$

   Note that the resultant fraction is stored in another fraction (d). The method _sub_ returns d.

4. _mul_

   The _mul_ helps in overloading the * operator. The statement

   ```
   prod=x*y
   ```

   calls the _mul_ of x and takes y as the "other" argument. Therefore, it must have two arguments: a positional parameter (self) and a fraction (other). The product of two fractions $\dfrac{a_1}{b_1}$ and $\dfrac{a_2}{b_2}$ is calculated as follows. The numerator is calculated using the following formula.

$$numerator = a_1 \times a_2$$

And the denominator is calculated as follows.

$$denominator = b_1 \times b_2$$

Note that the resultant fraction is stored in another fraction (m). The method `_mul_` returns m.

5. `_truediv_`

The `_truediv_` helps in overloading the / operator (which returns an integer). The statement

```
div = x/y
```

calls the `_truediv_` of x and takes y as the "other" argument. Therefore, it must have two arguments: a positional parameter (`self`) and a fraction (`other`).

The division of two fractions $\dfrac{a_1}{b_1}$ and $\dfrac{a_2}{b_2}$ is done as follows. The numerator is calculated using the following formula.

$$numerator = a_1 \times b_2$$

and the denominator is calculated as follows.

$$denominator = b_1 \times a_2$$

Note that the resultant fraction is stored in another fraction (answer). The method `_truediv_` returns the answer.

Illustration 12.4: Create a class called fraction having numerator and denominator as its members. Overload the following operators for the class

- +
- −
- *
- /

Create LCM and GCD methods in order to accomplish the above tasks. The LCM method should find the LCM of two numbers and the GCD method should find the GCD of the two numbers. Note that LCM(x, y) × GCD(x, y) = x × y.

Solution: The implementation has already been discussed. The following code performs the requisite tasks and the output follows.

Code

```
##fractions
class fraction:
    def __init__(self):
        self.num=0;
        self.den=1;
    def getdata(self):
        self.num=input("Enter the numerator\t:")
        self.den = input("Enter the denominator\t:")
    def display(self):
        print(str(int(self.num)),"/",str(int(self.den)))
    def gcd(first, second):
        if(first<second):
            temp=first
            first=second
            second=temp
        if(first%second==0):
            return second
    else:
        return(fraction.gcd(second, first%second))
        def lcm(first, second):
            ##print("GCD is",str(fraction.gcd(first,second)))
            return((first*second)/fraction.gcd(first,second))
    def _add_(self,other):
        s=fraction()
        lc=fraction.lcm(int(self.den), int(other.den))
            s.num=((lc/int(self.den))*int(self.num))+((lc/
                        int(other.den))*int(other.num))
        s.den=lc
        return(s)
    def _sub_(self,other):
        lc=fraction.lcm(int(self.den), int(other.den))
        d=fraction()
            d.num=((lc/int(self.den))*int(self.num))-((lc/
                        int(other.den))*int(other.num))
        d.den=lc
        return(d)
    def _mul_(self,other):
        m=fraction()
        m.num=int(self.num)*int(other.num)
```

```
            m.den=int(self.den)*int(other.den)
            return(m)
        def __truediv__(self,other):
            answer=fraction()
            answer.num=int(self.num)*int(other.den)
            answer.den=int(self.den)*int(other.num)
            return(answer)
x =fraction()
x.getdata()
print("First fraction\t:")
x.display()
y=fraction()
y.getdata()
print("Second fraction\t:")
y.display()
z=(x+y)
print("Sum\t:")
z.display()
t=x-y
print("Difference\t:")
t.display()
prod=x*y
print("Product")
prod.display()
div=x/y
print("Division")
div.display()
Output:
>>>
```

Output

```
== RUN C:/Python/Operator Overlaoding/Add/Fraction_add.py ==
Enter the numerator      :2
Enter the denominator    :3
First fraction   :
2 / 3
Enter the numerator      :4
Enter the denominator    :5
Second fraction   :
4 / 5
Sum    :
22 / 15
Difference   :
-2 / 15
```

```
Product
8 / 15
Division
10 / 12
>>>
```

Was it really needed?

Note that the above illustration has been included in the chapter to explain the overloading of binary operators. Python, as such, provides addition, subtraction, multiplication and division for fractions (refer to Chapter 2). The same task can be done without overloading the operators as follows:

```
>>> from fractions import Fraction
>>> X=Fraction(20,4)
>>> X
Fraction(5, 1)
>>> Y=Fraction(3,5)
>>> Y
Fraction(3, 5)
>>> X+Y
Fraction(28, 5)
>>> X-Y
Fraction(22, 5)
>>> X*Y
Fraction(3, 1)
>>> X/Y
Fraction(25, 3)
    >>>
```

12.5   OVERLOADING THE += OPERATOR

The += operator adds a quantity to the given object. For example if the value of "a" is 5, then a+=4 would make it 9. However, the operator works for integer, reals and strings. The use of += for integer, real and string has been shown as follows:

```
>>> a=5
>>> a+=4
>>> a
9
>>> a=2.3
>>> a+=1.3
```

```
>>> a
3.5999999999999996
>>> a="Hi"
>>> a+=" There"
>>> a
'Hi There'
>>>
```

However, in order to make it work for a user defined data type (or object), it needs to be overloaded. The _idd_ helps in accomplishing this task. The following illustration (Illustration 12.5) depicts the use of _idd_ for an object of the complex class. A complex number has a real part and an imaginary part. Adding another complex number to a given complex number adds their respective real parts and imaginary parts. The program follows. Note that, _iadd_ takes two arguments. The first being the positional parameter and the second another object called "other." The real part of "other" is added to the real part of the object and the imaginary part of "other" is added to the imaginary part. The _iadd_ returns "self." Likewise, the reader may overload the _iadd_ operator for his class, as per the requirements.

Illustration 12.5: Overloading += for complex class (Illustrations 12.1 and 12.3)

Code

```
##overlaoding += for Complex class
class Complex:
    def _init_(self, real, imaginary):
        self.real=real
        self.imaginary=imaginary
    def _iadd_(self, other):
        self.real+=other.real
        self.imaginary+=other.imaginary
        return self
    def display(self):
    print("Real part\t:",str(self.real)," Imaginary part\
                          t:",str(self.imaginary))
X=Complex(2,3)
Y=Complex(4,5)
X.display()
Y.display()
X+=Y
X.display()
X+=Y
X.display()
```

Output

```
>>>
======= RUN C:/Python/Operator Overlaoding/iadd.py =======
Real part    : 2   Imaginary part    : 3
Real part    : 4   Imaginary part    : 5
Real part    : 6   Imaginary part    : 8
Real part    : 10  Imaginary part    : 13
>>>
```

12.6   OVERLOADING THE > AND < OPERATORS

The greater than (>) and less than (<) operators work in the usual manner for the integers, fractions and some other predefined types. However to be able to use these operators for user defined classes, the programmer must overload the operators. In Python, greater than (>) and less than (<) can be overloaded using the _gt_ and _lt_. The _gt_ returns a true or a false depending upon whether the first object is greater than the second or not. Similarly, the _lt_ returns a true or a false depending upon whether the first object is less than the second or not.

The following example overloads the _gt_ and _lt_ for a class called Data. The Data class has a data member called "value." The _gt_ compares the value of the instance (self) and that of another instance (other). If the value of the instance is greater than that of the other instance then a true is retuned, otherwise a false is returned. Similarly, The _lt_ compares the value of the instance (self) and that of another instance (other). If the value of the instance is smaller than that of the other instance then a true is returned, otherwise a false is returned.

Illustration 12.6: Write a program to create a class called Data having "value" as its data member. Overload the (>) and the (<) operator for the class. Instantiate the class and compare the objects using _lt_ and _gt_.

Solution: The mechanism of the _gt_ and _lt_ has already been discussed. The program follows.

Code

```
class Data:
    def _init_(self, value):
        self.value=value
```

```
        def display(self):
            print("data is ",str(value))
        def _lt_(self,other):
            return(self.value<other.value)
        def _gt_(self,other):
            return(self.value>other.value)
X= Data(5)
Y= Data(4)
print(X>Y)
```

Output

```
>>> `
==== RUN C:/Python/Operator Overlaoding/Comparision.py ====
True
False
>>>
print(X<Y)
```

12.7 OVERLOADING THE _BOOLEAN_ OPERATORS: PRECEDENCE OF _BOOL_ OVER _LEN_

In using "if" and "while" the programmer checks the condition passed in "if" or "while." If the condition is true the block following "if" or "while" is executed, otherwise it is not executed. We can also define the Boolean operators for a user defined object. In order to accomplish this, the programmer will require some method that helps in the overloading. Python provides two Boolean operators - _bool_ and _len_. The _bool_ method returns a true if the requisite condition is met, otherwise it returns a false. The _len_ method finds the length of the data member and returns false if it is null. The Boolean condition can be checked using the _len_ method, only if the _bool_ for that class is not defined. In case both _len_ and _bool_ are defined in a class, _bool_ takes precedence over _len_.

For example in the following illustration, writing if (X), where X is an instance of the class returns a false if no argument is passed while instantiating the class. Note that the first listing uses _len_. The next illustration (Illustration 12.7) checks the length of the data member "value" to return a true if "value" is not null and false otherwise.

Illustration 12.7: The following illustration creates a class called data. If no argument is passed while instantiating the class a false is returned, otherwise a true is returned.

Program

```
class Data:
 def_len_(self): return 0
X=Data()
if X:
    print("True returned")
else:
    print("False returned")
```

Output

```
>>>
======== RUN C:/Python/Operator Overlaoding/len.py ========
False returned
>>>
```

Illustration 12.8: Another variant of the above example has `'value'` as its data member. If the `'value'` is null a false is returned, otherwise a `true` is returned.

Program

```
class Data:
   def_init_(self, value):
      self.value=value
   def_len__(self):
      if len(self.value)==0:
         return 0
       else:
         return 1
##X= Data()
##if X:
## print("True returned")
##else:
## print("False returned")

Y=Data("hi")
if Y:
    print("True returned")
```

```
else:
   print("False returned")
X= Data("")
if X:
   print("Ture returned")
else:
   print("False returned")
>>>
```

Output

```
======== RUN C:/Python/Operator Overlaoding/len.py ========
True returned
False returned
>>>
```

Also note that if _bool_ is also defined in the class, then it takes precedence over the _len_ method. The _bool_ returns a true or a false as per the given condition. Although overloading _bool_ may not be of much use as every object is either true or false in Python. Illustration 12.9 presents an example in which both _bool_ and _len_ are defined.

Illustration 12.9: An example in which both _bool_ and _len_ are defined.

Program

```
class Data:
  def_init_(self, value):
    self.value=value
  def_len__(self):
    if len(self.value)==0:
      return 0
    else:
      return 1
  def_bool__(self):
    if len(self.value)==0:
      print("From Bool")
      return False
    else:
      print("From Bool")
      return True
Y= Data("hi")
if Y:
  print("True returned")
```

```
else:
  print("False returned")
X= Data("")
if X:
  print("Ture returned")
else:
  print("False returned")
```

Output

```
====== RUN C:/Python/Operator Overlaoding/_bool_.py ======
From Bool
True returned
From Bool
False returned
>>>
```

12.8 DESTRUCTORS

Destructors are called automatically when the space of an object of a class is reclaimed. Destructors are complementary to constructors. Constructors are called when a new object is created and the destructors are called when its space is reclaimed. It may be noted that the destructors are not as important in Python as they are in some other object-oriented languages. In fact, many programmers consider the destructors as "obsolete." The reasons for this are as follows.

Garbage collection: Garbage collection is one of the characteristics of Python. That is, the memory allocated to an object is reclaimed as soon as the object (an instance of a class) is reclaimed. So, there is little need of an explicit destructor.

Moreover, it becomes difficult to predict the position at which the destructor needs to be called. For example, in the following listing the destructor is called as soon as a value is assigned to the object. But conceptually, the user may want to use the object in the remaining task.

No garbage collection: There is another reason for not using destructors. They, at times, hinder garbage collection. This is good, if deliberate, but bad if not used without due deliberation. Most of the time the garbage collection done by Python is good. The following illustration (Illustration 12.10) presents a class called Data, which has an explicit destructor (_del_). Note that when the memory is reclaimed, a destructor is called.

Illustration 12.10: Use of destructor

Code

```
>>> class Data:
    def_init_(self, value):
        self.value=value
    def display(self):
        print("Value\t:",str(self.value))
    def_del_(self):
        print("Destructor called")
>>>
>>> X=Data(5)
>>> X.display()
Value : 5
>>> X='Hi'
Destructor called
>>>
```

Having discussed the problems of destructor, it is always better to craft an explicit method for the termination activities rather than allowing a destructor to be called.

12.9   CONCLUSION

Overloading means *many meanings for the same symbol*. Primarily overloading can be segregated into two classes: name overloading and symbol overloading. An operator, which is a symbol that tells the compiler to perform some mathematical operation, can also be overloaded. That is, operator overloading can be defined as giving multiple definitions to an operator. Python allows operators to be overloaded for user defined data types. In Python, operator overloading can be accomplished by overriding the requisite methods and calling them as and when required. It may be stated here that the overload operator is a member of a class. This chapter introduces the concept of operator overloading and explains the idea using ample examples. The reader is expected to attempt the problems given in the exercise to get a clear insight and be able to use the methods introduced in the chapter in practical situations.

GLOSSARY

- **Operator overloading:** This is the mechanism of assigning a new meaning to an existing object.

POINTS TO REMEMBER

- Operator overloading helps the programmer to define an existing operator for user defined objects.
- In Python all expression operators can be overloaded.
- Operator overloading can be implemented using special methods.
- `_bool_` has higher priority over `_len_`.

EXERCISES

MULTIPLE CHOICE QUESTIONS

1. Using operator overloading, the programmer can
   (a) Define an existing operator for user defined data type
   (b) Create new operators
   (c) Both
   (d) None of the above

2. In Python, operator overloading can be implemented by
   (a) Defining corresponding methods in the class for which user defined objects would be made
   (b) Operators are redefined in the same way as in C++
   (c) Python has predefined methods for defining operators
   (d) None of the above

3. Can `_init_` be overloaded?
   (a) Yes   (b) No
   (c) It can be overloaded only for specific classes
   (d) None of the above

4. If the same _init_ is to be designed to accept varying number of arguments, which of the following is the correct representation?
   (a) def _init_ (self)   (b) def _init_ (self, *args)
   (c) def _init_ (self, args)   (d) Both (b) and (c)

5. The above task can be accomplished by
   (a) Not giving any arguments in _init_
   (b) Equating some of the arguments to NONE
   (c) Both   (d) None of the above

6. Which of the following methods is used to overload the + operator?
   (a) _add_   (b) _iadd_
   (c) _sum_   (d) None of the above

7. Which of the following is used to overload the − operator?
   (a) _diff_   (b) _sub_
   (c) _minus_   (d) None of the above

8. Which of the following is used to overload the * operator?
   (a) _prod_   (b) _mul_
   (c) Both   (d) None of the above

9. For which of the following, operator overloading is really needed?
   (a) Complex   (b) Fraction
   (c) Polar coordinates   (d) None of the above

10. Which of the following is overloaded using _iadd_?
    (a) +   (b) + =
    (c) ++   (d) None of the above

11. Can > and < operators be overloaded in Python?
    (a) Yes   (b) No
    (c) Only for specific classes   (d) None of the above

12. Which has more priority _bool_ or _len_?
    (a) _bool_   (b) _len_
    (c) Both   (d) None of the above

THEORY

1. What is operator overloading? Explain its importance.

2. Explain the mechanism of overloading operators in Python.

3. Can all Python operators be overloaded?

4. The membership can be tested using the `'in'` operator. The `contains` method can be used for testing the membership in Python. Create a class having three lists and overload the membership operator for the class.

5. Explain the following methods and explain operator overloading using the operators.
   - (*a*) `_add_`
   - (*b*) `_iadd_`
   - (*c*) `_sub_`
   - (*d*) `_mul_`
   - (*e*) `_div_`
   - (*f*) `_len_`
   - (*g*) `_bool_`
   - (*h*) `_gt_`
   - (*i*) `_lt_`
   - (*j*) `_del_`

6. The following methods have not been discussed in the chapter. Explore the following and use them for complex class.
   - (*a*) `_getitem_`
   - (*b*) `_setitem_`
   - (*c*) `_iter_`
   - (*d*) `_next_`

PROGRAMMING

1. Create a class called `Distance` having `meter` and `centimeter` as its data members. The member functions of the class would be `putData()`, which takes the values of meter and centimeter from the user; `putData()`, which displays the data members and add, which adds the two distances.

   The addition of two instances of distances (say *d*1 and *d*2) would require addition of corresponding centimeters (*d*1.centimeter +*s*2.centimeter), if the sum is less than 100, otherwise it would be (*d*1.centimeter +*s*2.centimeter)%100. The "meter" of the sum would be the sum of meters of the two instances (*d*1.meter +*d*2.meter), if (*d*1.centimeter +*d*2.centimeter)<100, otherwise it would be (*d*1.meter +*d*2.meter+1).

2. Overload the + operator for the above class. The + operator should carry out the same task as is done by the add function.

The subtraction of two instances of distances (say $d1$ and $d2$) would require the subtraction of corresponding centimeters ($d1$.centimeter $-s2$.centimeter). The "meter" of the difference would be the sum of meters of the two instances ($d1$.meter $- d2$.meter).

3. Overload the $-$ operator for the `distance` class. Assume that $d1$-$d2$, would always mean $d1 > d2$.

4. Overload the $+=$ operator for `Distance` class. The $+=$ operator (that is $d1 +=d2$) would require the addition of $d1$ and $d2$ (as explained earlier) and updating $d1$ with ($d1+d2$). Note that, the value of $d2$ is not altered.

5. Overload the $*$ operator for the `Distance` class.

    The government of a developing country intends to do away with the present currency and intends to introduce a barter system, in which 12 bottles of "Tanjali" would be equivalent to a unit of currency. This in turn would increase the sales of the company. Hari and Aslam have 37 and 92 bottles of 'Tanjali' and would like to exchange the bottles to buy tickets to a movie. If each ticket is 60 Units, would they be able to watch the movie?

6. Now, help the people of the country by developing a program having a class called `nat_currency` and overload the $+$ operator, which adds two instances of `nat_currency`.

7. For the above question, overload the $-$ operator.

8. For the `nat_currency` class of question 6, overload the $+=$ operator.

9. For the `nat_currency` class of question 6, overload the $*$ operator.

10. Create a class called `date` having members' dd, mm, and yyyy (date, month, and year). Overload the $+$ operator, which adds the two instances of the `date class`.

    A hypothetical number called `irr`, of the form $c\sqrt{b}$, has b constant. Two instances of `irr` can be added as follows. If the first `irr` number is $r_1 = a_1 + c_1\sqrt{b}$ and the second is $r_2 = a_2 + 2\sqrt{d}$, the addition of r_1 and r_2 would be $r = r_1 + r_2 = (a_1 + a_2) + (c_1 + c_2)\sqrt{d}$.

    The difference of r_1 and r_2 would be $r = r_1 - r_2 = (a_1 - a_2) + (c_1 - c_2)\sqrt{d}$.

    The product of r_1 and r_2 would be $r = r_1 \times r_2 = (a_1 a_2 + c_1 c_2\, d) + (a_1 c_2 + a_2 c_1)\sqrt{d}$.

11. Create a class called `irr` and overload the $+$ operator.

12. For the `irr` class, overload the – operator.

13. For the `irr` class, overload the += operator

14. For the `irr` class, overload the * operator.

 A vector is written as $a\hat{i} + b\hat{j} + c\hat{k}$, where $\hat{i}$ is a unit vector in the x axis, $\hat{j}$ is the unit vector in the y axis and $\hat{k}$ is the unit `vector` is the z axis. The addition of two `vectors` requires the addition of the corresponding $\hat{i}$ components, addition of the corresponding $\hat{j}$ components and the addition of the corresponding $\hat{k}$ components. That is, for two `vectors` $v_1 = a_1\hat{i} + b_1\hat{j} + c_1\hat{k}$ and $v_2 = a_2\hat{i} + b_2\hat{j} + c_2\hat{k}$, the sum would be $v = v_1 + v_2 = (a_1 + a_2)\hat{i} + (b_1 + b_2)\hat{j} + (c_1 + c_2)\hat{k}$. Likewise, the difference of two vectors requires the subtraction of the corresponding $\hat{i}$ components, subtraction of the corresponding $\hat{j}$ components and the subtraction of the corresponding $\hat{k}$ components. That is, for two vectors $v_1 = a_1\hat{i} + b_1\hat{j} + c_1\hat{k}$ and $v_2 = a_2\hat{i} + b_2\hat{j} + c_2\hat{k}$, the difference would be $v = v_1 - v_2 = (a_1 - a_2)\hat{i} + (b_1 - b_2)\hat{j} + (c_1 - c_2)\hat{k}$.

15. Create a class called vector having three data members a, b, and c. The class must have the `getData()` function to ask the user to enter the values of a, b, and c; the `putData()` function to display the `vector`.

16. Overload the + operator for the `vector` class.

17. Overload the – operator for the `vector` class.

18. Overload the += operator for the `vector` class.

13

EXCEPTION HANDLING

After reading this chapter, the reader will be able to

- Understand the concept of exception handling
- Appreciate the importance of exception handling
- Use **try/except**
- Manually throw exceptions
- Craft a program that raises user defined exceptions

13.1   INTRODUCTION

Writing a program is an involved task. It requires due deliberation, command over the syntax and problem solving capabilities. In spite of all efforts, there is a possibility of some error cropping up or of an unexpected output. These errors can be classified as follows. The first types of errors are those due to syntax or those which can be intercepted by the compiler. On compiling a program having such errors, some standard message appears. These can be handled by learning the syntax or changing the code as per the requirement of the problem at hand. The following is an example of a code having syntax error. Note that the *closing parenthesis* is missing in the statement fun1('Harsh'. The code is followed by the message that appears when executing the code.

Code

```
def fun1(a):
  print('\nArgument\t:',a)
  print('\nType\t:',type(a))
```

```
fun1(34)
fun1(34.67)
fun1('Harsh'
```

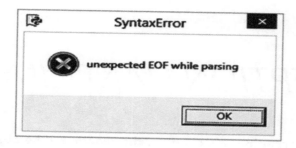

The second type is more complex. At times the program stops working or behaves in an undesirable way on execution. This may be due to incorrect user input, inability to open a file, accessing something which the program does not have authority to do and so on. These are referred to as exceptions. Exceptions are "events that modify the follow of the program"[1]. Python invokes these events when errors occur, or the programmer can explicitly invoke them.

Exceptions are used to handle some situations. So if something undeniable comes up, the programmer must have a place to go (part of the code) where that situation can be handled. In order to understand the point, consider the following example.

Suppose you intend to design a machine learning technique to identity whether a given EEG shows an epileptic spike. You decide the algorithm to be used, the language, and the tool, etc. However, you are not able to get the data. What will you do? Simply abandon the project and go to the exception handling part. That is, an exception is raised when situations like the above crop up. Let us consider one of the most common examples of exception handling. If one is crafting a program to divide two numbers entered by the user, an exception should be raised if the denominator entered is zero.

One of the most common ways of handling an exception is to craft a block, where one expects exception to occur. If somewhere in that block an exception is raised, the control goes to the part which handles the exception. The block where you expect the exception to come is the `try` block and the part where it is handled is the `expect` block. The chapter discusses some more ways to handle exceptions. However, the readers from C++ or C#

backgrounds will be familiar with the above technique and should find this easy and intuitive. Though Python has a mechanism to handle exceptions, the reader is expected to learn to code his own classes to handle exceptions. Therefore, the reader must revisit the chapter on classes and objects.

Exception handling in Python can be done using any of the following:

- try/expect
- try/expect/finally
- raise
- assert

This chapter concentrates on the first three. The chapter has been organized as follows. Section 13.2 discusses the importance and mechanisms of exception handling, Section 13.3 presents some of the built-in exceptions in Python, Section 13.4 summarizes the process by taking an example, Section 13.5 presents another example of exception handling and the last section concludes the chapter.

13.2   IMPORTANCE AND MECHANISM

Exception handling mechanisms can help the programmer to notify something. For example, consider the problem discussed in the previous section. You have the EEG of the patients and you want to find the epileptic spike in the EEG. If you are not able to find the spike, you can simply raise an exception. This technique is better than the conventional method of returning an integer code on being able to find something (or for that matter, not find something). Likewise, on detecting some special case or an unusual condition an exception can be raised.

At the runtime if an error crops up an exception is raised. This exception can be handled by the corresponding `expect` or can be simply ignored. Moreover, if there is no provision to handle the exception in the code then Python's default error handling mechanism comes into play. As stated earlier, on encountering an error condition the execution is restored after the try statement.

Python also has the `try/finally` statements to handle the termination condition. Those of you from a Java background will be familiar with `finally`. It is for handling the termination condition, whether or not an exception has occurred. For example in designing software the concluding screen must appear, whether or not an exception has occurred or for that matter the memory of objects must be reclaimed at the end. For such type of situations finally is immensely helpful.

13.2.1 An Example of Try/Catch

A list contains an ordered set of students. The first location contains the name of the students who got the highest marks, the second student's name is at the second position, and so on.

```
>>>L = ['Harsh', 'Naved', 'Snigdha', 'Gaurav']
```

In order to access an element at a given location, the user is asked to enter the index

```
>>>Index=input('Enter the index')
```

Now, the element at that position is accessed using the following statement

```
>>>print(L[int(index)])
```

So, if the user enters 1, 'Naved' would be the output, if he enters 2, "Snigdha" would be the output. However, the following message appears if he enters anything above 3.

```
Traceback (most recent call last):
 File "<pyshell#5>", line 1, in <module>
   print(L[int(index)])
IndexError: list index out of range
>>>
```

The error can be handled using try/catch as shown.

Code

```
def code:
    L = ['Harsh', 'Naved', 'Snigdha', 'Gaurav']
    try:
index=input('Enter index\t:')
print(L[index])
    except IndexError:
            print('List index out of bound')
print('This statement always executes')
```

Note that the try block contains the part of the code where the exception may come up. If a runtime error is there, the except part handles it. Also note that the except may have the name of the predefined exception. The statement after the except always executes, whether or not an exception has been raised. The reader is expected to take note of the fact that the control does not go back to the point where the expectation really occurred. It can only handle the exception in the requisite block, after which the normal execution continues. The syntax of the exception handling mechanism is as follows.

Syntax

```
try:
      ##code where exception is expected
except <Exception>:
      ##code to handle the exception
## rest of the program
```

13.2.2 Manually Raising Exceptions

The discussion so far has been concentrated on the situations wherein exceptions were raised and caught by Python itself. In Python, one can also manually raise the exceptions. The keyword 'raise' is used to explicitly trigger an exception. The keyword is followed by the <exception name> (same as that which is caught). The mechanism of handling such exceptions is the same as described above. That is, the corresponding expect would handle the thrown exception. The syntax is as follows.

Syntax

```
try:
      raise <something>
expect <something>:
      ##code which handles the exception
##rest of the code
```

If such exceptions are not caught, they are handled in the same fashion as in the above section. The examples in Section 13.4 present codes where the exceptions have been raised and caught.

13.3   BUILT-IN EXCEPTIONS IN PYTHON

If the programmer is able to raise specific exceptions, the program will be more effective. To be able to do so one must know the predefined exceptions in Python and then use these at appropriate places. This section presents some of the most common exceptions in Python. The following sections present the use of these exceptions:

- **AssertionError**
  When an assert statement fails, the AssertionError is raised.
- **AttributeError**
  When an assignment fails, the AttributeError is raised
- **EOFError**
  When the last word of the file is reached and the program attempts to read any further, the EOFError is raised.
- **FloatingPointError**
  This exception is raised when floating point operations fail.
- **ImportError**
  If the import statement written in the code cannot load the said module, this exception is raised. This is same as the `ModuleNotFoundError` in the later versions of Python.
- **IndexError**
  When the sequence is out of range, this exception is raised.
- **KeyError**
  If in a dictionary the key is not found, then this exception is raised.
- **OverflowError**
  Note that each data type can hold some value and there is always a maximum limit to what it can hold. When this limit is reached, the `OverflowError` is raised.
- **RecursionError**
  While executing a code that uses recursion, at times maximum iteration depth is reached. At this point in time, the `recursionError` is raised.
- **RuntimeError**
  If an error occurs and it does not fall in any of the said categories, then this exception is raised.
- **StopIteration**
  If one is using the `_next_()` and there are no more objects that can be processed, then this exception is raised.
- **SyntaxError**
  When the syntax of the code is incorrect, this exception is raised. For example, not writing the import statements or any such thing.
- **IntendationError**
  When incorrect use of indentation is done, then this exception comes up.
- **TabError**
  An inconsistent use of spaces or tabs leads to this type of error.

- **SystemError**
  If some internal error is found, then this exception is raised. The exception displays the problem that was encountered due to which the exception is raised.
- **NotImplementedError**
  If an object is not supported or the part that provides support has not been implemented, then the NotImplementedError is raised.
- **TypeError**
  If an argument is passed and is not expected, the TypeError is raised. For example, in a program that divides two numbers entered by the user, a character is passed, then TypeError is raised.
- **ValueError**
  When an incorrect value is passed in a function (or an attempt is made to enter it in a variable), the ValueError is raised. For example if a value which is outside the bounds of an integer is passed then this exception is raised.
- **UnboundLocalError**
  This exception is raised when a reference is made to a variable which does not have any value in that scope.
- **UnicodeError**
  This is raised when errors related to Unicode encoding or decoding come up.
- **ZeroDivisionError**
  The division and the modulo operation has two arguments. If the second argument is zero, this exception is raised.

13.4   THE PROCESS

This section revisits the division of two numbers and summarizes how to apply the concepts studied so far. Consider a function that takes two numbers as input and divides those two numbers. If the function is called and two integers are passed as arguments (say, 3 and 2), an expected output is produced if the second number is not zero. However if the second number is zero, a runtime error occurs and an error message (shown as follows) is produced. That is, Python handles exceptions automatically.

The program can be made user friendly by printing a user friendly, easy to understand message. This can be done by using exception handling.

Code

```
def divide(a,b):
  result =a/b
  print('Result is\t:',result)
divide(3,2)
divide(3,0)
>>>
```

Output

```
===== RUN C:/Python/Exception handling/No Exception.py =====
Result is   : 1.5
Traceback (most recent call last):
  File "C:/Python/Exception handling/No Exception.py",
                                      line 5, in <module>
  divide(3,0)
  File "C:/Python/Exception handling/No Exception.py",
                                      line 2, in divide
  result =a/b
ZeroDivisionError: division by zero
```

13.4.1   Exception Handling: Try/Except

The above problem can be handled by using the `try/except` construct to handle the run time error. The part of the code where the exception is likely to be raised is put in the `try` block. If an exception is raised, it will be handled in the `except` block. The `except` block can have the user friendly error message or the code which would handle the exception. The following code shows the use of the `try` block and displays how a run time error can be handled in the `except` block. Note the statement which divides the two numbers is in the `try` block. If the second number is zero an exception will be raised and the statements in the `except` block will be executed.

Code

```
>>>
def divide(a, b):
   try:
      d=a/b
      print('Result is\t:',str(d))
   except:
      print('Exception caught')
```

```
divide(2,3)
divide(2,0)
>>>
```

Output

```
======== RUN C:/Python/Exception handling/divide.py ========
Result is   : 0.6666666666666666
Exception caught
>>>
```

13.4.2   Raising Exceptions

One can also raise specific exceptions. For example, the following code raises the ZeroDivisionError if the second number is zero. Note that the corresponding except block catches this exception. This can be done if the user is sure which exception to raise in a given situation. Moreover, there is a chance that the programmer fails to raise the correct exception thus leading to the invocation of the automatic exception handling mechanism of Python.

Some of the common exceptions and their meanings have already been presented in Section 13.3. However, there are many more. The list of such exceptions can be found at the link provided in the references at the end of this book.

Code

```
def divide(a, b):
  try:
    if b==0:
      raise ZeroDivisionError
    d=a/b
    print('Result is\t:',str(d))
  except ZeroDivisionError :
    print('Exception caught:ZeroDivisionError ')
divide(2,3)
divide(2,0)
>>>
```

Output

```
===== RUN C:/Python/Exception handling/divide raise.py =====
Result is   : 0.6666666666666666
Exception caught:ZeroDivisionError
>>>
```

13.5   CRAFTING USER DEFINED EXCEPTIONS

So far we have seen the automatic exception handling capabilities of Python. That is, even if there is no `try/except`, Python handles exceptions. The use of `try/except` has also been discussed. The use of *raise* makes the exception handling more meaningful, as one can raise specific exceptions as per the needs. However, so far we have not seen how to deal with the situation, which requires us to raise a user defined exception. This section discusses the crafting and use of user defined exceptions.

Suppose there is a situation where a specific exception (as per the need of the program) is to be raised. However, there is no predefined exception to handle that situation. In such cases a class which would handle the exception that needs to be created. The said class should be a subclass of the `Exception` class, so that it can be used for raising exceptions. When the situation arises the exception can be raised, as shown in the following illustration. In the illustration that follows, a class called `My Error`, which is derived from `Exception`, is created. The _init_ of this class may contain the message which will be printed when the exception is raised. While raising the exception the keyword `raise`, followed by the name of the class is written. The reader is expected to observe the output and understand that first the message written in _init_ is printed, followed by the message in the `except` block. Though this is just a dummy example, it gives an idea as to how to craft classes that handle exceptions.

Code

```
class MyError (Exception):
  def_init__():
    print('My Error type error')
def divide(a, b):
  try:
    if b==0:
      raise MyError
  d=a/b
    print('Result is\t:',str(d))
  except MyError:
    print('Exception caught : MyError ')
divide(2,3)
divide(2,0)
>>>
```

Output

```
====== RUN C:\Python\Exception handling\MyException.py ======
Result is    : 0.6666666666666666
My Error type error
Exception caught: My Error
>>>
```

13.6   AN EXAMPLE OF EXCEPTION HANDLING

The following program finds the maximum number from a given list. The idea is simple. Initially, the first item is taken as "max." The items of the given list are then traversed. While traversing, if any element is greater than that stored in "max" then that number is stored in the variable "max." At the end the value of "max" is printed. The program and the corresponding output follow.

Code

```
def findMax(L):
  max=L[0]
  for item in L:
    if item>max:
      max =item
  print('Maximum\t:',str(max))
L=[2, 10, 5, 89, 9]
findMax(L)
>>>
```

Output

```
==== RUN C:/Python/Exception handling/Example/findMax.py ====
Maximum : 89
>>>
```

Note that if the contents of L are strings (e.g. L=["Harsh," "Nakul ," "Naved," "Sahil"]), the strings would be compared as per the rules and the largest ("Sahil") would be printed. That is the program works for integers, strings or floats. However, for the following list an exception would be raised:

```
L= [2, 'Harsh', 3.67]
```

Output

```
Traceback (most recent call last):
  File "C:/Python/Exception handling/Example/findMax.py",
                                    line 15, in <module>
    findMax(L)
  File "C:/Python/Exception handling/Example/findMax.py",
                                    line 4, in findMax
    if item>max:
TypeError: unorderable types: str() > int()
>>>
```

The problem can be handled by putting the part of the code where the problem is likely to come in the try block. Moreover, if all the items of the list are to be entered by the user then the possibility of a runtime error cropping up will be higher. In such cases the programmer must make sure that everything, including the input of items and calling the function, are in the try block. The following code presents the version of the program where items are entered by the user and exception handling is implemented. Note that the first run produces an excepted result, whereas the second run results in a runtime error and hence the exception handling mechanism is invoked.

Code

```
def findMax(L):
   max =L[0]
  for item in L:
     if item>max:
       max =item
 print('Maximum\t:',str(max))
L=[]
item=input('Enter items (press 0 to end)\n')
try:
  while int(item) !=0:
    L.append(item)
    item=input('Enter item (press 0 to end)\n')
  print('\nList \n')
  print(L)
    findMax(L)
except:
  print('Run time error')
```

Output (First run)

```
>>>
== RUN C:/Python/Exception handling/Example/findMax
                                      exception.py ==
Enter items (press 0 to end)
3
Enter item (press 0 to end)
2
Enter item (press 0 to end)
5
Enter item (press 0 to end)
12
Enter item (press 0 to end)
8
Enter item (press 0 to end)
98
Enter item (press 0 to end)
1
Enter item (press 0 to end)
0

List
['3', '2', '5', '12', '8', '98', '1']
Maximum     : 98
>>>
Output (Second run):
>>>
== RUN C:/Python/Exception handling/Example/findMax
                                      exception.py ==
Enter items (press 0 to end)
2
Enter item (press 0 to end)
8
Enter item (press 0 to end)
Harsh
Run time error
>>>
```

Also note that if a 'finally' is added to the code, the statements in finally are always executed whether or not an exception occurs. The code that contains both finally and except is presented as follows. Note that the first output produces the expected result and also prints the statements given in finally. The second output results in a runtime error and invokes exception handling mechanisms and also prints the message in finally. The reader is also expected to appreciate that there was no need whatsoever of the except as finally is already there. The code would have run correctly, as in handled the runtime error with a finally, however both have been included to bring home the point that expect does its intended job with a finally and finally can be used for cleanup actions or for de-allocating memory and so on.

Code

```
def findMax(L):
    max =L[0]
    for item in L:
      if item>max:
       max =item
print('Maximum\t:',str(max))
L=[]
item=input('Enter items (press 0 to end)\n')
try:
  while int(item) !=0:
    L.append(item)
    item=input('Enter item (press 0 to end)\n')
  print('\nList \n')
  print(L)
  findMax(L)
except:
  print('Run time error')
finally:
  print('This is always executed')
```

Output (first run)

```
>>>
== RUN C:/Python/Exception handling/Example/findMax
                                        exception.py ==
Enter items (press 0 to end)
1
Enter item (press 0 to end)
4
Enter item (press 0 to end)
2
```

```
Enter item (press 0 to end)
89
Enter item (press 0 to end)
3
Enter item (press 0 to end)
0
List
['1', '4', '2', '89', '3']
Maximum : 89
This is always executed
>>>
```

Output (second run)

```
>>>
== RUN C:/Python/Exception handling/Example/findMax
                                        exception.py ==
Enter items (press 0 to end)
3
Enter item (press 0 to end)
1
Enter item (press 0 to end)
7
Enter item (press 0 to end)
harsh
Run time error
This is always executed
>>>
```

13.7 CONCLUSION

The chapter presents a remarkable way to deal with exceptions. Though Python has an inbuilt mechanism to deal with exceptions, the knowledge of exception handling makes programming more effective, user friendly, and robust. The first step will be to identify the part of the code where exceptions are likely to come, and put that part in the `try` block. The exceptions can also be manually caught and handled in the `except` block. The `finally` block handles the unhandled exceptions and also executes even if there is no exception. The chapter also presents some of the most common exceptions that can be caught in Python. The reader is expected to use the concepts learned in this chapter in his/her programs. Happy programming!

GLOSSARY

```
try/except :Syntax
try:
        ##code where exception is expected
expect <Exception>:
        ##code to handle the exception
## rest of the program
```

```
Manually raising exceptions: Syntax
try:
        raise <something>
except <something>:
        ##code which handles the exception
##rest of the code
```

POINTS TO REMEMBER

- At the runtime, if an error crops up then an exception is raised.
- Exception handling in Python can be done using any of the following:
  - try/catch
  - try/finally
  - raise
  - assert
- In Python, one can also manually raise the exceptions.
- The part of the code where the exception is likely to be raised is put in the `try` block. If an exception is raised, it will be handled in the `except` block.
- The class that helps to raise user defined exceptions should be a subclass of the `Exception` class.
- The statements in `finally` are always executed, whether or not exceptions occur.

EXERCISES

MULTIPLE CHOICE QUESTIONS

1. Exception handling
   (a) Handles runtime errors in a program
   (b) Provides robustness
   (c) Both
   (d) None of the above

2. Exception handling is needed for
   (*a*) Syntax errors (*b*) Run time errors
   (*c*) Both (*d*) None of the above

3. Which of the following is not supported in Python?
   (*a*) Nested try (*b*) Re-throwing an exception
   (*c*) Both are supported (*d*) None of the above is supported

4. Which of the following is raised in the case of division by zero?
   (*a*) Divide (*b*) ZeroDivisionError
   (*c*) Both (*d*) None of the above

5. Which of the following is raised in the case when an IndexError is accessed?
   (*a*) Array index out of bound (*b*) Out of bound
   (*c*) Array (*d*) None of the above

6. Which of the following is true?
   (*a*) For each try there is exactly one catch
   (*b*) Every try must include a raise
   (*c*) A catch can handle any type of exception
   (*d*) A catch can handle the exception for which it is designed, unless it is catch all in which case it handles all the exceptions

7. How many "except's" can a try have?
   (*a*) Single (*b*) Two, only in specific conditions
   (*c*) Any number of catch (*d*) None of the above

8. Which type of exception can be raised?
   (*a*) Predefined (*b*) User defined
   (*c*) Both (*d*) None of the above

9. What is the base class of a class, of whose exception is to be raised?
   (*a*) Exception (*b*) Error
   (*c*) Both (*d*) None of the above

10. Which is the correct syntax of raise?
  (*a*) raise <name of the exception>
  (*b*) raise(<name of the exception>)
  (*c*) raise(new <user defined exception>)
  (*d*) All of the above

THEORY

1. What is the difference between compile time and runtime error?
2. What is exception handling?
3. Explain the mechanisms of exception handling.
4. Explain how to create a class that derives from the exception class. How is this class used to raise exceptions?
5. Explain the function of the following exception classes

PROGRAMMING

The roots of a quadratic equation $ax^2 + bx + c = 0$ are given by the formula $x = \dfrac{-b \pm \sqrt{b^2\, 4ac}}{2a}$. Write a program to ask the user to enter the values of a, b and c and calculate the roots.

1. Use try/except in the above question to handle the following situations.
  (*a*) Calculating the root of a negative number
  (*b*) Division by zero
  (*c*) Incorrect format
2. Create a class called negative_discriminant, which is a subclass of the exception class. Now in question 1 raise the negative_discriminant exception when the value of $b^2 - 4ac$ is negative.

   The division of two complex numbers is defined as follows. If $c_1 = a_1 + ib_1$ is the first complex number $c_2 = a_2 + ib_2$ and is the second complex number, then the complex number

   $$c = (a_1 \times a_2 - b_1 b_2)/(a_2^2 + b_2^2) + i(a_1 \times b_2 + b_1 a_2)/(a_2^2 + b_2^2)$$

3. Create a class called Complex and implement exception handling in the method that carries out division.

4. For the complex class defined in the previous question, use exception handling to prevent the user from entering a non-real number (as real or imaginary part).

5. In the complex class, create a function that converts complex numbers to the polar form.

6. Implement stacks using lists. Incorporate exception handling.

7. Implement queues using lists. Incorporate exception handling.

8. Implement the operations of linked list, and throw an exception when the number entered by the user is negative. Assume that the data part of the linked list would contain numbers only.

9. Write a program that takes the ppm of chorine in water from the user and finds whether the ppm is within permissible limits. If it is not, the program should raise an exception.

10. Write a program that finds the inverse of a given matrix. The program should raise an exception when the determinant of the matrix is zero.

INTRODUCTION TO DATA STRUCTURES

After reading this chapter, the reader will be able to

- Understand the importance of data structures
- Classify data structures
- Define stack, queue, tree, and graph
- Define algorithms and appreciate the characteristics of an algorithm
- Understand abstract data types
- Differentiate between iterative and recursive algorithms
- Implement bubble sort, selection sort, merge, and merge sort

14.1   INTRODUCTION

The last two sections introduced procedural and object-oriented programming. The concepts studied so far constitute the basis of programming. Having learned the basic concepts, let us move towards becoming a programmer. To become a programmer the knowledge of data structure is essential. In any project storing data, its organization and ways to access the data are some of the most important tasks. The organization of the data comes under what are generally referred to as **data structures**. The knowledge of these not only help us to make an efficient and effective program but also to solve various problems at hand by virtue of their inherent characteristics. This chapter briefly introduces the concept of data structures and discusses some of the algorithms of some of the most important data structures.

We begin with the classification of a data structure. Data structures may be **primary** or **secondary**. Primary data structures are those which are provided by the language. For example, in C, "int," "float," and "char" are primary data structures. The primary data structures or data types of Python have been discussed in Chapter 2 of this book.

The secondary data structures are formed from primary data structures. Stacks, queues, trees, and graphs are some examples of secondary data structures. The secondary data structures can further be classified as linear and nonlinear. Stacks and queues are linear data structures whereas trees and graphs are nonlinear data structures. The classification has been depicted in Figure 14.1.

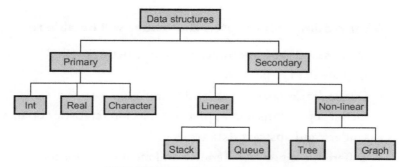

FIGURE 14.1 Classification of data structures

We begin our discussion with one of the simplest data structures, an **array**. An array consists of homogeneous elements at consecutive memory locations. Arrays are used to store elements which are similar, and accessing many such elements will take less time if they are stored in consecutive memory locations. Arrays are an integral part of languages like C, C++, Java, and C. In Python, however, arrays can be accessed using library. The formation, usage and applications of multi-dimensional arrays have been discussed in the following chapter - Chapter 18. Section 14.4 of this chapter discusses the various algorithms related to arrays in detail.

Definition

Array: An array consists of homogeneous elements at consecutive memory locations

A **stack** is a linear data structure, which follows the principle of Last In First Out (LIFO). In order to understand the concept of stacks, consider opening a document in Microsoft Word. When one opens a document using the "Open" dialog and finds the document using the "Browse" window, he cannot close the "Open" dialog until he closes the "Browse" window. Also the application can be closed only if one closes the "Open" dialog. The "Browse" window, which was opened at the end, has to be closed first. This is just like a pile of books, from which only the book which was kept the end can be taken out. Stacks are used in sub procedure calls and backtracking. The stacks are characterized by an index called TOP, which is initially -1. The value of TOP increases as and when the elements are added in the stack. The algorithms of stack and its applications are discussed in Chapter 15.

Definition

Stack: A stack is a linear data structure that follows the principle of Last In First Out (LIFO).

Queue is a data structure that follows the principle of First In First Out (FIFO). Customer services use the idea of Queue. The person who enters first is served earlier than the person who entered later. When we give many print commands to a printer, the commands are stored in a queue and the corresponding documents are printed in the order in which the command was given. Queues are used in scheduling algorithms by the operating systems, in spooling (*e.g.* for printer) and inapt many other places. The queues (static) are characterized by two indices - REAR and FRONT. The initial value of both the indices is -1. The value of REAR increases as elements are inserted in the queue and that of FRONT increases when elements are removed from the queue. The algorithms of insertion and deletion in a queue are presented in Chapter 15. The chapter also presents some of the important applications of queue.

Definition

Queue: A queue is a linear data structure that follows the principle of First In First Out (FIFO).

A graph may be defined as a set containing two finite sets: the set of vertices (V) and the set of edges (E). They are represented using two-dimensional arrays or linked lists. A graph can be weighted, in which case the corresponding matrix would have weights at the requisite positions. Graphs are traversed using methods like breadth first search or depth first search. Interestingly, these traversals use linear data structures like stacks and queues. Graphs are extensively used in many computational problems. In fact, there is a dedicated branch of algorithms for solving problems using graphs. The concept of algorithms and applications of graphs are discussed in Chapter 17 of this book.

Definition

Graph: A graph may be defined as G = (V, E), where V is a finite, non-empty set of vertices and E is a finite, non-empty set of edges. Each element of E is (x, y), where x and y belong to the set of vertices.

A tree is a graph which does not have any cycle or isolated vertex (or edges). A tree is a graph and therefore it has vertices and edges. The absence of cycles and isolated vertices makes it usable for many problems like searching, finding complexity, and so on. A tree is generally used for representing a hierarchical relationship. A special tree called a binary tree has only a maximum of two children at each level. Trees have been discussed in Chapter 17 of this book.

Definition

Tree: A tree is a graph that does not have any cycle or isolated vertex or edge.

In the following chapters, the concepts related to trees and graphs have been discussed. Trees are graphs and fall under the category of non-linear data structures. As stated earlier these are extensively used in searching, sorting, finding minimum spanning trees, and solving some of the most important problems in the field of computer science.

As well as the above there are other data structures like Plex, which are beyond the scope of this book. The concept of file has already been discussed in chapter 9 of this book. The organization of a file is a fascinating topic used in many fields, including data base management system.

The chapter has been organized as follows. This section has introduced the definitions of a data structures and their types. The definitions of linear data structures like stacks and queues and nonlinear data structures like graphs and trees have also been presented in this section. The second section discusses Abstract Data Types (ADT) and the third section discusses the definition of algorithms. Section 14.4 discusses arrays and Section 14.5 discusses iterative and non-iterative algorithms. The topic has been discussed by taking examples of three popular sorting techniques: selection sort, bubble sort, and merge sort. The last section concludes the chapter.

14.2 ABSTRACT DATA TYPE

Each language has predefined data types like int, float, etc. The operations that can be applied to these data types are also defined for each type. As stated earlier, user defined data types are needed so languages support such data types. Now, the operations that can be applied to these data types must be at least declared, if not defined for these types. The higher level abstraction makes the purpose and use of these data types clear.

Abstract Data Types contain elements along with the set of operations to manipulate the elements. The operations tell us what is to be done, not how it is to be done. That is, ADTs are not about implementation, as long as it is correct, but about the tasks. The higher level abstraction of the task is important. As a matter of fact, it is the designer's decision as to what operations will constitute the ADT. There is no hard and fast rule on the number of operations and the type of operations. An example of ADT is a stack. A stack, as explained earlier, is a linear data structure that follows the principle of Last In First Out (LIFO). A stack can be described with the help of the following operations:

- `push(item)`: Inserts `'item'` at the top of the stack
- `pop()`: Takes an element out of the stack
- `isfull()`: Returns true if the stack is full
- `isempty()`: Returns true if the stack is empty
- `overflow()`: Returns true if an overflow exception is raised
- `underflow()`: Returns true if an underflow exception is raised

Note that in the above description, the various functions are clear about what is to be done not how it is to be done. Other examples of ADTs include queues, lists, trees, graphs, etc. The reader may also note that languages like C++, Java, C#, Python, etc., support ADTs via classes.

The implementation of an ADT requires data structures. The choice of data structure, therefore, becomes one of the most contentious issues. An appropriate data structure must be chosen as per the problem at hand, keeping in view the efficiency part too.

For example, the stack data structure can be implemented using data structures like:

- Array
- Linked list

Having studied the definitions of data structures, let us shift our focus to the way a problem is solved. The next section introduces the notion of algorithms and the following section presents arrays.

14.3 ALGORITHMS

In order to accomplish any task, one needs to plan the chain of action. For example you are required to complete a task consisting of 4 subtasks, where each subtask can be performed only on the completion of the previous subtask. You would probably perform the first subtask, followed by the second, followed by the third and finally the fourth. An example of such a process follows. In the process, it is assumed that the person has ingredients required for the Indian recipe (of *kheer*) that follows.

Ingredients: 1 L milk, ¼ cup rice, 6 tablespoon sugar, some dry fruits (almonds, raisins, cashews).

The steps to make Indian *"kheer"* have been depicted in Figure 14.2.

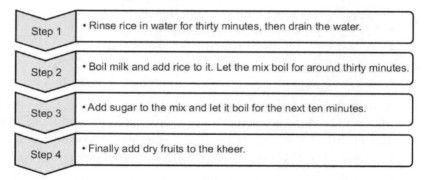

Step 1 • Rinse rice in water for thirty minutes, then drain the water.

Step 2 • Boil milk and add rice to it. Let the mix boil for around thirty minutes.

Step 3 • Add sugar to the mix and let it boil for the next ten minutes.

Step 4 • Finally add dry fruits to the kheer.

FIGURE 14.2 Making *Kheer*

A set of steps required to accomplish a particular task is called an algorithm. Though there can be many ways of achieving a particular task, the algorithm designer must look for the most efficient way of doing so; both in terms of space and time. However, this efficiency must not come at the expense of correctness. Moreover, each statement of an algorithm must be unambiguous. The characteristics of a good algorithm can be summarized as follows:

Correctness: An algorithm must produce correct results in all cases or it must explicitly state for which cases it will not work.

Unambiguous: Each statement of an algorithm must be deterministic.

Efficiency: The time required by the algorithm must be as low as possible, and the space required must also be also be as low as possible.

Finiteness: The number of steps in a given algorithm must be finite.

The time or space complexity of an algorithm can be stated in terms of asymptotic functions. These functions give an idea of an algorithm's comparative performance. As a matter of fact we are not interested in the exact equation which relates the time taken by the size of the problem, but only a function that tells us how the algorithm would behave with larger values of n.

Big Oh: The O (big Oh) notation depicts the upper bound of an algorithm. Formally, for a function $f(t)$, $O(f(t))$ is defined as follows:

$$g(t) = O(f(t)), \text{ if } g(t) \le cf(t) \text{ for some } n \ge n_0$$

Omega: The Ω(Omega) notation depicts the lower bound of an algorithm. Formally, for a function $f(t)$, $\Omega(f(t))$ is defined as follows:

$$g(t) = \Omega(f(t)), \text{ if } g(t) \ge cf(t) \text{ for some } n \ge n_0$$

Theta: The θ(big Oh) notation depicts the tight bound of an algorithm. Formally, for a function $f(t)$, $\theta(f(t))$ is defined as follows:

$$g(t) = \theta(f(t)), c_1 g(t) \le f(t) \le c_2 g(t) \text{ for some } n \ge n_0$$

14.4 ARRAYS

An array is a linear data structure that has the same type of elements. The elements of an array are stored in consecutive memory locations. Those of you from a C background will have already studied arrays. This section implements insertion and deletion from an array. An insertion can be done at the beginning, at the end and somewhere in-between. Likewise, a deletion can be done from the beginning, from the end and from anywhere in-between. Inserting an element at the beginning requires all elements to be shifted one position to the right, thus making way for the "item." After this, the element "item" is inserted at the first position and the length of the array in incremented by unity. That is,

```
##Shift each element of the array one position to the right
arr[0] = item
length = length +1
```

The first step requires O(*n*) time and the second and the third would require O(1) each. Therefore the complexity of inserting an element at the first position is O(*n*). Inserting an element at the end requires increasing the length of the given array by one. The task, thus becomes O(1), as we are keeping track of the number of elements in the variable "length."

```
arr[length] = item
length = length +1
```

Inserting an element after a certain position requires shifting all elements after that position by one, followed by putting the element at that position and increasing the length of the array by one.

```
#shift all elements after 'position' by one.
arr[pos] = item
length = length +1
```

The average case complexity of the above task would be O(*n*). Deleting an element from the beginning requires shifting all the elements, starting from the second element, to the right (by one) and then reducing the length of the array by one. That is,

```
#shift all the elements to the right (starting from the
                                     second element)
length = length -1
```

The complexity of shifting all the elements to one position to the right would be O(*n*) and hence the complexity of the procedure would be O(*n*). Deleting an element after a particular position requires shifting all the elements, starting from (position +1), to the right (by one) and then reducing the length of the array by one. That is,

```
#shift all the elements to the right (starting from
                                      position +1)
length = length -1
```

The complexity of shifting all the elements to one position to the right would be O(*n*) and hence the complexity of the procedure would be O(*n*). Deleting an element from the end requires reducing the length of the array by one. This takes O(1), time. That is,

```
length = length -1
```

The task can be done by using functions in C but it requires the use of pointers. The C program to implement insertion and deletion in an array is as follows.

Inserting an element in a given array, deleting an element from a given array (In C)

```c
void insert_end(int * arr,int * length, int item)
    {
    int i;
    *(arr+*length)=item;
    *length=*length+1;
    printf("\nAfter insertion\n");
    for(i=0;i<*length;i++)
        {
        printf("%d->",*(arr+i));
        }
    }
void insert_beg(int * arr, int *length, int item)
    {
    int i;
    for(i=*(length)-1; i>=0; i--)
        {
        *(arr+i+1)=*(arr+i);
        //printf("\nFrom %d to %d, shifting %d",i,
                                    i+1, *(arr+i));

        }
    *(arr+i+1)=item;
    *length=*length+1;
    printf("\nAfter insertion\n");
    for(i=0;i<*length;i++)
        {
        printf("%d->",*(arr+i));
        }
    }
void insert_after(int * arr, int *length, int position,
                                        int item)

    {
    int i;
    for(i=*(length)-1; i>=position+1; i--)
        {
        *(arr+i+1)=*(arr+i);
        //printf("\nFrom %d to %d, shifting %d",i,
                                    i+1,*(arr+i));

        }
    *(arr+i+1)=item;
    *length=*length+1;
```

```
        printf("\nAfter insertion\n");
        for(i=0;i<*length;i++)
            {
            printf("%d->",*(arr+i));
            }
        }
void del_beg(int *arr, int *length)
    {
    int i;
    if(*length!=0)
        {
        for(i=0;i<*(length); i++)
            {
            *(arr+i)=*(arr+i+1);
            }
        *length=*length-1;
        printf("\nAfter deletion\n");
        for(i=0; i<*length;i++)
            {
            printf("%d->",*(arr+i));
            }

        }
    else
        {
        printf("\nCannot delete\n");
        }
    }
void del_end(int *arr,int *length)
    {
    int i;
    if(*length !=0)
        {
        *length= *length-1;
        printf("\nAfter deletion\n");
        for(i=0; i<*length;i++)
            {
            printf("%d->",*(arr+i));
            }
        }
    else
        {
        printf("\nCannot delete");
        }
```

```
        }
void main()
        {
        int arr[20], i,length=0;
        clrscr();
        insert_end(arr, &length, 32);
        insert_end(arr, &length, 23);
        insert_beg(arr, &length, 19);
        insert_beg(arr, &length, 87);
        insert_after(arr, &length, 2, 78);
        del_beg(arr, &length);
        del_end(arr, &length);
        getch();
        }
```

Note that in C the modular approach used to accomplish the above task is complex and intricate. It requires the use of pointers and passing of both the address of the array and its length in each function. The insertion and deletion of an element in an array is simple in Python. It requires the use of the array class. The functions to accomplish different tasks have been presented in Table 14.1.

Table 14.1 Functions for array

Name of the function	Task
append	Adding an element at the end
insert	Adding the element at the specified position. The function has two arguments: first is the element and the second is the position
count	This counts the number of times the argument is repeated
pop	Takes out the top element from the array
remove	Removes the element from a given position
reverse	Reverses the order of elements in the array
tostring	Converts the given array into a string

```
from array import array
arr = array('i')
arr.append(3)
arr
Out[4]: array('i', [3])
arr.append(5)
arr
```

```
Out[6]: array('i', [3, 5])
arr.insert(1,23)
arr
Out[8]: array('i', [3, 23, 5])
arr.insert(0,32)
arr
Out[11]: array('i', [32, 3, 23, 5])
arr.count(3)
Out[12]: 1
arr.pop(2)
Out[13]: 23
arr
Out[14]: array('i', [32, 3, 5])
arr.remove(3)
arr
Out[16]: array('i', [32, 5])
arr.reverse()
arr
Out[18]: array('i', [5, 32])
arr.tostring()
Out[19]: b'\x05\x00\x00\x00 \x00\x00\x00'
arr.write(file)
```

```
AttributeError     Traceback (most recent call last)
<ipython-input-20-e7f729e1f6ad> in <module>()
----> 1 arr.write(file)
AttributeError: 'array.array' object has no attribute
                                               'write'.
```

14.5   ITERATIVE AND RECURSIVE ALGORITHMS

In order to understand the difference between an iterative and a recursive algorithm, we will consider the examples of three algorithms for sorting: bubble, selection, and   merge sort. The first two are examples of iterative algorithms and the third is an example of a recursive algorithm.

14.5.1   Iterative Algorithms

Iterative procedure is one in which each statement happens one after another. Linear search, bubble sort, and selection, etc., are examples of iterative algorithms.

Bubble Sort

In bubble sort the first element is compared with the second, the second with the third and so on; if the element to be compared is smaller than the first, the elements are swapped. After the first iteration, the maximum element is placed at the last position. The process is repeated for the second element and so on. The process has been presented in the following algorithm:

```
int [] bubble(a[], n)
    {
            for(i=0; i<n, i++)
            {
                    for(j=i+1; j<n;j++)
                    {
                    If( a[i]<a[j+1])
                        {
                                temp=a[j];
                                a[j]=a[j+1]
                                a[j+1]=temp;
                        }
                    }
            }
        return a;
        }
```

Analysis

The number of times each statement is executed has been presented in Table 14.2. The first statement is executed $(n+1)$ times and the statements inside the loop are executed n times. Each time the inner loop executes $(n-i)$ times therefore making the total number as $n(n-i-1)$. The execution of the if block depends on the data. Note that the total number of executions has n^2 as the highest degree term. Therefore the complexity of the algorithm is $O(n^2)$.

Table 14.2 Analysis of bubble sort

`Int [] selection(a[], n)`	Number of times statement executed
`{`	
`for(i=0; i<n, i++)`	$(n+1)$
`{`	
`    for(j=i+1; j<n;j++)`	$n(n-i)$

(Continued)

Table 14.2 (*Continued*)

Int [] selection(a[], n)	Number of times statement executed
{	
If(a[i]<a[j+1])	$n(n\text{-}i\text{-}1)$
{	
temp=a[j];	Depends on data, minimum 0, maximum $n(n\text{-}i\text{-}2)$
a[j]=a[j+1];	Depends on data, minimum 0, maximum $n(n\text{-}i\text{-}2)$
a[j+1]=temp;	Depends on data, minimum 0, maximum $n(n\text{-}i\text{-}2)$
}	
}	
}	
return a;	1
}	

First iteration

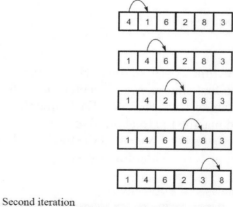

Second iteration

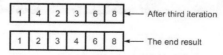

FIGURE 14.3 An example of bubble sort

Selection Sort

In selection sort the first element is compared with the rest of the elements and whichever is smaller is replaced with the first. This results in the minimum element coming at the first position. The process is repeated for the second element and so on. The process has been presented in the following algorithm:

```
Int [] selection(a[], n)
    {
        for(i=0; i<n, i++)
        {
            for(j=i+1; j<n;j++)
            {
            If( a[i]<a[j])
                    {
                        temp=a[i];
                        a[i]=a[j];
                        a[j]=temp;
                    }
                }
            }
        return a;
    }
```

Analysis: Note that the algorithm has a nested loop. The outer loop executes *n* times and the inner's execution makes the complexity O(n^2).

The process has been exemplified in Figure 14.3. The first position has 4, it is compared with the second position and since the second position has 1, the numbers are swapped. Now, 1 is compared with 6, 2, 8, and 3, one by one. Since none of these is smaller than 1, the numbers remain at their respective positions.

First iteration

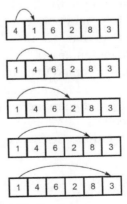

FIGURE 14.4 (*Continued*)

Second iteration

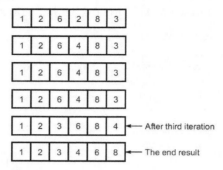

FIGURE 14.4 An example of selection sort

14.5.2 Recursive Algorithms

Recursive algorithms are those in which the procedure is called in the same procedure. Recursion requires a base case, the solution of which must be known. If the base case is not given the algorithms will not terminate, thus resulting in stack overflow when the program executes. Examples of recursive algorithms are binary search, merge sort, quick sort, etc.

Merge

Given two sorted lists $a1$ and $a2$, having $n1$ and $n2$ elements, the merged list is a sorted list having at most $(n1 + n2)$ elements. The procedure for merge is as follows.

The two lists are merged as follows. The pointer i is kept at the first index of the first list and j at the first index of the second list. The resultant array, c, is initialized to [ ] and pointer k points to the first position of c. If the element at a is less than that at b, the ith element of a is copied to c, and the pointers i and k are incremented. If the element at a is greater than that at b, the jth element of b is copied to c, and the pointers j and k are incremented. If the elements at a and b are equal, the ith element of a is copied to c, and the pointers i, j and k are incremented. The process is repeated till i becomes n_1 or j becomes n_2, after which the elements of the first array (if i$<n_1$) are copied to c. Otherwise (if j$<n_2$) the elements of the second array are copied to c.

```
Int [] Merge (a1, a2, n1, n2)
    {
    i=0;
    j=0;
```

```
k=0;
c=[];
      while((i<n1) && (j<n2))
            {
            if (a1[i] <a2[j])
                  {
                  c[k]= a1[i];
                  k++;
                  i++;
                  }
            else if (a2[j] <a1[i])
                  {
                  c[k]= a2[j];
                  k++;
                  j++;
                  }
            else if (a2[j] ==a1[i])
                  {
                  c[k]= a2[j];
                  k++;
                  j++;
                  i++;
                  }
}
      while( i<n1)
            {
            c[k++]=a1[i++];
            }
while(j<n2)
            {
            c[k++]=a2[j++];
            }
      return c;

      }
```

Merge Sort

Merge sort works as follows. Low points to the first index of the array and high points to the last index of the array to be sorted. If the value of low is equal to that of high, there is only one element in the array and hence the array is returned (an array having a single element is deemed to be sorted). Otherwise the array is split into two halves, merge sort is recursively applied to the two parts and the result is merged using the procedure explained above.

```
Merge_Sort(a, low, high)
    {
    If (low==high)
        {
        Return a;
        }
    else
        {
        mid = (low+ high)/2;
        a1=Merge_Sort(a, low, mid);
        a2= Merge_Sort(a, mid+1, high);
        a=merge(a1, a2, n/2, n/2);
        return a
}
}
```

Analysis

The complexity of merge is O(n) (note that there are loops which run one after another). The merge sort divides the array into two parts until a single element array is formed. Therefore, if the number of elements is initially n, after the first iteration the two parts will have $n/2$ elements each. In the next iteration, the number of elements in the two parts will be $n/4$ and so on. The process terminates if the number of elements becomes 1. That is $\dfrac{n}{2^i} = 1$. That is $i = \log_2 n$. The complexity of merge sort becomes O($n \log n$).

14.6 CONCLUSION

One of the most important things while designing a program is to do a task efficiently. The efficiency must be both in terms of space and time. Managing time complexity requires developing better algorithms whereas the space complexity can be managed with various factors. This chapter introduced the concept of data structures for efficient storage, management and access of data. The classification of algorithms has been discussed and definitions of various data structures have been presented. The chapter also introduces the concept of complexity. The examples of iterative and recursive algorithms have been given to explain the concept. The reader is expected to implement the concepts presented here. The following chapters take the discussion forward and explain various applications of stacks, queues, and implementation of linked lists. To conclude "Bad programmers worry about the code, good programmers worry about the data structures."

GLOSSARY

Array: An array consists of homogeneous elements at consecutive memory locations.

Stack: A stack is a linear data structure that follows the principle of Last In First Out (LIFO).

Queue: A queue is a linear data structure that follows the principle of First In First Out (FIFO).

Graph: A graph may be defined as G= (V, E), where V is a finite, non-empty set of vertices and E is a finite, non-empty set of edges. Each element of E is (x, y), where x and y belong to the set of vertices.

Tree: A tree is a graph that does not have any cycle or isolated vertex or edge.

Big Oh: The O (big Oh) notation depicts the upper bound of an algorithm. Formally, for a function $f(t)$, O($f(t)$ is defined as follows.

$$g(t) = O(f(t)), \text{ if } g(t) \leq cf(t) f \text{ or some } n \geq n_0$$

Omega: The (Omega) notation depicts the lower bound of an algorithm. Formally, for a function $f(t)$, $(f(t)$ is defined as follows.

$$g(t) = \Omega(f(t)), \text{ if } g(t) \geq cf(t) f \text{ or some } n \geq n_0$$

Theta: The θ(Big Theta) notation depicts the tight bound of an algorithm. Formally, for a function $f(t)$, $\theta(f(t)$ is defined as follows.

$$g(t) = \theta(f(t)), \text{ if } c_1 g(t) \leq f(t) \leq c_2 g(t) f \text{ or some } n \geq n_0$$

POINTS TO REMEMBER

- Algorithms should have the following features.
  - (a) Correctness
  - (b) Unambiguous
  - (c) Efficiency
  - (d) Finiteness

- An array is a linear data structure that has the same type of elements.
- Iterative procedure is one in which each statement runs after another.
- Linear search, bubble sort, selection sort, etc., are examples of iterative algorithms.
- The complexity of bubble sort is $O(n^2)$.
- The complexity of selection sort is $O(n^2)$.
- The complexity of merge sort is $O(n \log n)$.

EXERCISES

MULTIPLE CHOICE QUESTIONS

1. Which of the following is correct?

   (*a*) A data structure is used to organize elements.

   (*b*) Data structures may be used to access elements efficiently.

   (*c*) The knowledge of data structures helps the programmer to make efficient programs.

   (*d*) All of the above.

2. Which of the following is an example of a basic data structure?

   (*a*) int   (*b*) float

   (*c*) char   (*d*) All of the above

3. Which of the following might be a linear data structure?

   (*a*) Queue   (*b*) Stack

   (*c*) Tree   (*d*) All of the above

4. Which of the following is an example of a nonlinear data structure?

   (*a*) Tree   (*b*) Graph

   (*c*) Both   (*d*) None of the above

5. A linear data structure which follows the principle of First In First Out is

   (*a*) Queue   (*b*) Stack

   (*c*) File   (*d*) None of the above

6. A linear data structure which follows the principle of Last In First Out is
   - (*a*) Queue
   - (*b*) Stack
   - (*c*) File
   - (*d*) None of the above

7. Which queue is more efficient with respect to the available space utilization?
   - (*a*) Linear queue
   - (*b*) Circular queue
   - (*c*) Both are equally efficient
   - (*d*) No basis for comparison

8. A queue can be used in which of the following applications?
   - (*a*) Round robin scheduling
   - (*b*) Spooling
   - (*c*) Customer services
   - (*d*) All of the above

9. Which search uses queue?
   - (*a*) Depth first search
   - (*b*) Breadth first search
   - (*c*) Both
   - (*d*) None of the above

10. Which search uses stack?
    - (*a*) Depth first search
    - (*b*) Breadth first search
    - (*c*) Both
    - (*d*) None of the above

11. A tree
    - (*a*) May have an isolated edge.
    - (*b*) May have a loop.
    - (*c*) May have an isolated vertex.
    - (*d*) None of the above.

12. A graph
    - (*a*) May have a loop
    - (*b*) May have an isolated edge
    - (*c*) May have an isolated vertex
    - (*d*) All of the above

THEORY

1. What is a data structure? Explain the importance of data structures.

2. Classify data structures on the basis of basic and non-basic. Give examples of each type.

3. Classify data structures on the basis of linear and non-linear. Give examples of each type.

4. What is a queue? Write an algorithm for the static implementation of a queue.

5. What is a stack? Write an algorithm for the static implementation of a stack.

6. State a few applications of stack. Explain how a stack can be used in blind search.

7. Define a tree. What is the difference between a graph and a tree?

8. What is a graph? State a few applications of a graph.

9. Differentiate between iterative and recursive algorithms. Give an example of each.

10. What is an abstract data type? Explain with the help of an example.

11. What is an array? Write algorithms for the following.
    (a) Inserting an element at the beginning
    (b) Inserting an element at the end
    (c) Inserting an element after a given element
    (d) Deleting an element from the beginning
    (e) Deleting an element from the end
    (f) Deleting a given element from an array

12. Explain bubble sort. What is the complexity of bubble sort?

13. Suggest a change in bubble sort, so that the complexity can be improved.

14. Explain selection sort. What is the complexity of selection sort?

15. Suggest a change in selection sort, so that the complexity can be improved to $O(n \log n)$.

16. Write an algorithm to merge to sorted arrays. State its complexity.

17. Write an algorithm to implement merge sort. What is its complexity?

18. Which is better - bubble sort or selection sort?

19. Which is better - selection sort or merge sort?

20. Which is better in terms of space complexity - merge sort or selection sort?

PROGRAMMING EXERCISE

1. Write a program to implement a stack.

2. Write a program to implement a queue.

3. Write a program to carry out the following operations in an array
   (i) Inserting an element at the beginning
   (ii) Inserting an element at the end
   (iii) Inserting an element after a given element
   (iv) Deleting an element from the beginning
   (v) Deleting an element from the end
   (vi) Deleting a given element from an array

4. Write a program to implement bubble sort. What is the complexity of bubble sort?

5. Write a program to implement selection sort.

6. Write a program to implement to merge to sorted arrays. Write a program to implement merge sort.

7. Write a program to concatenate two given arrays.

8. Write a program to find the maximum element from a given array.

9. Write a program to find the second maximum element from a given array.

10. Write a program to reverse the order of elements of a given array.

STACKS AND QUEUES

After reading this chapter, the reader will be able to

- Understand the importance of stacks and queues
- Using dynamic tables for implementing stacks
- Understand postfix, prefix, and infix expressions
- Convert infix to postfix, infix, to prefix, and postfix to infix
- Understand the applications of stacks and queues

15.1 INTRODUCTION

Stacks and queues were introduced in the previous chapter. This chapter takes the topic forward and explains various implementations and applications of stacks and queues. The data structures are important as they find applications in recursive algorithms, conversion and evaluation of expressions, operating systems, and in popular CPU scheduling algorithms like round robin, etc. It may be stated here that Python provides libraries for both stacks and queues. However, a programmer is expected to know the implementations of the said data structures and to understand the advantages and problems associated with various implementations.

This chapter also introduces infix, postfix, and prefix expressions. Conversion and evaluation of expressions have been discussed in detail in this chapter. This topic finds applications in compiler design too. The linked list based implementation of stacks and queues have been deferred to the next chapter, as linked lists have been formally introduced in the next chapter.

This chapter has been organized as follows. Section 15.2 presents the basic terminology and array based implementation of stack. Section 15.3 discusses one of the dynamic implementations of stack and the discussion continues in the next section. Section 15.5 discusses two important applications of stacks: reversal of string and infix, postfix and prefix expressions. Section 15.6 presents the basics of queues and its implementation. The last section concludes the chapter. The reader is expected to revisit Chapter 14 before proceeding any further.

15.2 STACK

A stack is a linear data structure that follows the principle of Last In First Out (LIFO) or First In Last Out (FILO). A stack can be implemented using an array which has a fixed capacity (say n). The TOP denotes the position at which the element is to be inserted. Initially, the value of TOP is -1. As elements are inserted onto the stack, the value of TOP is increased by one until its value becomes (n-1), after which the 'Overflow' exception is raised. The insertion in a stack is referred to as 'push'. The algorithm for push has been presented as follows (Algorithm 15.1).

Algorithm 15.1

```
push(item):
     if TOP ==(n-1):
          print("Overflow")
     else:
          TOP=TOP+1
          a[TOP]=item
```

An element is deleted from the top of the stack if the value of TOP is not -1, in which case an underflow exception is raised. Otherwise, the element at TOP is returned and the value of TOP is decremented by 1. This operation is referred to as 'pop'. The algorithm for pop is as follows (Algorithm 15.2).

Algorithm 15.2

```
pop()
     if TOP == -1:
          print("Underflow")
     else
          temp=a[TOP]
          TOP=TOP-1
          return(temp)
```

The `push` and `pop` operations take O(1) time each. Supposing all the place-holders of the given stack are full and each element is to be popped, the total time would be $n \times O(1) = O(n)$.

The above implementation is static implementation. The following illustration implements the above algorithm (Illustration 15.1).

Illustration 15.1: Write a program to implement a stack.

Solution: The theory has already been discussed.

```
class Stack:
  def_init_(self,n):
  self.TOP=-1
  self.a=[]
  self.n=n
def overflow(self):
if self.TOP==(self.n-1):
  return True
else:
  return False
def underflow(self):
 if self.TOP==-1:
   discuss return True
discuss else:
discuss return False
def push(self, data):
 discuss if Stack.overflow(self):
   discuss print("Overflow...")
discuss else:
 discuss self.TOP=self.TOP+1
self.a.append(data)
print("TOP =",self.TOP)
def pop(self):
 if Stack.underflow(self):
 print("Underflow...")
   return (-1)
  else:
  temp=self.a.pop()
 self.TOP=self.TOP-1
 print("TOP=",self.TOP)
 return(temp)
 s= Stack(5)
 s.push(3)
 s.push(2)
```

```
s.push(4)
s.push(1)
s.push(21)
s.push(71)
i=0
while i<5:
    temp=s.pop()
 if temp!= -1:
 print(temp)
 else:
 print("Underflow")
 i+=1
```

Output

```
>>>
============= RUN C:\Windows\System32\stack.py =============
TOP = 0
TOP = 1
TOP = 2
TOP = 3
TOP = 4
Overflow...
TOP= 3
21
TOP= 2
1
TOP= 1
4
TOP= 0
2
TOP= -1
3
>>>
```

15.3   DYNAMIC IMPLEMENTATION OF STACKS

The problem with the above implementation is that as soon as the maximum limit is reached (of the maximum number of elements that the stack can have), overflow occurs. One of the ways of handling the problem is to increment the size of the stack by 1 as and when a new element is inserted after the limit is reached. However, this is not a very appropriate solution of the problem as each time a new array is created the values of the previous arrays are copied into the new array. So, for the first item a new array is created (initial array). The second insertion increases the size of the stack by 1 and copies the previous item in the new stack. This implies that there would be one copy operation and 1 insertion in inserting the second element. In the third insertion, there would be two copy operations and 1 insertion. Note that in the nth insertion, there would be $(n-1)$ copy operations and 1 insertion operation. In total there would be $O(n^2)$ copy operations.

```python
class Stack:
def init_(self,n):
    self.TOP=-1
    self.a=[]
    self.n=n
def check(self):
    if self.TOP==(self.n-1):
      self.resize()
def underflow(self):
    if self.TOP==-1:
      return True
else:
      return False

def push(self, data):
    Stack.check(self)
    self.TOP=self.TOP+1
    self.a.append(data)
    print("TOP =",self.TOP)

def pop(self):
    if Stack.underflow(self):
      print("Underflow...")
      return (-1)
else:
    temp=self.a.pop()
    self.TOP=self.TOP-1
    print("TOP=",self.TOP)
    return(temp)
def resize(self):
    self.n=self.n+1

s= Stack(5)
s.push(3)
```

```
s.push(2)
s.push(4)
s.push(1)
s.push(21)
s.push(71)
i=0
```

Output

```
====== RUN C:/Python/Data Structure/Stack_dynamic1.py ======
TOP = 0
TOP = 1
TOP = 2
TOP = 3
TOP = 4
TOP = 5
TOP= 4
71
TOP= 3
21
TOP= 2
1
TOP= 1
4
TOP= 0
2
>>>
```

15.4   DYNAMIC IMPLEMENTATION: ANOTHER WAY

The problem with the above implementation can be handled by doubling the size of the array after the limit is reached. This solution is better than other solutions where the size of the array is incremented by 1, as the number of copy operations using this method is O(n). So, for the first item, a new array is created (initial array). The second insertion increases the size of the stack by 1 and copies the previous item into the new stack. This implies that there will be one copy operation and 1 insertion in inserting the second element. In the third insertion, a new stack of size 4 is created and there would be two copy operations and 1 insertion. In the fourth insertion, there is no need to create a new stack. The reader is expected to carry out the mathematical analysis. Note that this gives you an idea of amortized analysis. Those of you interested may refer to the links at the end of this book. The following code presents the implementation.

Code

```
class Stack:
  def_init_(self,n):
    self.TOP=-1
    self.a=[]
    self.n=2*n
  def check(self):
    if self.TOP==(self.n-1):
      self.resize()
def underflow(self):
    if self.TOP==-1:
      return True
else:
    return False

def push(self, data):
  Stack.check(self)
  self.TOP=self.TOP+1
  self.a.append(data)
  print("TOP =",self.TOP)
def pop(self):
  if Stack.underflow(self):
    print("Underflow...")
    return (-1)
else:
  temp=self.a.pop()
  self.TOP=self.TOP-1
  print("TOP=",self.TOP)
  return(temp)
def resize(self):
  self.n=self.n+1
```

The implementation of stacks using linked lists has been dealt with in the next chapter. We now move on to some of the applications of a stack.

15.5   APPLICATIONS OF STACKS

Stacks can be used to carry out a variety of tasks like reversing a string, evaluation of a postfix expression, conversion of infix to postfix, and evaluation of postfix. Let us begin with reversing a string of characters.

15.5.1 Reversing a String

A string can be reversed using a stack by adopting the procedure that follows. From a given string one character is taken at a time and put in the stack. When all the characters are over, we start popping out characters from the stack. For example if the input string is "harsh," the process of reversing the string using a stack has been depicted in Figure 15.1.

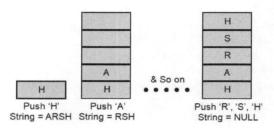

FIGURE 15.1 A stack can be used to reverse the order of characters of a string

Illustration 15.1: Ask the user to enter a string and reverse the string using a stack (use a list as stack).

Solution: The theory has already been discussed. The program is as follows.

Code

```
str= input('Enter a string\t:')
rev_string=''
a=[]
for i in str:
  a.append(i)
i=0
while i<len(str):
  x=a.pop()
  rev_string=rev_string+ x
  i=i+1

print(rev_string)
```

Output

```
>>>
========== RUN C:/Python/Data Structure/reverse.py ==========
Enter a string    :harsh
hsrah
>>>
```

Illustration 15.2: Reverse a line entered by the user using stacks. The stack need not be implemented. You can use a list as a stack.

Solution: The process remains same. However, to split a line into words the `split()` function is used.

```
line=input('Enter a line\t:')
a=[]
rev_line=''
words=line.split()
print(words)
for i in words:
  a.append(i)
i=0
while i<len(words):
  rev_line+=a.pop()
  rev_line+=' '
  i+=1
print(rev_line)
```

Output

```
>>>
========== RUN C:/Python/Data Structure/revline.py ==========
Enter a line        :I am Harsh
['I', 'am', 'Harsh']
Harsh am I
>>>
```

15.5.2 Infix, Prefix, and Postfix Expressions

Another important application of stack is to convert an infix expression to that in postfix and prefix. In order to understand this, let us first see what postfix, prefix, and infix expressions are. When a binary operator is between two operands, the expression is referred to as infix. If the operator is after the two operands, the expression is in the postfix form. If the operator is before the operands, the expression is in the prefix form. For example, the addition of "a" and "b" can be written as follows, in different forms:

Infix: $a + b$
Postfix: $ab +$
Prefix: $+ ab$

The evaluation of a postfix expression can be done by employing the following procedure.

Evaluation of Postfix

Step 1: Initialize the postfix expression, P by NULL and let the stack be initially empty.

Step 2: For an incoming symbol, s, in expression E

Repeat the following steps till there is a symbol in the given string

If it is a operand, put in the stack

Else if it is an operator pop two symbols from the stack (say x; and y, in that order)

Apply the operator as $x + y$, and put the result in the stack.

In order to understand the above procedure, let us consider an expression E

$$E = ab + c \times d/$$

The steps of evaluation of this postfix expression have been depicted in Table 15.1, shown as follows.

Table 15.1 An example of conversion of a postfix expression to that in prefix

Symbol	Stack	Processing
a	A	push(a)
b	a, b	push(b)
+	.	x = pop(), y = pop(), $x+y$
.	$(a+b)$	push($(a+b)$)
c	$(a+b), c$	push(c)
X	.	x = pop(), y = pop(), $x+y$
.	c X $(a+b)$	(push($(c$ X $(a+b))$))
d	$(c$ X $(a+b)), d$	push(d)
/	.	x = pop(), y = pop(), $x+y$
.	$(c$ X $(a+b))/d$	.push($(c$ X $(a+b))/d$)

We now come to the conversion of an infix expression to that in postfix. The conversion of an infix expression to that in postfix can be carried out by employing the following procedure.

Postfix Conversion

- Put a closing parenthesis at the end of the given expression E.
- Put an opening parenthesis at the top of the stack.
- Initialize P to NULL.
- Repeat the following steps until there is a symbol remaining in E.
- For each symbol, *s*.
  If "*s*" is an operand, put it in P
  If "*s*" is an opening parenthesis, put in the stack
  If "*s*" is an operator,
  Put "*s*" in stack, if the top of the stack contains an operator having a lower priority operator (or for that matter, no operator).
  Otherwise pop the topmost symbol from the stack, put it in P and push the incoming operator in the stack.
- If "*s*" is closing parentheses, continue popping symbols from the stack until an opening parentheses is found (including the opening parentheses).

The conversion of an infix expression to that in postfix is similar. However, the given string needs to be reversed first. This is followed by the application of the above procedure, after which the resulting string should be reversed. The conversion of an infix expression to that in prefix can be carried out by employing the following procedure.

Prefix Conversion

- Reverse the given expression E, call it E'.
- Put a closing parenthesis at the end of the given expression E'.
- Put an opening parenthesis at the top of the stack.
- Initialize P to NULL.
- Repeat the following steps till there is a symbol remaining in E.
  For each symbol, s.
    If "*s*" is an operand , put it in P
    If "*s*" is an opening parenthesis, put in the stack
    If "*s*" is an operator,
- Put "*s*" in stack, if the top of the stack contains an operator having a lower priority operator (or for that matter, no operator).
- Otherwise pop the topmost symbol from the stack, put it in P and push the incoming operator in the stack.
- If "*s*" is a closing parenthesis, continue popping symbols from the stack until an opening parenthesisis found (including the opening parenthesis).

Reverse the output obtained P, call it P'.

15.6 QUEUE

As stated in the first section, a queue is a linear data structure that follows the principle of First In First Out (FIFO). A queue is characterized by FRONT and REAR. Initially, the value of FRONT and REAR are both -1. When a new element is added to a queue, the value of REAR is incremented, if the value of REAR is not (n-1). When an element is deleted from the queue, the value of FRONT is incremented by 1 if FRONT is not -1. In the first insertion REAR and FRONT are both incremented and the value of REAR (and FRONT) become 0. In the case of deletion where the value of REAR and FRONT are same, the value of REAR and FRONT become -1. The algorithms for insertion in a queue and deletion from a queue are as follows:

```
Insert(item)
   {
   if( REAR == (n-1)):
         {
         print ("overflow");
         }
else
         {
         if(FRONT == -1)
               {
               FRONT = REAR = 0;
               a[REAR] =item;
               }
         else
               {
               REAR = REAR +1;
               a[REAR] = item;
               }
         }
   }
```

The algorithm (both places) for the deletion from a queue is as follows. The algorithm (both places) returns the value which is deleted from the queue. If a "-1" is returned, it indicates an underflow.

```
int delete()
     {
     if (FRONT == -1)
             {
             print("Underflow")
             }
```

```
      else if (FRONT == REAR)
              {
              temp = a[FRONT];
              REAR =-1;
              FRONT = -1;
              return temp;
              }
              else
              {
              temp= a[FRONT];
              FRONT = FRONT + 1;
              return temp;
              }
          }
```

The following illustration depicts the static implementation of a queue.

Illustration 15.3: Implement queue using a list.

Solution: In the program that follows, the queue has been implemented using a list called "a." The initial values of FRONT and REAR are both -1 .

```
class Queue:
  def_init_(self,n):
    self.FRONT=-1
    self.REAR=-1
    self.a=[]
    self.n=n
def overflow(self):
  if self.REAR==(self.n-1):
    return True
  else:
    return False
def underflow(self):
  if self.FRONT==-1:
    return True
  else:
    return False

def insert(self, data):
  if Queue.overflow(self):
    print('Overflow')
  elif self.FRONT==-1:
    self.FRONT=self.FRONT+1
    self.REAR=self.REAR+1
    self.a.append(data)
```

```
            print("Front = ",str(self.FRONT), "\tRear", str(self.
                    REAR),"\tData\t:",str(self.a[self.REAR]))
        else:
            self.REAR=self.REAR+1
            self.a.append(data)
            print("Front = ",str(self.FRONT), "\tRear", str(self.
                    REAR),"\ tData\t:",str(self.a[self.REAR]))

    def delete(self):
      if self.FRONT==-1:
        return (-1)
    elif self.FRONT==self.REAR:
      temp=self.a[self.FRONT]
      print("FRONT=",self.FRONT)
      self.FRONT=-1
      self.REAR=-1
      return temp

    else:
      temp=self.a[self.FRONT]
      self.FRONT=self.FRONT+1
      print("FRONT=",self.FRONT)
      return(temp)

q= Queue(5)
q.insert(3)
q.insert(2)
q.insert(4)
q.insert(1)
q.insert(21)
q.insert(71)
i=0
while i<6:
  temp=q.delete()
  if temp!= -1:
    print(temp)
else:
  print("Underflow")
i+=1
```

Output

```
>>>
========== RUN C:/Python/Data Structure/Queue.py ==========
```

```
Front = 0      Rear  0    Data  : 3
Front = 0      Rear  1    Data  : 2
Front = 0      Rear  2    Data  : 4
Front = 0      Rear  3    Data  : 1
Front = 0      Rear  4    Data  : 21
Overflow
FRONT= 1
3
FRONT= 2
2
FRONT= 3
4
FRONT= 4
1
FRONT= 4
21
Underflow
```

15.7   CONCLUSION

Many researchers consider data structures more important than the procedure. Stacks and queues are the most important aspects of these important things. The implementations of stacks and queues have been discussed in this chapter. The conversion of a postfix expression to that in infix, infix to postfix, infix, to prefix have not been implemented and have been left as an exercise for the reader. The reader is also expected to visit the links provided at the end of this book to find some more applications of stacks and queues and try to implement them. Lastly, the linked list based implementation has been discussed in this chapter.

GLOSSARY

Stack: A linear data structure which follows the principle of Last in First out (LIFO).

Queue: A linear data structure which follows the principle of First in First out (FIFO).

IMPORTANT POINTS

- Complexity of insertion and deletion in both stack and queue is O(1).
- If the value of TOP is -1, stack is empty.
- In the static implementation, if the value of TOP is $(n\text{-}1)$, the stack is full, where n is the maximum number of elements a stack can hold.
- On inserting an element, in a stack the value of TOP increases by 1.
- On removing an element from a stack, the value of TOP decreases by -1.
- Evaluation of postfix expression, conversion of infix to postfix, and that to prefix requires stack.
- Applications of queues include customer services, round robin, printer spooling, etc.

EXERCISES

MULTIPLE CHOICE QUESTIONS

1. Books are kept one over another such that the book which is kept at the end would be picked up first. Which data structure resembles this structure?

   (a) Stacks   (b) Queues

   (c) Graphs   (d) Trees

2. What is the time complexity of a POP operation in the static implementation of stack?

   (a) O(1)   (b) O(n)

   (c) O(n^2)   (d) None of the above

3. What is the time complexity of a PUSH operation in the static implementation of stack?

   (a) O(1)   (b) O(n)

   (c) O(n^2)   (d) None of the above

4. What is the space complexity of a PUSH operation in the static implementation of stack?

   (a) O(1)   (b) O(n)

   (c) O(n^2)   (d) None of the above

5. In the dynamic implementation of stack which data structure can be used?

   (*a*) Graphs   (*b*) Trees

   (*c*) Linked lists   (*d*) None of the above

6. Which one is more flexible - static or dynamic implementation of stack?

   (*a*) Static   (*b*) Dynamic

   (*c*) Both of the above   (*d*) Cannot determine

7. What is the prefix form of the expression: $((a\text{-}b) \times c)/d$.

   (*a*) /×-1bcd   (*b*) –abcx/d

   (*c*) /×-abcd   (*d*) None of the above

8. What is the postfix form of the above expression?

   (*a*) ab-c × d/   (*b*) ab-cd × /

   (*c*) abc+-/   (*d*) None of the above

9. Which of the following is true?

   (*a*) The prefix of an expression is just the reverse of the postfix

   (*b*) Conversion of an infix expression to postfix and that to prefix follows similar procedures

   (*c*) Both the statements are true

   (*d*) None of the statements is true

10. Evaluation of postfix requires which of the following data structures?

    (*a*) Stacks   (*b*) Queues

    (*c*) Graphs   (*d*) Trees

11. Customer services resemble which of the following data structures?

    (*a*) Stacks   (*b*) Queues

    (*c*) Graphs   (*d*) Trees

12. Round robin algorithm requires which of the following data structures?

    (*a*) Stacks   (*b*) Queues

    (*c*) Graphs   (*d*) Trees

13. What is the time complexity of the addition of an element in the static implementation of a queue?
    (*a*) O(1)   (*b*) O(*n*)
    (*c*) O(n^2)   (*d*) None of the above

14. The dynamic implementation of queue requires which of the following data structures?
    (*a*) Graphs   (*b*) Trees
    (*c*) Linked lists   (*d*) None of the above

15. Which of the following is an application of circular queue?
    (*a*) Traffic lights   (*b*) Memory management
    (*c*) Adding large integers   (*d*) All of the above

THEORY

1. Write an algorithm for static implementation of a stack. What are the problems in the implementation?

2. State any two methods to address the above problems.

3. State any two applications of stack. Implement any one.

4. Write an algorithm to implement a queue from two stacks.

5. State a few applications of a queue. How is a queue useful in scheduling using a round robin algorithm? Explain.

6. What is a circular queue? Write an algorithm for implementing a circular queue.

7. What is a doubly ended queue?

8. Write an algorithm for converting an infix expression to a postfix expression.

9. Write an algorithm for converting an infix expression to a prefix expression.

10. Write an algorithm for converting a postfix expression to an infix expression.

NUMERICAL

1. Evaluate the following postfix expressions:
   (a) $ab - c \times$
   (b) $ab - cd / \times$
   (c) $ab + cd / - f +$
   (d) $ab \cdot c -$
   (e) $x\text{Sin}$

2. Convert the following to postfix:
   (a) $(a + b) - (c / d) \times f$
   (b) $(a / b) \times (c + d)$
   (c) $a /(b + c)) - d$
   (d) $(c \cdot d) \times ((a + b) / f)$
   (e) $a + ((b / c) \times (d \cdot f))$

3. Convert the following into prefix:
   (a) $a - ((b / d) \times f)$
   (b) $a / (b \times (c + d))$
   (c) $(b /(a + c)) \times (d - f)$
   (d) $c \cdot ((d \times (a - b)) / f)$
   (e) $(a + b) / c \times (d \cdot f)$

PROGRAMMING EXERCISES

1. Write a program for static implementation of a stack.

2. Write a program to implement a queue from two stacks.

3. Implement a round robin algorithm.

4. What is a circular queue? Write a program for implementing a circular queue.

5. Write a program for converting an infix expression to a postfix expression.

6. Write a program for converting an infix expression to a prefix expression.

7. Write a program for converting a postfix expression to an infix expression.

USEFUL LINK

1. Lecture notes: *https://www.cs.cmu.edu/~rjsimmon/15122-s13/09-queuestack.pdf.*

CHAPTER 16

LINKED LISTS

After reading this chapter, the reader will be able to

- Understand the need and importance of linked lists
- Insert and delete an item in a given linked list
- Implement stack and queue using a linked list
- Understand the problems associated with linked lists

16.1 INTRODUCTION

The previous chapter introduced two of the most important data structures; namely stack and queue. Stacks follow the principle of Last In First Out (LIFO) whereas queues are linear data structures which follow the principle of First In First Out (FIFO). That is, an element can be added or removed only from a specific position in these data structures. The data structure introduced in this chapter is far more flexible in terms of the insertion and removal of elements. The previous chapter also discussed the static implementation of stacks and queues. But the discussion on the dynamic implementation using linked lists was deliberately delayed. The linked list discussed in this chapter will help the user in the dynamic implementation of stack and queue. Here, it may be stated that Python provides functions for creation of linked lists and supported operations. The purpose of this chapter is to make the user familiar with the mechanism of the operations.

Linked list is a data structure whose basic unit is node. Each node has two parts namely: DATA and LINK. The DATA part contains the value whereas the LINK part has the address of the next node (Figure 16.1).

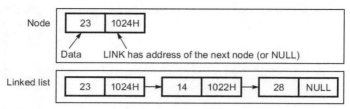

FIGURE 16.1 The basic unit of a linked list is a node. A linked list may have any number of nodes. The last node has NULL in its LINK part.

Linked lists are used in many problems like the implementation of dynamic stacks and queues and implementing non-linear data structures like trees and graphs. It may be stated here that although the use of linked lists makes the dynamic implementation easy, they come with their own problems. In some cases linked lists are not used in the implementation of trees. In implementing non-linear data structures the need of linked lists must be deliberated upon. For example, if we have a balanced binary tree or a heap then the use of arrays is much better than a linked list.

A linked list consists of nodes connected together via LINK. As stated earlier, each node has data and a LINK, where data may be a primary or even a secondary data structure and the LINK is a pointer to the next node. The first node of a linked list will henceforth be denoted by HEAD. It may also be noted that the LINK of the last node is NULL, indicating that there is no node after the last node. Therefore it becomes easy to identify the first and the last node in a linked list. The following operations can be carried out in a linked list:

1. Insertion at beginning

2. Insertion at middle

3. Insertion at end

4. Deletion at beginning

5. Deletion at middle

6. Deletion at end

The following section explains each of the above operations in detail. Each algorithm is followed by a figure, which exemplifies the procedure explained in the example.

16.2 OPERATIONS

A linked list can be used in various applications. However, to be able to use them, one must be equipped with the procedures to insert and delete elements at the beginning, at the end and at the specified position. The following discussion throws light on the requisite procedures.

Insertion at beginning

In order to insert a node at the beginning, a new node (say TEMP) is created and the data is inserted in the DATA part of the TEMP. Now, the NEXT of TEMP would point to the HEAD of the linked list and finally, TEMP becomes the new HEAD. The insert_beg(VALUE) presents the algorithm to insert a node at the beginning and Figure 16.2 presents the implementation of this process.

Algorithm

```
    insert_beg (VALUE)
{
//Create a node called TEMP.
   TEMP = node()
//Now put the given value (VALUE) in the data part of TEMP.
   TEMP->DATA = VALUE
//Set the LINK part of TEMP to FIRST.
   TEMP->LINK = FIRST
   Rename TEMP to FIRST.
}
```

The algorithm has been explained in the following figure (Fig. 16.2).

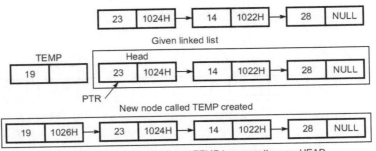

FIGURE 16.2 Inserting a node at the beginning

Insertion after a particular node

In order to insert a node after a particular node, a node pointer called PTR is created. Initially PTR points to the HEAD. The LINK of PTR becomes the LINK of the current node until the current node has the value after which we intend to insert the new node. A new node called TEMP is created and VALUE is inserted in its DATA part. Let the LINK of PTR be PTR1. Finally, the LINK of PTR will point to TEMP and the LINK of TEMP will point to the PTR1. The insert_middle(VAL, VALUE) presents the algorithm to insert a node after a given node (having data VAL) and Figure 16.3 shows an example of this process.

Algorithm

```
    Insert_middle (VAL, VALUE)
{
    PTR = FIRST
    while (PTR->DATA != VAL)
    {
    PTR=PTR-> LINK
    }
    PTR1=PTR ->LINK
//Create a new node called TEMP
    TEMP = node()
    TEMP->DATA = VALUE
    TEMP->LINK = PTR1
    PTR->LINK = TEMP
}
```

The algorithm has been explained in the following figure (Figure 16.3).

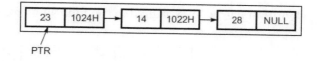

Given Linked List

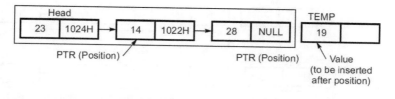

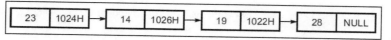

FIGURE 16.3 Insertion after a particular position

Insertion at the end

In order to insert a node at the end, a node pointer called PTR is created. Initially PTR points to the HEAD. The LINK of PTR becomes the LINK of the current node till the current node's LINK is NULL. A new node called TEMP is created and VALUE is inserted in its data part. Finally, the LINK of PTR will point to TEMP and the LINK of TEMP will be NULL. The insert_end(VALUE) presents the algorithm to insert a node after a given node and Figure 16.4 shows an example of this process.

Algorithm

```
   Insert_end (VALUE)
 {
   PTR = FIRST
   while (PTR->LINK != NULL)
          {
           PTR=PTR-> LINK
              }
//Create a new node called TEMP
      TEMP->DATA = VALUE
      PTR->LINK = TEMP
      TEMP->LINK = NULL
 }
```

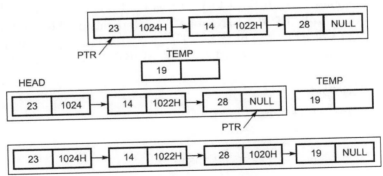

FIGURE 16.4 Insertion at the end

Deletion From the Beginning

In order to delete a node from the beginning, the LINK of HEAD becomes the new HEAD. Also, if required, the DATA of HEAD may be stored in some memory location. The del_beg() presents the algorithm to delete the first node of the linked list and Figure 16.5 shows an example of this process.

Algorithm

```
Delete_beg ()
{
Set backup = HEAD->DATA
Rename HEAD->LINK as HEAD
}
```

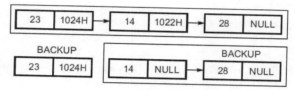

FIGURE 16.5 Deleting a node from the beginning

Deletion of a node after a particular node (having VALUE = VAL)

In order to delete a node which is after a particular node, the following procedure is employed. A node pointer PTR is created, which initially points to the HEAD. The LINK of PTR becomes PTR→LINK till the PTR→DATA becomes VAL. If the LINK of this PTR point to PTR1 and PTR1's LINK points to PTR2, the LINK of PTR will point to PTR2 and, if required, the DATA of PTR1 can be saved. The `del_middle()` presents the algorithm to accomplish the above task and Figure 16.6 shows an example of this process.

Algorithm

```
del_middle(VAL)
{
        PTR = HEAD
        while ((PTR->LINK)->DATA != VAL))
                }
                PTR=PTR->LINK
                }
PTR->NEXT = PTR1
PTR1->NEXT PTR2
PTR->NEXT = PTR2
        }
```

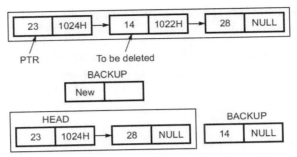

FIGURE 16.6 Deleting a node from a particular position

Deletion of a node from the end

In order to delete a node from the end, the following procedure is employed. A node pointer PTR is created, which initially points to the HEAD. The LINK of PTR becomes PTR->LINK till the PTR->LINK->LINK becomes NULL. Finally, the LINK of PTR will point to NULL. If required the DATA of PTR->LINK can be saved. The del_end() presents the algorithm to accomplish the above task and Figure 16.7 shows an example of this process.

Algorithm

```
del_end ()
{
     PTR = FIRST
        while ((PTR->NEXT)->NEXT != NULL)
                {
                PTR=PTR->LINK
                }
        Set backup = (PTR->NEXT)->DATA
        PTR->NEXT = NULL

}
```

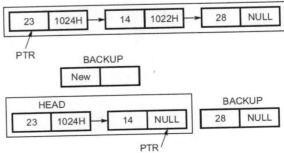

FIGURE 16.7 Deleting a node from the end

Illustration 16.1: Write a program to implement various operations of a singly linked list.

Code: The algorithm of each operation has already been discussed. The following code presents the Python implementation of the above code. Note that the code has 6 functions (in the linked list class), each implementing the corresponding algorithm.

```python
class Node:
  def __init__(self):
      self.data=None
      self.link=None

  def setVal(self, val):
      self.data=val
  def getVal(self):
      return self.data

  def setNext(self, next1):
      self.link=next1

  def getNext(self):
      return self.link

  def hasNext(self):
      if self.link!=None:
          return True
      else:
          return False

class LinkedList:
  def _init_(self):
    self.head=None
    self.length=0

  def listLength(self):
    current=self.head
    count=0
    while current!=None:
        count=count+1
        current=current.getNext()
    return count

  def insertBeg(self,val):
    tempNode=Node()
    tempNode.setVal(val)
    if self.length==0:
      self.head=tempNode
```

```
    else:
      tempNode.setNext(self.head)
          self.head=tempNode
          self.length+=1

  def insertEnd(self, val):
    tempNode=Node()
    tempNode.setVal(val)
      current=self.head
      while current.getNext()!=None:
            current=current.getNext()
            current.setNext(tempNode)
          self.length+=1

  def insertAfter(self, val1, val):
    tempNode=Node()
    tempNode.setVal(val)
    current=self.head
    while current.data!=val1:
        current=current.getNext()
    current1=current.getNext()
    current.setNext(tempNode)
    tempNode.setNext(current1)

  def del_beg(self):
    current=self.head
    if current!=None:
      current=self.head
      next1=current.link
      self.head=next1
      self.length=self.length-1
    else:
      print('Cannot delete')

  def del_end(self):
    current=self.head
    if current!=None:
        while (current.link).link!=None:
          current=current.link
        current.link=None
      else:
        print('Cannot delete')

  def del_after(self, val):
    flag=0
    current=self.head
```

```
            while current.data!=val:
              current=current.link
            current1=current.link
            current2=current1.link
            current.link=current2
            self.length=self.length-1
        def clear(self):
          self.head=None

        def traverse(self):
          current=self.head
          while current!=None:
            print(current.data,end=" ")
            current=current.getNext()
L = LinkedList()
print('\nList');
L.traverse()
L.insertBeg(2)
print('\nList');
L.traverse()
L.insertBeg(5)
print('\nList');
L.traverse()
L.insertBeg(7)
print('\nList');
L.traverse()
L.insertAfter(5,8)
print('\nList')
L.traverse()
L.insertEnd(9)
print('\nList')
L.traverse()
print('\nLength\t',str(L.listLength()))
L.del_beg()
print('\nList')
L.traverse()
L.del_after(8)
print('\nList')
```

```
L.traverse()
L.del_end()
print('\nList')
L.traverse()
L.clear()
print('\nList');
L.traverse()
L.del_beg()
L.traverse()
```

Output

```
List
List
2
List
5 2
List
7 5 2
List
7 5 8 2
List
7 5 8 2 9
Length      5

List
5 8 2 9
List
5 8 9
List
5 8
List
Cannot delete
>>>
```

The above linked list is referred to as a singly linked list. There are other variants as well, such as a doubly linked list. In a doubly linked list, each node has two pointers PREVIOUS and NEXT along with the data part. The PREVIOUS connects the node to the previous node and the NEXT connects the node to the next node. Also the NEXT of the last node is NULL, indicating that this node is not connected to any other node. The first node of a doubly linked list is also given a special name.

For example, if A and B are connected as shown in the figure then the "NEXT" of A is address of B and the "PREVIOUS" of B is the address of A (Figure 6.8).

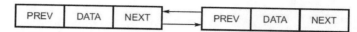

FIGURE 16.8 Node of a doubly linked list are connected via two pointers: NEXT and PREV

In a doubly linked list the following operations can be carried out:

1. Insertion at beginning
2. Insertion at middle
3. Insertion at end
4. Deletion at beginning
5. Deletion at middle
6. Deletion at end

There is another variant of a linked list, which is a circular linked list. In a circular linked list last node is connected to the first node. That is, the "NEXT" of the last node contains the address of the first node.

16.3 IMPLEMENTING STACK USING A LINKED LIST

A stack, as explained earlier, supports only two operations: insertion at the end and deletion from the end. The implementation of a stack using a linked list, therefore, requires only these two operations to be implemented. A linked list having only two operations insert_end (VAL) and del_end (Section 16.2) would be a stack. The first operation is equivalent to push and the second is equivalent to pop (). Illustration 16.2 presents the implementation of a stack using linked list.

Illustration 16.2: Write a program to implement stack using linked list.

Code

```
class Node:
  def_init_(self):
    self.data=None
    self.link=None
```

```
    def setVal(self, val):
        self.data=val

    def getVal(self):
        return self.data

    def setNext(self, next1):
        self.link=next1

    def getNext(self):
        return self.link

    def hasNext(self):
        if self.link!=None:
            return True
        else:
            return False

class Stack:
    def _init_(self):
        self.head=None
        self.length=0

    def Length(self):
        current=self.head
        count=0
        while current!=None:
            count=count+1
            current=current.getNext()
        return count

    def push(self, val):
        tempNode=Node()
        tempNode.setVal(val)
        current=self.head
        if current!=None:
            while current.getNext()!=None:
                current=current.getNext()
            current.setNext(tempNode)
            self.length+=1
        else:
            self.head=tempNode

    def pop(self):
        current=self.head
        if current!=None:
            while (current.link).link!=None:
```

```
                current=current.link
            data=current.data
            current.link=None
        else:
            print('Underflow')
            data=-1
        return data

    def traverse(self):
        current=self.head
        while current!=None:
            print(current.data,end=" ")
            current=current.getNext()
S = Stack()
print('\nStack')
S.traverse()
S.push(2)
print('\nStack')
S.traverse()
#[2]
S.push(5)
print('\nStack');
S.traverse()
#[2,5]
S.push(3)
print('\nStack');
S.traverse()
#[2,5,3]
val=S.pop()
if val!=-1:
    print('\n',str(val), 'popped')
print('\nStack')
S.traverse()
#[2,5]
val=S.pop()
if val!=-1:
    print('\n',str(val), 'popped')
print('\nStack')
S.traverse()
#[2]
```

Output

```
>>>
========== RUN C:/Python/Data Structures/Stack.py ==========
```

```
Stack
Stack
2
Stack
2 5
Stack
2 5 3
 5 popped

Stack
2 5
 2 popped

Stack
2
>>>
```

16.4   QUEUE USING A LINKED LIST

A queue, as explained earlier, supports only two operations: insertion at the end and deletion from the beginning. The implementation of a queue using a linked list, therefore, requires only these two operations to be implemented. A linked list having only two operations Insrt_end(VAL) and del_beg, would be a queue. The first operation is the same as en_queue and the second is the same as the de_queue(). Illustration 16.3 presents the implementation of a queue using linked list.

Illustration 16.3: Write a program to implement queue using linked list.

Code

```
class Node:
  def_init_(self):
    self.data=None
    self.link=None

  def setVal(self, val):
    self.data=val

  def getVal(self):
    return self.data

  def setNext(self, next1):
    self.link=next1
```

```python
    def getNext(self):
      return self.link

    def hasNext(self):
      if self.link!=None:
          return True
      else:
          return False
class Queue:
  def_init_(self):
    self.head=None
    self.length=0

  def Length(self):
    current=self.head
    count=0
    while current!=None:
        count=count+1
        current=current.getNext()
    return count

  def enqueue(self, val):
    tempNode=Node()
    tempNode.setVal(val)
    current=self.head
    if current!=None:
  while current.getNext()!=None:
    current=current.link
    current.link=tempNode
    tempNode.link=None
    self.length+=1
else:
    self.head=tempNode
    self.length=self.length+1

  def dequeue(self):
    current=self.head
    if current!=None:
      current=self.head
      next1=current.link
      self.head=next1
      self.length=self.length-1
else:
    print('Cannot delete')
```

```
    def traverse(self):
        current=self.head
        while current!=None:
            print(current.data,end=" ")
            current=current.getNext()
Q = Queue()
print('\nQueue')
Q.traverse()
Q.enqueue(2)
print('\nQueue')
Q.traverse()
#[2]
Q.enqueue(5)
print('\nQueue')
Q.traverse()
#[2,5]
Q.enqueue(7)
print('\nQueue');
Q.traverse()
#[2,5,7]
Q.dequeue()
print('\nQueue');
Q.traverse()
#[5,7]
Q.dequeue()
print('\nQueue');
Q.traverse()
#[7]
```

Output

```
>>>
========== RUN C:/Python/Data Structures/Queue.py ==========
Queue
Queue
2
Queue
2 5
Queue
2 5 7
Queue
5 7
Queue
7
>>>
```

16.5   CONCLUSION

A linked list contains connected nodes. Each node has two parts: the DATA part and the LINK part. The DATA part may contain a basic or a complex data structure. The LINK part contains the address of the next node. The last node, therefore, has NULL in its LINK part. One can have linked lists of integers, float, char, or even strings. The reader is expected to explore the linked lists of user defined data structures and use them in solving problems. Problems related to polynomial addition and subtraction have been discussed in the references given at the end of the book. The reader is expected to go through the theory and implement the operations using a linked list. Moreover, the algorithms of a doubly and a circular linked list may be developed in a way similar to that of a singly linked list given in the chapter. Having studied linked lists and arrays the reader is also encouraged to find the advantages of using linked lists and also its disadvantages (for example extra overhead, pointers, etc.). The most important attribute of a linked list is its flexibility.

GLOSSARY

Node: A node is the basic unit of linked list. It has two parts: data and link. The link points to the next node.

POINTS TO REMEMBER

- The link of the last node of a linked is NULL
- Complexities of operations, discussed in the chapter

Operation	Complexity
Insertion at the beginning	O(1)
Insertion at end	O(n)
Insertion in the middle	O(n)
Deletion from the beginning	O(1)
Deletion from the end	O(n)
Deletion from the middle	O(n)

EXERCISES

MULTIPLE CHOICE QUESTIONS

1. The last element of a singly linked list points to
   (*a*) The first element
   (*b*) NULL
   (*c*) Any element
   (*d*) None of the above

2. A linked list can
   (*a*) Grow
   (*b*) Shrink
   (*c*) Both
   (*d*) None of the above

3. In a problem we need a maximum of 100 items; which data structure would be best suited if only the last element of the data structure is to be accessed?
   (*a*) Stack
   (*b*) Queue
   (*c*) Linked list
   (*d*) Both stack and linked list

4. In a linked list an element can be inserted at
   (*a*) The first position
   (*b*) The last position
   (*c*) At any position
   (*d*) None of the above

5. Which of the following makes arrays less advantageous when compared to linked lists?
   (*a*) Array have a fixed size
   (*b*) The elements of an array are stored at consecutive memory locations
   (*c*) It is difficult to add/delete an element from a given position
   (*d*) All of the above

6. What is the complexity of indexing in a linked list?
   (*a*) O(*n*)
   (*b*) O(1)
   (*c*) O(n^2)
   (*d*) None of the above

7. What is the complexity of indexing in a dynamic array?
   (*a*) O(1)
   (*b*) O(*n*)
   (*c*) O(n^2)
   (*d*) None of the above

8. What is the complexity of inserting an element at the end in an array?
   (a) O(1)   (b) O(n)
   (c) O(n^2)   (d) None of the above

9. What is the complexity of inserting an element at the end in a linked list?
   (a) O(1)   (b) O(n)
   (c) O(n^2)   (d) None of the above

10. When wasted space is concerned (pointers etc.), what is space complexity in a linked list?
    (a) O(1)   (b) O(n)
    (c) O(n^2)   (d) None of the above

11. When wasted space is concerned (pointers etc.), what is space complexity in an array?
    (a) O(1)   (b) O(n)
    (c) O(n^2)   (d) None of the above

12. When wasted space is concerned (pointers etc.), what is space complexity in a dynamic table?
    (a) O(1)   (b) O(n)
    (c) O(n^2)   (d) None of the above

13. Which is better in terms of time complexity for the operation that adds an element in the middle?
    (a) Array   (b) Linked List
    (c) Both   (d) None of the above

14. Which is better in terms of time complexity for the operation that adds an element at the end?
    (a) Array   (b) Linked List
    (c) Both   (d) None of the above

15. In a circular linked list the last element points to
    (a) The first element   (b) The middle element
    (c) NULL   (d) None of the above

THEORY

1. What is a linked list? Write an algorithm for the following
   (*a*) Inserting an element at the beginning of a linked list
   (*b*) Inserting an element at the end of a linked list
   (*c*) Inserting an element after a given element of a linked list
   (*d*) Deleting an element from the beginning of a linked list
   (*e*) Deleting an element from the end of a linked list
   (*f*) Deleting an element after a given element from a linked list

2. Derive the time complexity of each of the above.

3. What is a doubly linked list? Write an algorithm for the following
   (*a*) Inserting an element at the beginning of a doubly linked list
   (*b*) Inserting an element at the end of a doubly linked list
   (*c*) Inserting an element after a given element of a doubly linked list
   (*d*) Deleting an element from the beginning of a doubly linked list
   (*e*) Deleting an element from the end of a doubly linked list
   (*f*) Deleting an element after a given element from a doubly linked list

4. Derive the complexity for each of the above algorithms.

5. Write an algorithm to implement a stack using a linked list.

6. Write an algorithm to implement a queue using a linked list.

7. Write an algorithm to invert a linked list.

8. Write an algorithm to implement a queue using two stacks.

9. Write an algorithm to find whether a given string is a palindrome.

10. Write an algorithm to find the maximum element in a linked list.

PROGRAMMING

Implement Q1, Q3, & Q5-Q10 of the above section.

EXPLORE

The chapter gives an introduction to linked lists. The reader is expected to read and implement the algorithms of doubly linked lists and circular linked lists.

For doubly linked lists, the reader may refer to:

- *https://www.cs.cmu.edu/~guna/15-123S11/Lectures/Lecture11.pdf*

## CHAPTER 17

BINARY SEARCH TREES

After reading this chapter, the reader will be able to

- Understand the terminology and representation of trees and graphs
- Understand the importance of a binary search tree
- Implement insertion, searching, and traversal in a BST

17.1   INTRODUCTION

Consider the hierarchical structure of your college. The college should have the head under which the deans of various faculties work. The faculty is made up of various departments, which have their respective heads. These heads take the help of the chairs of various committees. This heretical structure can be viewed as a tree with the head of the institute at the 0th level, the deans at the first level, and the heads of the departments at the second level and so on.

Let us take another example, that of tic-tac-toe. At the beginning, the first player may fill any of the 9 cells in a 3 × 3 grid. After this move the second user may fill the other symbol in any of the remaining squares, keeping in mind the constraints. The game can thus be represented as a tree. Likewise, a tournament can be represented using a tournament tree.

In the case of machine learning, the decision trees help us to learn. The heap, a type of tree, helps us to find the maximum or minimum in $O(1)$ time.

There are numerous applications of trees and graphs. This chapter introduces trees and graphs and concentrates on a specific type of tree called the binary search tree, which is important in searching and is the basis of many other important topics.

The chapter has been organized as follows. The second section presents the definition, terminology, and representation of trees and graphs. The third section discusses the binary search trees (BST) and the last section concludes the chapter.

17.2   DEFINITION AND TERMINOLOGY

So far linear data structures, like stacks and queues, have been discussed. The data structures, their implementations and applications were presented in the previous chapter. However, there are many applications where nonlinear data structures are required. This chapter introduces two nonlinear data structures; namely graphs and trees. However, the focus of this chapter will be on trees - mainly a specific kind of tree called a binary search tree. Let us begin with the definition of a graph and its representation.

17.2.1   Graphs: Definition and Representation

Graph: A graph is a set (V, E), where V is a finite, non-empty set of vertices. The set E consists of tuples (x, y), where x and y belong to the set V. Figure 17.1 shows a graph G = (V, E), where V is (A, B, C, D) and the set E is {(A, B), (A, D), (B, C), (B, D), (C, D)}.

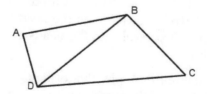

FIGURE 17.1 A graph G = (V, E), V = {A, B, C, D} and
E= {(A, B), (A, D), (B, C), (B, D), (C, D)}

The edges of a graph may have weights, in which case the graph is referred to as a weighted graph. A graph may be represented using a matrix or a linked list. The element at the ith row and the jth column in the matrix will be 1, if an edge exists between the vertex i and the vertex j, otherwise the element will be zero. In the case of a weighted graph, these elements may represent the weights of the corresponding edges. The matrix corresponding to the graph of Figure 17.1 is as follows:

$$\begin{bmatrix} 0 & 1 & 0 & 1 \\ 1 & 0 & 1 & 1 \\ 0 & 1 & 0 & 1 \\ 1 & 1 & 1 & 0 \end{bmatrix}$$

Note that the element at the first row and the second column is 1, as there is an edge between the first vertex (A) and the second vertex (B). Likewise there is an edge between A and D, hence the element at the first row and fourth column is 1. Graphs may also be represented using a set of linked lists, in which each linked list will point to the vertices connected to the corresponding vertex. The linked list representation of the graph of Figure 17.1 is as follows (Figure 17.2). Note that the list of A contains B and D as A is connected to B and D. Likewise, the list of B contains A, C, and D.

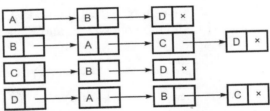

FIGURE 17.2 The linked list representation of the graph presented in Figure 17.1

Graph is one of the most important data structures. This data structure has applications in a wide variety of tasks like finding the shortest paths, ranking of web pages, etc. As a matter of fact, there is a dedicated subject on graph algorithms.

17.2.2   Trees: Definition, Classification, and Representation

Tree: A tree is a non-linear data structure. It is basically a graph which does not form any cycle and does not have isolated edges or vertices. Figure 17.3 (*a*) shows an example of a graph which is not a tree, as there exists a cycle in the graph. The Figure 17.3 (*b*) is a tree as it does not contain any cycle or isolated vertex or edge. The graph of Figure 17.3 (*c*) is not a tree, as it contains an isolated edge.

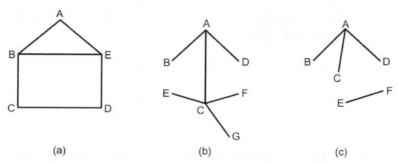

(a)   (b)   (c)

FIGURE 17.3 The examples of graphs, which are not trees
((a) and (c)) and an example of a tree (b)

Trees can be classified on the basis of the number of children of a node. If each node of a tree has a maximum of two children, it is called a binary tree. If each node of a tree has two children except for the last level at which a node has no child, it is called a complete binary tree. Figure 17.5 shows a complete binary tree. The root of a tree is always at level 0, the children of the root at level 1 and so on. The tree of Figure 17.4 is a binary tree, as each node has 0, 1, or 2 children. Note that the node A is at level 0, the nodes B and C are at level 1, and the nodes D, E, and F are at level 2.

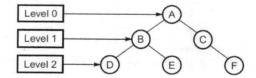

FIGURE 17.4 Binary tree; each node has 0, 1, or 2 children

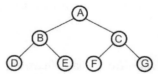

FIGURE 17.5 Complete binary tree; each node has 2 children except for the nodes at the last level, at which each node has 0 children

The number of nodes in a complete binary tree having two levels is 3, that having three levels is 7 and that having four levels is 15. A complete binary tree having n levels has $2n+1$ nodes. In the tree shown in Figure 17.5, A is the root of the tree as it is at level 0. The nodes B and C are siblings, as they have the same parent (A). Also, the nodes D and E are siblings and so are F and G.

The nodes D, E, F, and G are the leaves, as they have no children. The following table (Table 17.1) presents the terminology of a tree.

Table 17.1 Terminology of a tree

Edge: A line which connects two nodes.
Parent: A node from which the given node has been derived.
Root: A node which does not have a parent is called the root.
Degree of a node: The degree of a node is the number of children of a given node.
Degree of a tree: The degree of a tree is represented by the maximum number of children.
Level of a tree: The root of a tree is at level 0, the children of root are at level 1 and so on.

17.2.3 Representation of a Binary Tree

A binary tree can be stored in a computer using an array or a linked list. The array representation of a binary tree requires the root to be stored at the 0th index. For each node stored at the nth index, its left child would be stored at the $(2n+1)^{th}$ index and the right child at $(2n+2)^{th}$ index.

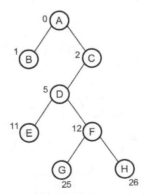

FIGURE 17.6 Calculation of index for the array representation of a binary search tree

For example, in the above tree (Figure 17.6) the root would be stored at the 0th index.

- The left child of the root (B) would be stored at the index, given by the formula

$$2 \times n + 1 = 2 \times 0 + 1 = 1$$

- The right child of the root would be stored at the index, given by the formula
$$2 \times n + 2 = 2 \times 0 + 2 = 2$$
- That is B would be stored at the 1st index and C at the 2nd index
- Likewise the left child of C would be stored at the index, given by the formula
$$2 \times n + 1 = 2 \times 2 + 1 = 5$$

The left child of D would be stored at the 11th index and the right child would be stored at the 12th index. Finally, the left and the right child of F would be stored at the 25rd and the 26th index. The array representation of the tree of Figure 17.6 is therefore as follows:

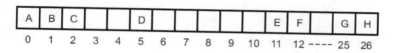

As is evident from the above array, this representation suffers from wastage of space. That is a lot of space is wasted if the given tree is not a completely balanced tree. Note that in the case of a completely balanced tree, no space would be wasted in the array representation.

There is another way in which a binary tree can be stored, which is by using a doubly linked list. In the representation, a node's left child's address is stored at the previous pointer and its right child's address is stored at the next pointer. The following figure (Figure 17.7) shows the linked list representation of the tree in Figure 17.6.

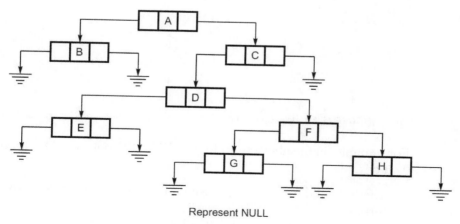

Represent NULL

FIGURE 17.7 Doubly linked list representation of a binary tree

17.2.4   Tree Traversal: In-order, Pre-order, and Post-order

A tree can be traversed in in-order, pre-order, and post-order.

In the in-order traversal, the root of a tree is given as an input to the algorithm. The algorithm works as follows. The left child of the root is given as the input to the same algorithm (recursion). This is followed by the processing of the root, following which the right child of the root is given as an input to the same algorithm (recursion). The algorithm has been presented as follows. The implementation has been presented in the next section. Though there is a corresponding non-recursive procedure to accomplish the task, it has not been discussed in this chapter. The reader may refer to the links at the end of this book for a more detailed study.

```
In-order(root)
    {
       if((root->left == NULL)&& (root->right == NULL))
           {
           print (root->data);
           }
       else
           {
           In-order(root ->left);
           print (root->data);
           In-order(root->right);
           }
    }
```

In the pre-order traversal, the root of a tree is given as an input to the algorithm. The algorithm works as follows. The data of the root is processed first. This is followed by the output obtained by giving the left child of the root as an input to the same algorithm (recursion), following which the right child of the root is given as an input to the same algorithm (recursion). The algorithm has been presented as follows. The implementation has been presented in the next section. Though there is a corresponding non-recursive procedure to accomplish the task, it has not been discussed in the chapter. The reader should refer to the links at the end of this book for a more detailed study.

```
In-pre(root)
    {
       if((root->left == NULL)&& (root->right == NULL))
           {
           print (root->data);
           }
```

```
else
    {
    print (root->data);
    pre-order(root ->left);
    pre-order(root->right);
    }
}
```

In the post-order traversal, the root of a tree is given as an input to the algorithm. The algorithm works as follows. The output obtained by giving the left child of the root to the algorithm itself is followed by the output obtained by giving the right child of the root as an input to the same algorithm (recursion) after which the root is processed. The algorithm has been presented as follows. The implementation has been presented in the next section. Though there is a corresponding non-recursive procedure to accomplish the task, it has not been discussed in this chapter.

```
In-post(root)
    {
      if((root->left == NULL)&& (root->right == NULL))
         {
         print (root->data);
         }
    else
         {
         post-order(root ->left);
         post-order(root->right);
        print (root->data);
         }
    }
```

17.3   BINARY SEARCH TREE

One of the advantages of trees is that they help in efficient searches. One of the variants of binary tree called binary search tree helps to find an element in O(log n) time (average case). A binary search tree is a binary tree in which each node satisfies the following property:

$$\text{node} \to \text{data} > (\text{node} \to \text{left}) \to \text{data and}$$
$$\text{node} \to (\text{data}) < (\text{node} \to \text{right}) \to \text{data}$$

The tree shown in Figure 17.8 is a binary search tree, whereas that shown in Figure 17.9 is not.

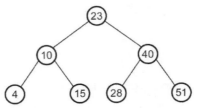

FIGURE 17.8 An example of a binary search tree; note that each node's left child has value less than the value in the data part and its right child has data greater than the node's data

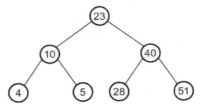

FIGURE 17.9 An example of a tree which is not a binary search tree, note that right child of node having data 10 is less than 10

17.3.1 Creation and Insertion

The creation of a BST is simple. The first value becomes the data part of the root. To insert a new value in the tree a new node is created, its correct position is found and the new node is placed at its correct position. The algorithm for inserting a new node in a BST is as follows.

```
Init( value)
    {
    root = node();
    root->data = value;
    root->right = NULL;
    root->left = NULL;
    }
Insert( value)
    {
    ptr = root;
    root1 = root;
    while( ptr ! = NULL)
        {
        if( value  > ptr->data)
            {
            root1=ptr;
```

```
            ptr = ptr->right;
            }
    else
            {
            root1=ptr;
            ptr = ptr->left;
            }
        }
    if (value > root1->data)
        {
        Node1 = node();
        Node1 = data;
        Node1->left = NULL;
        Node1 ->right = NULL;
        root1->right = Node1;
        }
    else
        {
        Node1 = node();
        Node1 = data;
        Node1->left = NULL;
        Node1 ->right = NULL;
        root1->left = Node1;

        }
    }
```

In order to understand the procedure, let us consider Illustration 17.1. This illustration is followed by another which implements the algorithm for the insertion in a BST.

Illustration 17.1: Insert 47, in the BST of Figure 17.10.

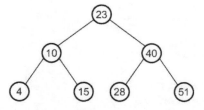

FIGURE 17.10 Binary Search Tree for Illustration 17.1

Solution: The process has been depicted in Figure 7.11 (*a*) to 7.11 (*d*). The reader is expected to follow the steps and map them to those given in the algorithm.

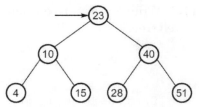

FIGURE 17.11(a) The search begins at the root. Since the value to be searched is greater than that at root, the right sub tree is searched

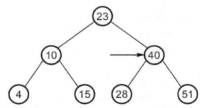

FIGURE 17.11(b) The root of the right sub tree is 40. Since the value to be searched (47) is greater than that at root, the right sub tree of this node is searched

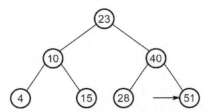

FIGURE 17.11(c) The root of the right sub tree is 51. Since the value to be searched (47) is less than that at ptr, the left is searched

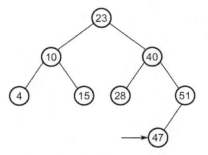

FIGURE 17.11(d) 47 is inserted

Illustration 17.2: Write a program to insert the value entered by the user in the binary search tree.

Program

```
class node:
  def_init_(self, data=None):
    self.data=data
    self.left= None
    self.right=None
class BST:
  def init (self,data):
    self.root=node(data)
  def InsertNode(self, val):
    ptr=self.root
    root1=self.root
    while(ptr!=None):
      if (val>ptr.data):
        root1=ptr
        ptr=ptr.right
      elif (val<ptr.data):
        root1=ptr
        ptr=ptr.left
      if (ptr==None):
        if (val<root1.data):
        Node=node(val)
        ptr=node()
        ptr.left=None
        ptr.data=val
        ptr.right=None
        root1.left=ptr
else:
        Node = node(val)
        ptr=node()
        ptr.right=None
        ptr.data=val
```

```
            ptr.right=None
            root1.right=ptr
def traverse(root):
            ptr=root

     if (ptr.left!=None):
         BST.traverse(ptr.left)
     print(" ",str(ptr.data),end='')
     if (ptr.right!=None):
         BST.traverse(ptr.right)
new_bst=BST(10)
print('\nTree\t:')
BST.traverse(new_bst.root)
new_bst.InsertNode(20)
new_bst.InsertNode(5)
print('\nTree\t:')
BST.traverse(new_bst.root)
new_bst.InsertNode(2)
new_bst.InsertNode(1)
new_bst.InsertNode(15)
new_bst.InsertNode(17)
print('\nTree\t:')
BST.traverse(new_bst.root)
```

Output

```
>>>
============ RUN C:\Python\Data Structure\BST.py ============

Tree  :
  10
Tree  :
  5   10   20
Tree  :
  1   2   5   10   15   17   20
>>>
```

17.3.2 Traversal

As stated in the previous section, a binary tree can be traversed in three ways: In-order, pre-order, and post-order traversal. The following illustration implements in-order, pre-order, and post-order traversal of a binary search tree.

Illustration 17.3: Write a program to implement pre-order, post-order, and in-order traversal of a binary search tree.

Program

```
class node:
  def _init_(self, data=None):
     self.data=data
     self.left=None
     self.right=None
class BST:
  def _init_(self,data):
     self.root=node(data)
  def InsertNode(self, val):
     ptr=self.root
     root1=self.root
     while(ptr!=None):
     if (val>ptr.data):
     root1=ptr
     ptr=ptr.right
   elif (val<ptr.data):
     root1=ptr
     ptr=ptr.left
   if (ptr==None):
     if (val<root1.data):
        Node=node(val)
        ptr=node()
        ptr.left=None
        ptr.data=val
        ptr.right=None
        root1.left=ptr
    else:
        Node = node(val)
        ptr=node()
        ptr.right=None
        ptr.data=val
```

```
            ptr.right=None
            root1.right=ptr
def inorderTraverse(root):
        ptr=root

        if (ptr.left!=None):
            BST.inorderTraverse(ptr.left)
        print(" ",str(ptr.data),end='')
        if (ptr.right!=None):
        BST.inorderTraverse(ptr.right)
    def preorderTraverse(root):
        ptr=root
        print(" ",str(ptr.data),end='')
        if (ptr.left!=None):
            BST.preorderTraverse(ptr.left)

        if (ptr.right!=None):
            BST.preorderTraverse(ptr.right)
def postorderTraverse(root):
        ptr=root
        if (ptr.left!=None):
            BST.postorderTraverse(ptr.left)

        if (ptr.right!=None):
            BST.postorderTraverse(ptr.right)
        print(" ",str(ptr.data),end='')
new_bst=BST(10)
new_bst.InsertNode(20)
new_bst.InsertNode(5)
new_bst.InsertNode(2)
new_bst.InsertNode(1)
new_bst.InsertNode(15)
new_bst.InsertNode(17)
print('\nIn-order Traversal of the BST\t:')
BST.inorderTraverse(new_bst.root)
print('\nPre-order Traversal of the BST\t:')
BST.preorderTraverse(new_bst.root)
print('\nPost-order Traversal of the BST\t:')
BST.postorderTraverse(new_bst.root)
```

Output

```
>>>
====== RUN C:\Python\Data Structure\Tree Traversal.py ======
```

```
In-order Traversal of the BST :
   1   2   5   10   15   17   20
Pre-order Traversal of the BST :
  10   5   2   1   20   15   17
Post-order Traversal of the BST :
   1   2   5   17   15   20   10

>>>
```

17.3.3   Maximum and Minimum Elements

The maximum element can be found by finding the rightmost element of the tree. The pointer is first set to the root and iteratively set to the root of the right sub tree, until ptr reaches terminal node. Logic can be extended to the complementary problem of finding the minimum element from the tree.

Illustration 17.4: Write a program to find the maximum and the minimum element from a binary search tree.

Program

```python
class node:
  def _init_(self, data=None):
    self.data=data
    self.left= None
    self.right=None

class BST:
  def _init_(self,data):
    self.root=node(data)
  def InsertNode(self, val):
    ptr=self.root
    root1=self.root
    ##flag=None;
    ##print(' Ptr =', str(ptr.data),' Root 1 :',str(root1.
                                                 data))
  while(ptr!=None):
    if (val>ptr.data):
      root1=ptr
      ptr=ptr.right
    ##flag='right'
    ##print('Right')
    elif (val<ptr.data):
      root1=ptr
      ptr=ptr.left
```

```
        ##flag='left'
        ##print('left')
    if (ptr==None):
      if (val<root1.data):
      Node=node(val)
      ptr=node()
      ptr.left=None
      ptr.data=val
      ptr.right=None
      root1.left=ptr
      ##print('Inserted ',str(val))
    else:
      Node = node(val)
      ptr=node()
      ptr.right=None
      ptr.data=val
      ptr.right=None
      root1.right=ptr
      ##print('Inserted ',str(val))

def maximum(root):
      ptr=root
      max1=ptr.data
      while(ptr.right!=None):
      ptr=ptr.right
      max1=ptr.data
      print('Maximum \t:',str(max1))

def minimum(root):
      ptr=root
      min1=ptr.data
      while(ptr.left!=None):
      ptr=ptr.left
      min1=ptr.data
      print('Minimum \t:',str(min1))

new_bst=BST(10)
new_bst.InsertNode(20)
new_bst.InsertNode(5)
new_bst.InsertNode(2)
new_bst.InsertNode(1)
new_bst.InsertNode(15)
new_bst.InsertNode(17)
BST.maximum(new_bst.root)
BST.minimum(new_bst.root)
```

Output

```
>>>
========== RUN C:\Python\Data Structure\BST max.py ==========
Maximum    : 20
Minimum    : 1
>>>
```

17.4   CONCLUSION

The chapter introduces one of the most important data structures called a tree. Since the set of trees is a subset of graphs, the definition and representation of graphs have also been included in the chapter. Moreover, the programs given in the chapter use linked list representations of a tree as the array based implementation becomes inefficient in terms of space if the tree is not a completely balanced tree. Trees can be traversed in variety of ways. The in-order, post-order, and the pre-order traversal have been described in the chapter. One of the most important trees called binary search trees has been introduced in the chapter. The algorithm and the corresponding program for searching an element in a binary search tree and insertion have also been included and exemplified. The reader is expected to visit the links given at the end of the chapter and explore the algorithm for deleting a node from a binary search tree. The appendix of this book discusses some of the important graph algorithms also. Moreover, this is just a beginning of the topic; explore trees and dive into the exciting world of problem solving through trees.

GLOSSARY

Graph: A graph is a set (V, E), where V is a finite, non-empty set of vertices. The set E is a set consisting of tuples (x, y), where x and y belong to the set V.

Tree: A tree is a non-linear data structure. It is basically a graph which does not form any cycle and which does not have isolated edges or vertices.

Edge: A line which connects two nodes.

Parent: A node from which the given node has been derived.

Root: A node which does not have a parent is called the root.

Degree of a node: The degree of a node is the number of children of a given node.

Degree of a tree: The degree of a tree is the maximum degree of any node of the tree.

Level of a tree: The root of a tree is at level 0, the children of root are at level 1 and so on.

Binary Search Tree: It is a binary tree in which each node satisfies the following property:

$$\text{node} \rightarrow \text{data} > (\text{node} \rightarrow \text{left}) \rightarrow \text{data and}$$
$$\text{node (data)} < (\text{node} \rightarrow \text{right}) \text{ data}$$

POINTS TO REMEMBER

- The complexity of insertion in a binary search tree is $O(\log n)$, if the tree is balanced.
- A tree can be represented using arrays. In this representation, the root is placed at the 0th index, the right child of a node at the nth index is at $(2n + 2)^{\text{th}}$ index and the left child at the $(2n + 1)^{\text{th}}$ index.
- The linked list representation of a tree is efficient in terms of space.
- From a binary search tree, the complexity of finding the maximum/minimum element is $O(\log n)$, if the tree is balanced.
- From a binary search tree, the complexity of finding the maximum/minimum element is $O(\log n)$, if the tree is skewed.

EXERCISES

MULTIPLE CHOICE QUESTIONS

1. Which of the following is true?

    (*a*) Every tree is a graph

    (*b*) Every graph is a tree

    (*c*) A tree cannot have a cycle

    (*d*) A tree cannot have an isolated edge

2. If G is the set of all the graphs, T is the set of all the trees and BST is the set of all the binary search trees, then which of the following is false?
   (a) $G \subseteq T$
   (b) $T \subseteq G$
   (c) $BST \subseteq T$
   (d) $BST \subseteq G$

3. What is the depth of a balanced tree having n nodes?
   (a) O(n)
   (b) O(log n)
   (c) O(1)
   (d) None of the above

4. What is the depth of a skewed tree having n nodes?
   (a) O(n)
   (b) O(log n)
   (c) O(1)
   (d) None of the above

5. In which of the following applications trees can be sued?
   (a) Searching
   (b) Sorting
   (c) Priority queues
   (d) All of the above

6. What is the best case complexity of insertion in a binary search tree?
   (a) O(1)
   (b) O(log n)
   (c) O(n)
   (d) None of the above

7. What is the average case complexity of insertion in a binary search tree?
   (a) O(1)
   (b) O(log n)
   (c) O(n)
   (d) None of the above

8. What is the worst case complexity of insertion in a binary search tree?
   (a) O(1)
   (b) O(log n)
   (c) O(n)
   (d) None of the above

9. A BST is created out of sorted list of n numbers; what is the complexity of inserting an element in the tree?
   (a) O(1)
   (b) O(n)
   (c) O(log n)
   (d) None of the above

10. A balanced BST is given, what is the complexity of inserting an element?
    (a) O(1)
    (b) O(n)
    (c) O(log n)
    (d) None of the above

NUMERICAL

1. Create a BST out of the following list of numbers
   (*a*) 2, 23, 14, 29, 35, 28, 19, 1, 3, 7, 16, 15
   (*b*) 1, 2, 3, 4, 5, 6, 7
   (*c*) 10, 8, 6, 4, 2, 1
   (*d*) 10, 15, 18, 17, 16, 19, 14, 21
   (*e*) 1, 2, 3, 4, 10, 9, 8, 7

2. Which of the above is balanced?

3. Which of the above (Q1) is skewed?

4. The list (*b*) (Q1) is a sequence; find the nth element of the sequence and the complexity to insert the *n*th element

5. In Q1 (*d*), what is the average complexity of inserting an element?

6. Write the in-order traversal of (*a*) to (*e*) (Q1).

7. Write the post-order traversal of (*a*) to (*e*) (Q1).

8. Write the pre-order traversal of (*a*) to (*e*) (Q1).

9. In Q1, use the in-order and post-order traversal of (*a*) to recreate the tree.

10. In Q1, use the in-order and pre-order traversal of (*b*) to recreate the tree.

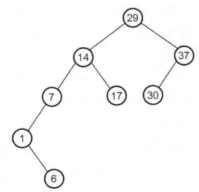

FIGURE 17.12 A Binary Search Tree

11. Write the in-order traversal of the tree in Figure 17.12.

12. Write the pre-order traversal of the tree in Figure 17.12.

13. Write the post-order traversal of the tree in Figure 17.12.

14. Write the level order traversal of the tree in Figure 17.12.

15. Insert the following in the tree in Figure 17.12 and show the new tree in each step.

  (a) 2   (b) 5

  (c) 32   (d) 31

  (e) 29

PROGRAMMING

1. Write a program to create a binary search tree from a list of numbers entered by the user.

2. Write a program to traverse the above tree in
   (a) In-order traversal
   (b) Post-order traversal
   (c) Pre-order traversal

3. Write a program to find a given element from a binary search tree.

4. Write a program to find the maximum element from a binary search tree.

5. Write a program to find the minimum element from a binary search tree.

6. Write a program to find the second maximum element from a given binary search tree.

7. Write a program to find the sum of elements of a binary search tree.

8. Write a program to find the depth of a binary search tree.

9. Write a program to find the sibling of an element from a binary tree.

10. Write a program to find the parent of an element from a binary tree.

11. Write a program to find all ancestors of a given element of a binary search tree.

12. Write a program to find all children of a given node of a binary tree.

13. Write a program to delete an element from a given binary tree.

14. Write a program to find the rightmost child of the left sub tree of a node in a given binary tree.

15. Write a program to find the leftmost child of the right sub tree of a node in a given binary tree.

18

INTRODUCTION TO NUMPY

After reading this chapter, the reader will be able to

- Understand the downside of Dynamic Typing
- Understand the importance of NumPy
- Create unidimensional and multi-dimensional arrays
- Understand broadcasting
- Understand the importance and creation of structured arrays

18.1   INTRODUCTION

One of the most important features of Python is dynamic typing. In C, the programmer declares the type of variable and then starts working on it. Though some amount of typecasting is possible, in general one cannot change the type of the variable in the program. For example if the programmer declares a variable, say num, of integer type, and assigns some value to it, he cannot assign a string (say) to it.

```
int num;
num=5;
printf("%d", num);
num="Harsh";//error
```

However, in the case of Python, one needs not declare the type of variable. For example, in the following code, 5 is assigned to num and the value of num is printed. In the succeeding statements the string "Harsh" is assigned to num and the value stored in num is printed. Note that the code executes just fine.

```
num = 5
print( num )
num = 'Harsh'
print( num)
```

This is due to dynamic typing, which makes Python stand apart from its other counterparts. However, this comes at a cost. Each time the variable is assigned a value the operations that can be applied to that variable must be elucidated, which takes time. If in a particular situation the type of a variable would not change, there is hardly any need for such maneuveration. This is also relevant for procedures which deal with numbers and scientific and statistical calculations. In such situations, the codes can be made efficient by casting them to defined types and manipulating them. This chapter throws light on a package which comes to our rescue in such situations. The package is NumPy.

The chapter has been organized as follows. The second section introduces NumPy and discusses the creation of a basic array. The section also throws light on the data types provided by the package. The third section discusses some of the standard functions for generating sequences. The fourth section discusses some important aggregate functions. The concept of broadcasting has been introduced in the fifth section. The sixth section discusses structured arrays and the last section concludes the chapter.

18.2 INTRODUCTION TO NUMPY AND CREATION OF A BASIC ARRAY

NumPy is a Python package, which stands for Numerical Python. NumPy contains multidimensional array objects and the routines which process these arrays. The package was created by Travis Oliphant. It has almost all the features of Numeric, its predecessor, and Numarray. One of the greatest advantages of NumPy (when used along with SciPy, Scientific Python, and MATPLOTLIB) is its ability to perform operations similar to those in MATLAB. Note that NumPy is open source as against MATLAB. The package can be easily installed ON your computer from *htpps://www. continuum.io*. You can download Anaconda, which is a free distribution software for SciPy and related packages.

Using NumPy, multidimensional arrays can be subjected to mathematical and logical operations, transforms like Fourier Transforms and operators related to linear algebra and random numbers. The ability to manipulate multidimensional arrays assumes importance as they are used in various algorithms including those of machine learning.

The ndarray is the most important object in NumPy, as it helps to create an array. These arrays are zero based indexed. The elements of the array are assigned consecutive memory locations. These elements are then arranged in the row major style (as in the case of C) or column major style (as in the case of FORTRAN). In Python a basic array can be created using the numpy.array function. The function takes the following arguments:

- **Object:** It returns an array or nested sequence
- **dtype:** The data type of the array is represented by dtype
- **copy:** The object is copied if the value of this argument is true
- **order:** An array can be row major (C) or column major (F) or any (A)
- **subok:** Returned array forced is to be a base class array
- **ndmin:** This argument specifies the minimum number of dimensions

In order to understand the concept, let us have a look at some simple examples. In the code that follows, the NumPy package is imported as 'np'. The array function of np is then used to create an array ([7, 14, 21, 28, 35]). Finally, the value of the array1 is displayed:

```
>>>import numpy as np
>>>array1 = np.array([7, 14, 21, 28, 35])
>>>array1
array([ 7, 14, 21, 28, 35])
```

Let us have a look at another example. In the following code, the NumPy package is imported as 'np'. The array function of np is then used to create a two dimensional array ([1, 2, 3], [4, 5, 6], [7, 8, 9]). That is the first row of the array is [1, 2, 3]; the second row is [4, 5, 6] and the third row is [7, 8, 9]. Finally, the value of the array2 variable is displayed:

```
>>>array2=np.array([[1,2,3],[4,5,6],[7,8,9]])
>>>array2
array([[1, 2, 3],
       [4, 5, 6],
       [7, 8, 9]])
```

An array of string type can be created by specifying the datatype (dtype = str) in the array function of np. The procedure has been depicted in the following snippet:

```
>>>array2=np.array([[1,2,3],[4,5,6],[7,8,9]], dtype=str)
>>>array2
```

```
array([['1', '2', '3'],
       ['4', '5', '6'],
       ['7', '8', '9']],
dtype='<U1')
```

One of the most obvious questions is why the need to use these arrays in place of those provided by Python? The first reason is the wide variety of data types provided by NumPy. The variety of data types provided by the package makes the task at hand easy.

Some of the important data types provided by NumPy are as follows:

- `bool_` : Boolean
- `int_` : default integer type
- `intc`: Same as that of 'C'

NumPy also provides `int8`, `int16`, `int32`, and `int64` data types. The first (`int8`) uses 8 bits and hence can store (-2^7) to (2^7-1) (that is -128 to +127). `int16` takes 16 bits and hence can store values from -32,768 to +32,767. Likewise `int32` and `int64` take 32 and 64 bits. The corresponding unsigned integers are `unit8`, `uint16`, `uint32`, and `uint64`. The difference between `int` and `uint` is that in the former, one bit is reserved for sign and in the latter all the bits are used for storing the numbers, and hence the unsigned integers can store larger values. For example `unit8` can store values from 0 to 255. The data types for floating point numbers are as follow:

- `float_`
- `float16`: It has 10 bit mantissa
- `float32`: It has 23 bit mantissa
- `flaot64`: It has 52 bit mantissa

The data types for complex numbers are as follows:

- `complex_`
- `complex64`
- `complex128`

Here it may be stated that the data type object describes the interpretation of fixed blocks of memory. It has information about:

- Type of data
- Size
- Order
- The shape and data type in case of a subarray

18.3   FUNCTIONS FOR GENERATING SEQUENCES

Having gone through the basics of `NumPy` arrays, let us visit some of the remarkable functions which help when creating useful arrays.

18.3.1   `arange()`

The `arange` function helps to print a sequence, having some initial value (`start`), some final value (`stop`), the difference between the consecutive terms (`step`), and the datatype (`dtype`). The syntax of the function is as follows. The description of each of the parameters follows:

```
numpy.arange(start, stop, step, dtype)
```

- `Start:` The starting value of the sequence
- `Stop:` The value up to which the sequence is generated (not inducing the value itself)
- `Step:` The difference between the consecutive values
- `dtype:` The data type

The above function has been exemplified in the following code which generates an arithmetic progression having first term 3, the last term 23 (less than 25), and the difference between the two consecutive terms 2. The data type of the elements is `'int'`.

```
>>a=np.arange(3,25,2, int)
>>a
array([3, 5, 7, 9, 11, 13, 15, 17, 19, 21, 23])
```

`arange` can also take a single argument. Writing `np.arange(6)` will generate a sequence having first value 0, the difference between the consecutive terms as 1, and the last term 5, that is:

```
>>b=np.arange(6)
>>b
array([0, 1, 2, 3, 4, 5)]
```

In the `arange` function one can also specify the data type along with the above, in order to change the default data type of the elements.

```
>>c=np.arange(6, dtype=float)
>>c
array([0., 1., 2., 3., 4., 5.])
```

18.3.2 `linspace()`

The `linspace` function divides the given range into a specified number of segregations and returns the sequence so formed. The function takes the following parameters:

- `start`: The first value of the sequence
- `stop`: The last value (included until endpoint = `False`)
- `num`: The number of items
- `endpoint`: If endpoint is False then the "stop" value is not included in the sequence
- `retstep`: If this is True, the step size is returned
- `dtype`: The data type of the elements of the sequence; if not specified then the data type is inferred by the start and the stop values

Example: In the sequence generated by the following code the first number of the sequence is 1 and the last value is 27. The number of elements in the sequence is 11.

```
>>d=np.linspace(11, 227, 11)
>>d
array([11., 12.6, 14.2, 15.8, 17.4, 19., 20.6, 22.2,
                                    23.8, 25.4, 27.])
```

If the value of the "endpoint" argument is false, the last value (in this case, 27) is not included.

```
>>e=np.linspace(11, 227, 11, endpoint=False)
>>e
array([11., 12.45454545, 13.90909091, 15.36363636,
       16.01010102, 18.27272727, 19.72727273, 21.10101010,
              22.63636364, 24.09090909, 25.54545455])
```

The value of the step can be viewed by assigning "True" to the retstep; argument. For example, in the sequence generated by dividing the range 11-26 in 12 parts, the gap (the last argument of the result) is 1.45454545454546.

```
>>f=np.linspace(11, 227, 11, endpoint=False, retstep=True)
>>f
(array([11., 12.45454545, 13.90909091, 15.36363636,
       16.01010102, 18.27272727, 19.72727273, 21.10101010,
              22.63636364, 24.09090909, 25.54545455]),
                                    1.4545454545454546)
```

18.3.3 `logspace()`

The `logspace` function generates a sequence which is equally spaced in the logspace. That is the elements of the sequence will be between base^{start} and base^{stop} "," where the value of the base is provided in the argument. The default value of base is 10. The `dtype` signifies the data type of the elements. Like in the case of the previous function, endpoint= False would exclude base^{stop} NumPy.

`logspace (start, stop, num, endpoint, base, dtype)`

18.4   AGGREGATE FUNCTIONS

The `numpy` module contains many aggregate functions. The various functions along with a brief explanation are as follows:

- **numpy.sum** This finds the sum of the elements of the argument (*e.g.* a list or an array)
- **numpy.prod** This finds the product of the elements of the argument (*e.g.* a list or an array)
- **numpy.mean** This finds the mean of the elements of the argument (*e.g.* a list or an array)
- **numpy.std** This finds the standard deviation of the elements of the argument
- **numpy.var** This finds the variance of the elements of the argument
- **numpy.max** This finds the maximum element of the argument. In the case of a list or a 1D array, the maximum element will be displayed. However, in the case of a 2D array the axis along which the maximum element is desired can also be mentioned. Here, axis=0 indicates columns and axis=1 indicates rows.
- **numpy.min** This finds the minimum element of the argument. In the case of a list or a 1D array, the minimum element will be displayed. However, in the case of a 2D array the axis along which the minimum element is desired can also be mentioned. Here, axis=0 indicates columns and axis=1 indicates rows.
- **numpy.argmin** This finds the position (index) of the maximum element
- **numpy.argmax** This finds the position of the minimum element
- **numpy.median** This finds the median of the elements of the argument
- **numpy.percentile** This finds the percentile of the elements of the argument. The percentile (25 etc.) is the second argument.

- **numpy.any** This finds if any element of the given argument is there
- **numpy.all** This finds if all the arguments of the given argument are there

The following code exemplifies the above functions by generating a set of 50 values. The values are between 0 and 100 (the np.random.random(50) has been multiplied by 100). The maximum, minimum, argument of the maximum, argument of the minimum, average, median, standard deviation, variance, 25th percentile, and 75th percentile of the elements have been found using the above functions.

```
import numpy as np
Values1=100*(np.random.random(50))
Values1
```

Output

```
array([  7.89901504e+01,   3.10353272e+01,   4.55247975e+01,
2.09271021e+01,      1.28704552e+01,      8.83259317e+01,
4.34685519e+01,      6.47957990e+01,      3.94568075e+01,
8.14517974e+01,      1.30191468e+01,      8.69577211e+01,
9.94997332e+01,      5.33860103e+01,      5.67079066e+01,
9.98534029e+01,      3.22963592e+01,      4.98089020e+01,
6.68875653e+01,      9.65255635e+01,      4.94490583e+01,
7.37397326e+01,      3.40551969e+01,      4.37639703e+01,
4.48223897e+01,      3.25917428e+01,      9.59794929e+01,
5.87367182e+01,      9.87710458e+01,      4.37364340e+01,
1.97519881e+00,      6.03630476e+01,      8.92749410e-02,
9.06113729e+01,      7.97883172e+01,      8.95203320e+01,
1.69638876e+01,      8.40854179e+00,      3.45767708e+01,
3.24516258e+01,      9.71498648e+01,      1.29033485e+01,
7.12565243e+01,      3.77831919e+01,      6.59571908e+01,
6.80006473e+01,      3.69824712e+00,      9.23685114e+01,
3.10464585e+01,   3.48051930e+01])
Max=np.max(Values1)
Max_Index=np.argmax(Values1)
Min=np.min(Values1)
Min_Index=np.argmin(Values1)
Sum=np.sum(Values1)
Prod=np.prod(Values1)
Mean=np.mean(Values1)
SD=np.std(Values1)
Variance=np.var(Values1)
Med=np.median(Values1)
```

```
Per25=np.percentile(Values1,25)
Per75=np.percentile(Values1,75)
print("Max\t:",Max,"\nIndex\t:",Max_Index,"\nMin\t:",Min,
      "\nIndex\t:",Min_Index,"\nAverage\t:",Mean,"\nStad
Deviation\t:",SD,"\nVariance\t:",Variance,"\nMedian
      t:",Med,"\nPercentile 25\t:",Per25,"\nPercentile
                                        75\t:",Per75)
```

Output

```
Max     : 99.8534028512
Index : 15
Min     : 0.0892749410473
Index : 32
Average      : 53.3430471879
Stad Deviation    : 29.5561768206
Variance    : 873.567588252
Median      : 49.6289801762
Percentile 25     : 32.4866550288
Percentile 75     : 79.5887755051
```

The data can be visualized using the `matplotlib` module discussed in the next chapter. The following code plots the histogram of the above data.

```
plt.hist(Values1)
plt.title('Values Generated')
plt.xlabel('Values')
plt.ylabel('Number')
plt.show()
```

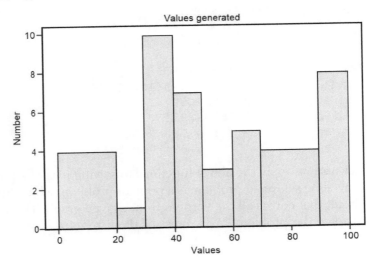

The above functions can also be applied on 2 dimensional arrays, as stated earlier. The following code exemplifies the above functions by generating a 2 dimensional array having three rows and three columns. The values are between 0 and 1. The maximum, minimum, argument of the maximum, argument of the minimum, average, median, standard deviation, variance, 25th percentile, and 75th percentile of the elements have been found using the above functions.

```
Max=np.max(B)
Max_Index=np.argmax(B)
Min=np.min(B)
Min_Index=np.argmin(B)
Sum=np.sum(B)
Prod=np.prod(B)
Mean=np.mean(B)
SD=np.std(B)
Variance=np.var(B)
Med=np.median(B)
Per25=np.percentile(B,25)
Per75=np.percentile(B,75)
print("Max\t:",Max,"\nIndex\t:",Max_Index,"\nMin\t:",Min,
      "\nIndex\t:",Min_Index,"\nAverage\t:",Mean,"\nStad
Deviation\t:",SD,"\nVariance\t:",Variance,"\nMedian\
      t:",Med,"\nPercentile 25\t:",Per25,"\nPercentile
                                   75\t:",Per75)
```

Output

```
Max    : 0.960839776764
Index  : 3
Min    : 0.0795636675955
Index  : 1
Average      : 0.533217195093
Stad Deviation    : 0.345312622379
Variance     : 0.119240807174
Median       : 0.653392931307
Percentile 25     : 0.180674642779
Percentile 75     : 0.884705912786
```

Let us now apply the above functions to solving part of a popular problem. Travelling salesman problem is a popular problem, which finds the shortest circuit that covers all the vertices from a given graph. There are many ways to solve the problem. Well, most of them require large amounts of time.

However, a method that uses dynamic programming finds the reduced matrix of the given matrix. The reduced matrix can be found as follows. First of all, the minimum element from all the columns is found. The minimum of a column is then subtracted from the elements of that particular column. The result of this step will be a matrix having at least one zero in each column. Likewise the minimum element of each row is found. This element is then subtracted from each element of the row. The result of this step will be a matrix having at least one zero in each row. The resultant matrix will be henceforth referred to as the reduced matrix. In Python this task can be accomplished easily. The first part of the process has been shown in the following snippet. The reader is expected to repeat the task for each row as well.

```
Min_Indeces_Col=np.argmin(B,axis=0)
Min_Col=np.min(B,axis=0)
print(Min_Col)
print(Min_Indeces_Col)
Output:
[ 0.18067464  0.07956367  0.14794398]
[0 0 2]
print(B-Min_Col)
print(np.sum(Min_Col))
```

Output

```
[[ 0.          0.          0.08625532]
 [ 0.78016513  0.80514225  0.50544895]
 [ 0.57876706  0.81862917  0.        ]]
0.408182293092
```

18.5 BROADCASTING

If two arrays of same dimensions are added together, an element of the resultant array is the sum of the corresponding elements of the two arrays. For example, if

$$A = [1, 2, 3]$$
$$B = [3, 4, 5]$$
then, $$A + B = [4, 6, 8]$$

Likewise, if

$$A = \begin{bmatrix} 1 & 2 & 1 \\ 0 & 3 & 2 \\ 4 & 2 & 5 \end{bmatrix}$$

$$B = \begin{bmatrix} 2 & 1 & 3 \\ 1 & 1 & 1 \\ 2 & 3 & 4 \end{bmatrix}$$

$$A + B = \begin{bmatrix} 3 & 3 & 4 \\ 1 & 4 & 3 \\ 6 & 5 & 9 \end{bmatrix}$$

It may be stated here that the above result is obvious. However, Python applies the operations element by element not only in addition or subtraction, but also in the case of multiplication and division. The following snippet shows the results when two row arrays are added, subtracted, multiplied, or divided. (Note that in each case the resultant array is obtained by applying the operation in the corresponding elements).

```
import numpy as np
A=np.array([1,2,3])
B=np.array([7,8,9])
Sum=A+B
Diff=A-B
Prod=A*B
Div=A/B
print("Sum\t:",Sum,"\nDifference\t:",Diff,"\nProduct\
                        t:",Prod,"Div\t:",Div)
```

Output

```
Sum : [ 8 10 12]
Difference : [-6 -6 -6]
Product : [ 7 16 27] Div : [ 0.14285714 0.25 0.33333333]
```

The above examples give expected results as the dimensions of the arrays on which the operations were applied had appropriate dimensions. What if two arrays of different dimensions are added together? Python has a way to deal with such situations. This is called broadcasting. It may be stated here that broadcasting does not always work. It works in the situations discussed as follows. For example, if a row array (say, [1, 2, 3]) is added to a column array (say [[7], [8], [9]]), then the following procedure is employed:

$$
\begin{matrix}
1 & 2 & 3 \\
1 & 2 & 3 \\
& 1\,2\,3 &
\end{matrix}
+
\begin{matrix}
7 & 7\,7 \\
8 & 8\,8 \\
9 & 9\,9
\end{matrix}
=
\begin{matrix}
8 & 9 & 10 \\
9 & 10 & 11 \\
10 & 11 & 12
\end{matrix}
$$

That is the row matrix is converted to a two dimensional matrix by copying the elements of the first row to all other rows. Here the number of rows would be equal to the number of elements in the column matrix. Likewise the column matrix is also converted into a two dimensional matrix by copying the elements of the column to all other columns. Here, the number of columns would be equal to the number of elements in the row matrix. Likewise the results of subtraction, multiplication, and division can be evaluated. The program follows:

$$
\begin{matrix}
1 & 2 & 3 \\
1 & 2 & 3 \\
1 & 2 & 3
\end{matrix}
-
\begin{matrix}
7 & 7 & 7 \\
8 & 8 & 8 \\
9 & 9 & 9
\end{matrix}
=
\begin{matrix}
-6 & -5 & -4 \\
-7 & -6 & -5 \\
-8 & -7 & -6
\end{matrix}
$$

$$
\begin{matrix}
1 & 2 & 3 \\
1 & 2 & 3 \\
1 & 2 & 3
\end{matrix}
*
\begin{matrix}
7 & 7 & 7 \\
8 & 8 & 8 \\
9 & 9 & 9
\end{matrix}
=
\begin{matrix}
7 & 14 & 21 \\
8 & 16 & 24 \\
9 & 18 & 27
\end{matrix}
$$

```
C=B[:,np.newaxis]
C
array([[7],
       [8],
       [9]])
Sum=A+C
Diff=A-C
Prod=A*C
Div=A/C
print("Sum\t:\n",Sum,"\nDifference\t:\n",Diff,"\nProduct\t:\
                              n",Prod,"\nDiv\t:\n",Div)
```

Output

```
Sum :
  [[ 8  9 10]
   [ 9 10 11]
   [10 11 12]]
Difference :
   [[-6 -5 -4]
```

```
    [-7  -6  -5]
    [-8  -7  -6]]
Product       :
    [[ 7  14  21]
     [ 8  16  24]
     [ 9  18  27]]
Div :
    [[ 0.14285714   0.28571429   0.42857143]
     [ 0.125        0.25         0.375       ]
     [ 0.11111111   0.22222222   0.33333333]]
```

If a row array is added to a two dimensional array, the addition is carried out by converting the first array into a two dimensional array by copying the elements of the row to all other rows, the number of rows being the same as that in the second array. That is,

$$
\begin{matrix}
\mathbf{1} & \mathbf{2} & \mathbf{3} \\
1 & 2 & 3 \\
1 & 2 & 3
\end{matrix}
\;+\;
\begin{matrix}
1 & 2 & 3 \\
4 & 5 & 6 \\
7 & 8 & 9
\end{matrix}
\;=\;
\begin{matrix}
2 & 4 & 6 \\
5 & 7 & 9 \\
8 & 10 & 12
\end{matrix}
$$

Likewise the subtraction, multiplication, and division can be carried out. The following snippet shows the results of these operations:

```
D=[[1,2,3],[4,5,6],[7,8,9]]
Sum=D+A
Diff=D-A
Prod=D*A
Div=D/A
print("Sum\t:\n",Sum,"\nDifference\t:\n",Diff,"\nProduct\t:\
                        n",Prod,"Div\t:\n",Div)
```

Output

```
Sum :
    [[ 2   4   6]
     [ 5   7   9]
     [ 8  10  12]]
Difference    :
    [[0  0  0]
     [3  3  3]
     [6  6  6]]
Product    :
    [[ 1   4   9]
     [ 4  10  18]
     [ 7  16  27]]
```

```
Div    :
   [[ 1.   1.    1. ]
    [ 4.   2.5   2. ]
    [ 7.   4.    3. ]]
```

If a column array is added to a two dimensional array, the addition is carried out by converting the first array into a two dimensional array by copying the elements of the columns to all other columns, the number of columns being the same as that in the second array. The results of addition, subtraction, multiplication, and division of B and D are as follows (B and D above).

```
D=[[1,2,3],[4,5,6],[7,8,9]]
Sum=D+B
Diff=D-B
Prod=D*B
Div=D/B
print("Sum\t:\n",Sum,"\nDifference\t:\n",Diff,"\nProduct\
                              t:\n",Prod,"Div\t:\n",Div)
```

Output

```
Sum    :
   [[ 8 10 12]
    [11 13 15]
    [14 16 18]]
Difference  :
   [[-6 -6 -6]
    [-3 -3 -3]
    [ 0  0  0]]
Product    :
   [[ 7 16 27]
    [28 40 54]
    [49 64 81]]  Div :
    [[ 0.14285714  0.25       0.33333333]
     [ 0.57142857  0.625      0.66666667]
     [ 1.          1.         1.        ]]
```

The above discussion can be summarized as follows:

- If two arrays have different dimensions, the one with lesser dimensions is padded with the one on the leading side.
- If one of the arrays is either row (or column matrix) the elements of the row (or column) are copied to all other rows (or columns) and then the operation is applied.
- If the dimensions do not match, an error is raised.

18.6   STRUCTURED ARRAYS

The structured arrays help us to create an array having a structure as its element. This not only helps in maintaining the information easily but also helps with easy access and manipulation. In order to understand the concept, let us take an example. Suppose that you have been asked to store the data of employees: their names, ages, and salaries. Now, you make three different arrays: name, age, and salary, having the following data:

```
name=['Harsh','Naved','Aman','Lovish']
age=[100,70,24,18]
salary=[75500.00,65500.00,55500.00,45500.00]
```

Since it is difficult to handle individual arrays, we create a structured array containing the above information. In order to do that we can create an array in which each element is a tuple containing three values: name, which is a Unicode string of size 10; age, which is an integer of 4 bytes and salary, which is float (8 bytes), using the following statement:

```
data=np.zeros(4,dtype={'names':('name','age','salary'),'
                        formats':('U10','i4','f8')})
```
This is followed by associating the attributes with the above arrays.
```
data['name']=name
data['age']=age
data['salary']=salary
```
The following code depicts an example of creating a structured array.
```
import numpy as np
name=['Harsh','Naved','Aman','Lovish']
age=[100,70,24,18]
salary=[75500.00,65500.00,55500.00,45500.00]
data=np.zeros(4,dtype={'names':('name','age','salary'),
                       'formats':('U10','i4','f8')})
data['name']=name
data['age']=age
data['salary']=salary
print(data)
```

Output

```
[('Harsh', 100, 75500.0) ('Naved', 70, 65500.0) ('Aman', 24,
                                                     55500.0)
('Lovish', 18, 45500.0)]
```

Once a structured array is created, the data can be accessed in the usual way. For example, to display the value of a particular attribute, we can simply mention the name of the attribute in single quotes inside the square brackets.

```
data['name']
```

Output

```
array(['Harsh', 'Naved', 'Aman', 'Lovish'], dtype='<U10')
data['age']
array([100, 70, 24, 18])
data['salary']
array([ 75500., 65500., 55500., 45500.])
data[1]
('Naved', 70, 65500.0)
```

These structured arrays can be used to access more complicated information from the data as well. For example, to see the name of the last employee of the list we can write:

```
data[-1]['name']
```

Output

```
'Lovish'
```

18.7   CONCLUSION

The NumPy package helps a programmer to deal with the multidimensional arrays in the most sophisticated way. The package allows us to create arrays of all types. The package provides a wide range of aggregate functions to deal with the elements and analyze the data. Here it may be noted that unlike conventional matrices, the elements of an array can also be operated upon in a unique fashion, discussed in the last but one section of this chapter. The chapter also sheds light onto the importance and usage of multidimensional arrays. The next chapter uses the matplotlib package to visualize the data and analyze the results. The reader is expected to go through the next chapter and deal with the problems given in the appendix of this book.

POINTS TO REMEMBER

- `NumPy` is a Python package, which stands for Numerical Python.
- `NumPy` contains multidimensional array objects and the routines which process these arrays.
- The `ndarray` helps in creating an array. These arrays are zero based indexed.
- The elements of an array are assigned consecutive memory locations.
- The elements of an array can be arranged in the row major style (as in the case of "C") or column major style (as in the case of Fortran).
- A basic array can be created using the `numpy.array` function.
- The `linspace(), logspace()` and `arange()` functions help to create arrays which have specific sequences.
- The structured arrays help us to create an array having a structure as its element.
- Broadcasting helps in applying arithmetic operations to arrays that have different dimensions
- Broadcasting does not always work

EXERCISES

MULTIPLE CHOICE QUESTIONS

1. In which of the following cases is dynamic typing redundant?
   (*a*) When the type of the variable would not change
   (*b*) When an object needs to hold more than one type of data
   (*c*) Both
   (*d*) None of the above

2. NumPy is
   (*a*) Numeric Python   (*b*) Numeric
   (*c*) Number Python   (*d*) None of the above

3. NumPy primarily deals with
   (*a*) Multidimensional arrays   (*b*) Graphics
   (*c*) Animations   (*d*) None of the above

4. Which of the following was the predecessor of NumPy?
   (*a*) Numeric
   (*b*) Number
   (*c*) MATLAB
   (*d*) None of the above

5. Which package provides MATLAB-like capabilities to Python?
   (*a*) NumPy
   (*b*) re
   (*c*) math
   (*d*) None of the above

6. Consider the following code
   ```
   A = np.array([4, 2, 1])
   B = np.array([3, 9, 27])
   C = B[:np.newaxis]
   sum = A+C
   ```
   Which of the following options is sum?
   (*a*) [[7, 5, 4], [13, 11, 10], [31, 29, 28]]
   (*b*) The arrays cannot be added
   (*c*) [7, 11, 28]
   (*d*) [[0, 0, 0], [0, 0, 0], [0, 0, 0]]

7. In the above question, if diff = A–C, which of the following options is diff?
   (*a*) [[1, –1, 2], [–5, –7, –8], [–23, –25, –26]]
   (*b*) The arrays cannot be added
   (*c*) [1, –7, –26]
   (*d*) [[0, 0, 0], [0, 0, 0], [0, 0, 0]]

8. In the above question, if prod = A * C, which of the following options is prod?
   (*a*) [[12, 6, 1], [36, 18, 9], [108, 54, 27]]
   (*b*) The arrays cannot be added
   (*c*) [12, 18, 27]
   (*d*) [[0, 0, 0], [0, 0, 0], [0, 0, 0]]

9. If A = [3, 4, 5] and B = [[0, 1, 2],[3, 4, 5], [6, 7,8]], find A–B
   (*a*) The arrays cannot be subtracted
   (*b*) [[3, 3, 3,], [0,0,0], [-3, -3, -3]]
   (*c*) [0, 0, 0]
   (*d*) [[0, 0, 0], [0, 0, 0], [0, 0, 0]]

10. In Python an array can have tuple as its element. Which of the following is true with respect to this statement?
    (*a*) Such arrays are called structured arrays
    (*b*) An array must have a single data type
    (*c*) This is possible in the case of lists not arrays
    (*d*) None of the above

11. In Python, which of the following is true with respect to broadcasting?
    (*a*) It is used when the dimensions of the arrays do not match
    (*b*) It is not always possible
    (*c*) Both
    (*d*) None of the above

12. In Python, which function can be used to generate a sequence?
    (*a*) `arange`   (*b*) `linspace`
    (*c*) `logspace`   (*d*) All of the above

13. The aggregate function in `NumPy` can be used to find
    (*a*) `Mean`   (*b*) `Median`
    (*c*) `Maximum`   (*d*) `Minimum`

14. Which of the following is true for `NumPy`?
    (*a*) It is a package which deals with multidimensional arrays
    (*b*) It is useful for carrying out statistical analysis
    (*c*) It works well with `MatPlotLib`
    (*d*) All of the above

15. One can create a histogram of the given data using
    (*a*) `re`   (*b*) `Matplotlib`
    (*c*) Both   (*d*) None of the above

THEORY

1. Explain the importance of the NumPy module.

2. Explain how a one dimensional array containing zeros is generated using NumPy. Also explain the creation of a 2 dimensional array.

3. Write a short note on aggregate functions in NumPy. State the functions used to find the following:
   - Mean
   - Maximum
   - Minimum
   - Standard deviation
   - Median
   - Percentile

4. Explain how an array can be generated in NumPy. Explain the syntax and usage of the following functions:
   - Linspace
   - Logspace
   - Arange

5. What is broadcasting in NumPy? Explain the rules of broadcasting.

6. What is a structured array? How is a structured array created in Python?

7. Explain the concept of dynamic typing in Python.

8. Explain the need to have the data type of a variable.

9. Explain the procedure of plotting a histogram of a given data.

10. Explain the use of `NumPy` in generating arithmetic progression and geometric progression.

APPLICATIONS/ NUMERICAL

1. Ask the user to enter the value of n. Now create an array, a, containing integers from 0 to (n-1).

2. Create another array, b, from the above array containing all the even numbers of the original array.

3. Create an array, c, from an array containing all the odd numbers of the original array.

4. Now add b and c and divide each element of the resultant array by 2. Check if the result is same as a.

5. Create a one-dimensional array containing 500 random numbers.

6. Find the mean, standard deviation, median, 25th percentile, 75th percentile of the numbers.

7. Create a histogram of the above data with 10 bins.

8. Implement linear search. Also use the requisite method of NumPy and compare the running time of both.

9. Sort the elements of the array. Also use the requisite method of NumPy and compare the running time of both.

10. Create an array of 500 random numbers. Find the product of the numbers using loops and by using the functions of numpy and compare the running time by the two methods.

11. From the above array find the maximum element by the following methods:

    (*a*) Using the maximum function of NumPy

    (*b*) Using loops in O(n) time

    (*c*) Using divide and conquer in O(log n) time

12. Create a two-dimensional array having n rows and m columns containing:

    (*a*) All ones

    (*b*) All zeros

    (*c*) 1's at the diagonal

    (*d*) 0-(m-1) at the diagonal

    (*e*) Random numbers

13. Create a two-dimensional array having 7 rows and 7 columns such that an element aij (element at the ith row and the jth column) is $(i+j)^2$.

14. Find the sum of elements at the diagonals.   (Refer to Q. 13)

15. Find the maximum element in each row.   (Refer to Q. 13)

16. Find the maximum element in each column.   (Refer to Q. 13)

17. Sort the elements of each row.   (Refer to Q. 13)

18. Sort the elements of each column.   (Refer to Q. 13)

19. From this array create an array having elements of alternate rows and alternate columns.   (Refer to Q. 13)

20. Create another array, from the original array, having elements from the 4th row onwards.   (Refer to Q. 13)

21. Create three arrays having the names, age, and roll numbers of students of an institute.

22. Create a structured array having a tuple as its element, containing name, age and roll number. Now carry out the following tasks vis-à-vis the structured array:

    (*a*) Display the names of all the students

    (*b*) Display the ages of all the students

    (*c*) Display the roll numbers of all the students

    (*d*) Display the name of the last student

    (*e*) Display the name of the eldest student

    (*f*) Display the name of the youngest student

    (*g*) Display the names and roll numbers of all the students having an age entered by the user.

INTRODUCTION TO MATPLOTLIB

After reading this chapter, the reader will be able to

- Understand the importance of MATPLOTLIB
- Create the plots for lines, curves, etc.
- Understand subplotting
- Create three dimensional plots using MATPLOTLIB

19.1   INTRODUCTION

In the previous chapter, the methods and procedures used to deal with the data were discussed. The chapter introduced `numpy` which helps to accomplish numerous tasks. It is important to be able to visualize the data as well. Visualization gives an insight of the results and may help to uncover the underlying patterns. `Matplotlib` is a package that helps to plot various types of graphs and visualize the data. This chapter primarily discusses the `pyplot` package of `matplotlib`.

The `pyplot` collection of the `matplotlib` provides a set of functions which help programmers to perform various tasks associated with plotting. These functions provide MATLAB like capabilities to Python programmers. `pyplot` provides functions to plot a figure, create a plotting area, assign labels, etc. The `pyplot` keeps an account of the current figure and the area and hence can direct the functions to the requisite axes. The following sections discuss some of the most important functions in `pyplot` and present some interesting examples.

The chapter has been organized as follows. Section 19.2 introduces basic plotting, Section 19.3 discusses sub-plotting and Section 19.4 presents 3D plots. The last section concludes the chapter.

19.2   THE PLOT FUNCTION

We start by plotting the values of a list. In order to generate a basic plot, a list L, having n values (index: 0 to (*n*-1)), can be passed to the `plot` function. In the generated plot, the x-axis will have values from 0 to (*n*-1) and the Y-axis will have the values in the given list. The `xlabel` function associates a label with the X-axis. The argument of the `xlabel` function is a string. The `ylabel` function associates a label with the Y-axis. The `show` function displays the figure. One can also save the figure using the `savefig` function. The `savefig` function takes two arguments: the figure to be plotted and the `dpi`. In the following example, the list L =[1, 4, 8, 10] is passed to the plot function. The string "X Axis" is passed to the `xlabel` function and "Y Axis" is passed to the `ylabel` function. Note that in the figure, the X axis has values from 0 to 3 (the indices of the values of the list) and the Y axis ranges from 0 to 10 (from 0 to the maximum value of the list). This can be changed using the `axis` function, which takes a list as an argument. The function has the following arguments:

- x_{min}
- y_{min}
- x_{max}
- y_{max}

The figure is saved as a `png` file using the `savefig` function. The function takes two arguments: the name of the figure and the `dpi`. Figure 19.1 shows the output of the program.

```
plt.plot([1,4,8,10])
plt.xlabel("X Axis")
plt.ylabel("Y Axis")
plt.show()
plt.savefig("line.png",dpi=80)
```

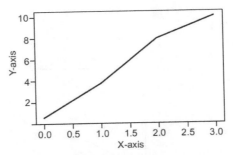

FIGURE 19.1 If a list is passed to the plot function, the values
are plotted against the indices of the list

In the above example, the plot function takes one argument. However, it
can also take two arguments indicating the values of X and Y. The following
example plots $y = 2x^2 - 3$ (Figure 19.2).

```
for x in [-5, -4, -3, -2, -1, 0, 1, 2, 3, 4, 5].
X=[-5,-4,-3,-2,-1,0,1,2,3,4,5]
Y= [2*x*x-3 for x in X]
plt.plot(X,Y)
plt.xlabel("X Axis")
plt.ylabel("Y Axis")
plt.show()
plt.savefig("line.png",dpi=80)
```

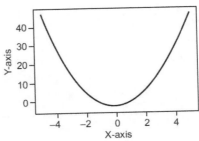

FIGURE 19.2 The plot function can also take two arguments; the second argument's
values can be generated using generators or comprehensions

One can even pass a two dimensional array (or list of lists) in plot, in which
case the first element of each row (or list) would be plotted as a separate plot
and the second as a separate plot. Figure 19.3 shows the output of the plot.

```
X=[[2,3,1],[4,6,3],[6,9,7],[8,10,5],[9,11,7],[10,18,12],
                                            [11,23,14]]
```

```
X
plt.plot(X)
plt.show()
```

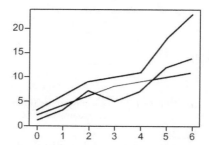

FIGURE 19.3 The plot function can take a two-dimensional array as arguments for plotting multiple lines

The plot function can have an additional argument stating the color of the plot. The default color is blue and it can be changed as follows. The `color` argument of the plot function can be set to a particular value, say `'red'` (`color = 'red'`) in order to generate a plot of the desired color. In the following example, the x-axis would now span from 0 to 6 and y-axis would span from 0 to 15, owing to the arguments of the axis function. The output of the following code would be same as that of the first one, except for the color of the plot and the axis (Figure 19.4).

```
plt.plot([1,4,8,10], color='red')
plt.xlabel("X Axis")
plt.ylabel("Y Axis")
plt.axis([0,6,0,15])
plt.show()
plt.savefig("line.png",dpi=80)
```

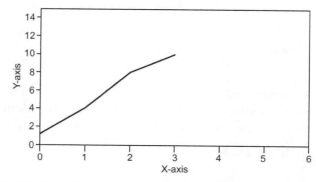

FIGURE 19.4 The plot function can also have an argument to set the color of the plot

If one wants to plot only the points and not the lines, an additional argument "*o*" can be passed to the plot function, shown as follows. Likewise, the plots indicated by a square and a triangle can be plotted by giving "*s*" and "*^*." The code follows and the output of the program has been shown in Figures 19.5 and 19.6.

```
plt.plot([1,3,4],[7,8,3],'o')
plt.show()
```

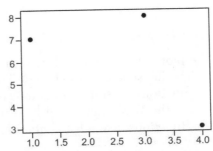

FIGURE 19.5 The plot function can also plot circles using an additional "o" argument

```
plt.plot([1,3,4],[7,8,3],'o')
plt.plot([1,2,3,4],[2,1,3,5],'s')
plt.plot([1,5,6],[9,10,11],'^')
plt.show()
```

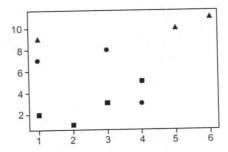

FIGURE 19.6 The plot function can also plot squares and triangles using additional "s" or "^" as argument

The following example shows the procedure for plotting the sine and cosine functions using `Matplotlib`. The `plot`, `show`, and `savefig` functions have already been explained in the above examples. In the following code, the X-axis is divided into 256 parts (from -22/7 to 22/7). The `linespace` function helps to accomplish this task. The sine of the X values can be calculated using the `sin` function of `numpy`. Likewise, the cosine can be calculated using the `cosine` function. Both the plots are plotted in the same area. The output has been shown in Figure 19.7.

```
from matplotlib import pyplot as plt
import numpy as np
X = np.linspace(-np.pi, np.pi, 256, endpoint=True)
C, S = np.sin(X), np.cos(X)
plt.plot(X,C)
plt.plot(X,S)
plt.show()
plt.savefig("SinCos.png", dpi=72)
```

The color of the plots can be changed by setting the color attribute to the requisite value. The linestyle can also be set. The `pyplot` also provides the `xlim` and `ylim` functions for setting the limits of the X- and the Y-axis. The ticks on the X- and the Y-axis can be set by using the `xticks` and `yticks` functions. These functions take a list containing the values to be displayed on the axes.

```
plt.figure(figsize=(8, 6), dpi=80)
plt.subplot(1, 1, 1)
X = np.linspace(-np.pi, np.pi, 256, endpoint=True)
C, S = np.cos(X), np.sin(X)
plt.plot(X, C, color="blue", linestyle="-")
plt.plot(X, S, color="red", linestyle="-")
plt.xlim(-4.0, 4.0)
plt.xticks(np.linspace(-4, 4, 9, endpoint=True))
plt.ylim(-1.0, 1.0)
plt.yticks(np.linspace(-1, 1, 5, endpoint=True))
plt.savefig("SinCos.png", dpi=180)
plt.show()
```

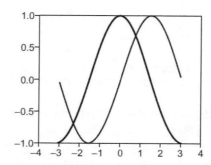

FIGURE 19.7 The sine and cosine function in the same plot

The following code prints the plot for the `log` function of numpy. The only difference in the previous and the following example is the use of the `log` function of numpy in place of the `sin` of the `cosine` function. The output of the code has been shown in Figure 19.8.

```
plt.figure(figsize=(8, 6), dpi=80)
plt.subplot(1, 1, 1)
X = np.linspace(0.1,2, 100, endpoint=True)
L = np.log(X)
plt.plot(X, L, color="blue", linestyle="-")
plt.xlim(0, 2)
plt.xticks(np.linspace(0, 2, 100, endpoint=True))
plt.ylim(-1.0, 1.0)
plt.yticks(np.linspace(-1, 1, 21, endpoint=True))
# Save figure using 80 dots per inch
plt.savefig("Log.png", dpi=180)
# Show result on screen
plt.show()
```

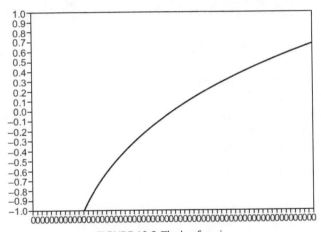

FIGURE 19.8 The log function

The `imshow` function of the `matplotlib` shows the image. The following example plots the magnitude and the phase of complex number between -2π to 2π. The output of the code has been shown in Figure 19.9.

```
import matplotlib.pyplot as plt
x = np.linspace(-2*np.pi, 2*np.pi, 100)
xx = x + 1j * x[:, np.newaxis]
out = np.exp(xx)
plt.subplot(121)
```

```
plt.imshow(np.abs(out),extent=[-2*np.pi, 2*np.pi, -2*np.
                                              pi, 2*np.pi])
plt.title('Magnitude of exp(x)')
plt.subplot(122)
plt.imshow(np.angle(out),extent=[-2*np.pi, 2*np.pi,
                                  -2*np. pi, 2*np.pi])
plt.title('Phase (angle) of exp(x)')
plt.show()
```

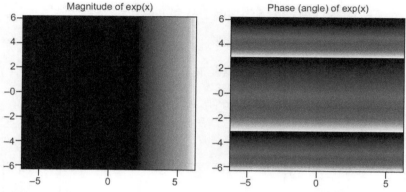

FIGURE 19.9 The use of implot to generate the magnitude and phase of a complex number

The plots described above are an excellent way of comparing the functions (say x^2, x^3 and x^4) by using the power function of numpy. The plot function has a label argument stating the type of curve. The limits of the x-axis are set from 1 to 20 and that of y-axis is from 0 to 800. The output of the code is shown in Figure 19.10.

```
x = np.linspace (0, 10, 50)
y1 = np.power(x, 2)
y2=np.power(x,3)
y3 = np.power(x, 4)
plt.plot(x, y1, label='$x^2$')
plt.plot(x, y2, label='$x^3$')
plt.plot(x, y3, label='$x^4$')
plt.xlim((1 , 20))
plt.ylim((0 , 800))
plt.xlabel('X Axis')
plt.ylabel('Y : Powers')
plt.title('First :$x^2$ Second:$x^3$ Third:$x^4$')
#plt.legend()
plt.savefig("powers.png",dpi=80)
plt.show()
```

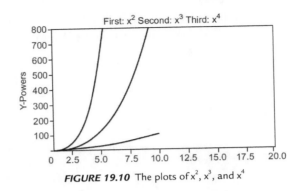

FIGURE 19.10 The plots of x^2, x^3, and x^4

The `pyplot` function can also be used to plot a histogram. The `hist` function can be used to accomplish the task. The `hist` function has data as an argument. The `color` argument of the function associates the color to the histogram. The optional `commutative` argument, if `True`, plots a commutative histogram. The number of bins indicates the segregations on the x-axis. The following code exemplifies the function. The output has been shown in Figure 19.11.

```
data = np.random.randn(100)
f , (ax1, ax2) = plt.subplots(1,2,figsize=(6,3))
ax1.hist(data,bins=10,normed=True,color='blue')
ax2.hist(data,bins=10,normed=True,color='red',cumulative=True)
plt.savefig('histogram.png')
plt.show()
```

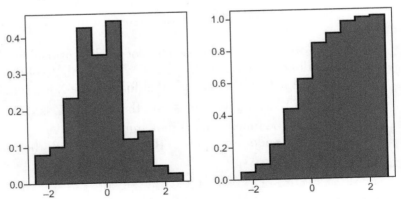

FIGURE 19.11 A histogram can be plotted using the `hist` function of `pyplot`

The `imshow` function plots the data passed as the argument. The matrix generated by the `random` function (10 rows and 10 columns) is passed as the argument in the `imgshow` function. The `colorbar` function of the `matlpotlib` is then invoked and is finally shown. The following code exemplifies the function and the output follows (Figure 19.12).

```
Img = np.random.random((10, 10))
plt.imshow(Img)
plt.colorbar()
plt.savefig('imageplot.png')
plt.show()
```

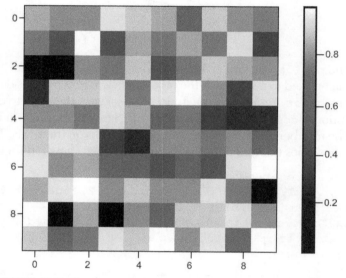

FIGURE 19.12 The `colorbar` function can be used to plot the required plots

The `matplotlib` can also be used to plot a 3 dimensional function. In order to plot a 3 dimensional plot, the `projection` attribute of the subplot function is set to `'3d'`. In the example that follows, the X is a set of 500 random numbers, the Y axis has `sin` of X and the value of Z is $\sqrt{1-(x^2+y^2)}$. The `plot_wireframe` function takes four arguments: `X`, `Y`, `Z`, and `linewidth`. The following code exemplifies the function and the output follows (Figure 19.13)

```
from mpl_toolkits.mplot3d import axes3d
ax = plt.subplot(111, projection='3d')
X=np.random.random(500)
Y=np.sin(X)
temp=np.absolute(1-(X**2 + Y**2))
Z=np.sqrt(temp)
```

```
plt.xlim(-1 ,1)
plt.ylim(-1,1)
ax.plot_wireframe(X, Y, Z, linewidth=0.1)
plt.savefig('wire.png')
plt.show()
```

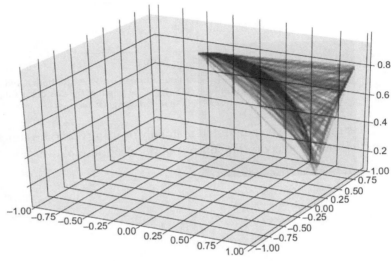

FIGURE 19.13 Plotting 3D graphs in MATPLOTLIB

19.3   SUBPLOTS

Suppose you want to compare the results of two different experiments. Having two figures side by side would greatly ease the task of comparing the results. In such situations the subplots come to our rescue. The idea is to have smaller axes in a single figure; in fact any sort of layouts in a given figure. This task can be accomplished in a number of ways. One of the simplest ways to use the matplotlib.axes function in matplotlib; -this is taking advantage of the fact that standard axes can be created using the matplotlib. axes() function. This function can also take a list of four numbers depicting the left, bottom, width, and height respectively. The mechanism of creating a subplot is as follows. The first two coordinates specify the origin of the new axes, considering the original axes to be of a unit's length. For example in the following figure (Figure 19.14), the origin of the subplot is (0.5,

0.5) and the axes are 40% of the length of the original axes. The arguments of the axes function in this case would be, therefore, (0.5, 0.5, 0.4, 0.4).

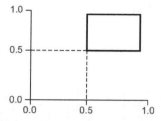

FIGURE 19.14 The axis (original) range from 0.0 to 1.0 (for both X and Y axes). The origin of the subplot is (0.5, 0.5). The length of the axes of the subplot are 40% of that of the original axes.

The subplots can be generated manually by using the `axes` function as shown in the following code. The output of the program follows (Figure 19.15).

```
import matplotlib.pyplot as plt
import numpy as np
axis1=plt.axes()
axis2=plt.axes([0.5,0.5,0.4,0.4])
plt.show()
```

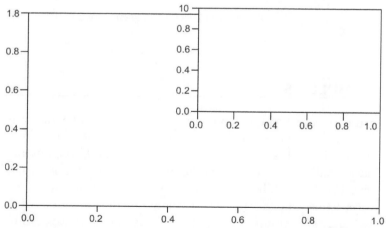

FIGURE 19.15 Creating a new subplot manually, using the `axes` function

To divide the given plot into two plots by creating another horizontal axis (that is dividing the graph, vertically, into two subplots), the `add_axes` function can be used. The function takes four arguments in a list as shown in the following example. The two subplots are plotted on two axes. Both the axes are created using the `add_axis` function. The `sin` function of `numpy` is used to plot a `sin` curve on the first axis and a `cosine` curve on the second axis. The values of X (50 in number, from 0 to 10) are obtained using the `linspace` function. The output of the code has been shown in Figure 19.16.

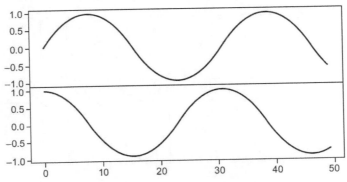

FIGURE 19.16 The first subplot has a sine curve and the second subplot shows a cosine curve

```
fig=plt.figure()
axis1=fig.add_axes([0.0,0.5,0.8,0.4])
axis2=fig.add_axes([0.0,0.1,0.8,0.4])
X=np.linspace(0,10,50)
axis1.plot(np.sin(X))
axis2.plot(np.cos(X))
plt.show()
```

The `subplot` function of `matplotlib.pyplot` helps to create a subplot with a grid. The function takes three arguments: the number of rows, the number of columns and the index. The following example shows nine subplots in a grid. Note that the arguments of the nine functions are as follows:

- (3, 3, 1)
- (3, 3, 2)
- (3, 3, 3)
- (3, 3, 4)
- (3, 3, 5)
- (3, 3, 6)
- (3, 3, 7)
- (3, 3, 8)
- (3, 3, 9)

The index of the subplot has been displayed in the subplot. Figures 19.17 and 19.18 show the output of the following codes.

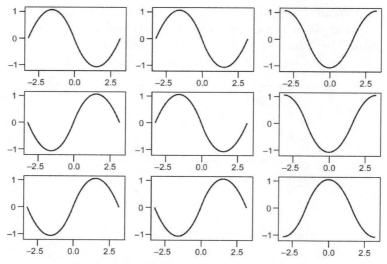

FIGURE 19.17 The subplots can be shown individually

```
X=np.linspace(-np.pi, np.pi, 100)
for i in range(1,10):
  plt.subplot(3,3,i)
  Y=np.sin(X+i*(np.pi/2))
  plt.plot(X,Y)
  plt.show()
plt.show()
```

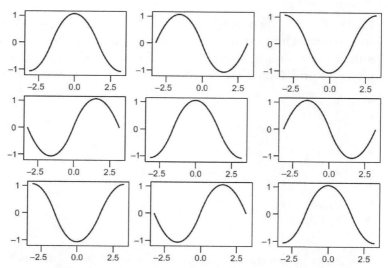

FIGURE 19.18 The subplots can be shown as a single plot also

Note that the distances between various axes of the subplots are not too much and hence the plot is not that clean. In order to handle such saturations, the `add_subplot` function can be used in the `pyplot.figure` to create axes. The horizontal and vertical spaces between the various subplots can be specified using the `subplots_adjust` function. The following code exemplifies the above functions and the output follows (Figure 19.19).

```
fig=plt.figure()
fig.subplots_adjust(hspace=0.4, wspace=0.4)
for i in range(1,10):
    axis=fig.add_subplot(3,3,i)
    Y=np.sin(X+i*(np.pi/2))
    axis.plot(X,Y)
plt.show()
```

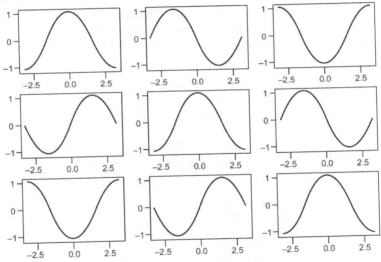

FIGURE 19.19 Using hspace and wspace in plotting subplots

As a matter of fact, `matplotlib` provides functions to plot the whole grid in one go too. The `pyplot.GridSpec` allows more complicated arguments for sophisticated options. However, both these are beyond the scope of this book.

19.4 3 DIMENSIONAL PLOTTING

Initially `MatPlotLib` supported only 2 dimensional plotting. However, the `mplot3d` toolkit has helped `matplotlib` evolve and pose a serious challenge to MATLAB. The toolkit allows the creation of a 3D space by setting the argument projection (of the axes function) to '3d'. The following codes show examples of 3D plotting. Note that most of the functions used in the following codes have already been explained. Each code follows the output (Figure 19.20).

```
from mpl_toolkits import mplot3d
fig = plt.figure()
axis=plt.axes(projection='3d')
plt.show()
```

The toolkit helps the programmer to plot sophisticated figures by passing the values of X, Y, and Z to the scatter 3D function of the pyploy.axes. The function has two more arguments: a and cmap. The cmap argument can be set to, say, 'Greens' or 'binary' or any other value (see the following tip). In the following example, the Z has 200 values from 0 to 20. The sine of these values constitute X and the square of the values of Z constitute Y. The code that follows exemplifies the function and the output follows (Figure 19.21).

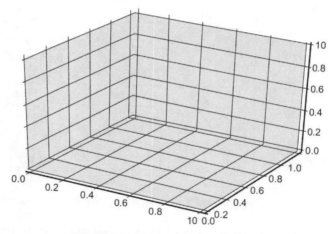

FIGURE 19.20 A basic 3-dimensional plot

Tip

Possible values of cmap

```
Accent, Accent_r, Blues, Blues_r, BrBG, BrBG_r, BuGn, BuGn_r,
BuPu, BuPu_r, CMRmap, CMRmap_r, Dark2, Dark2_r, GnBu, GnBu_r,
Greens, Greens_r, Greys, Greys_r, OrRd, OrRd_r, Oranges,
```

Oranges_r, PRGn, PRGn_r, Paired, Paired_r, Pastel1, Pastel1_r, Pastel2, Pastel2_r, PiYG, PiYG_r, PuBu, PuBuGn, PuBuGn_r, PuBu_r, PuOr, PuOr_r, PuRd, PuRd_r, Purples, Purples_r, RdBu, RdBu_r, RdGy, RdGy_r, RdPu, RdPu_r, RdYlBu, RdYlBu_r, RdYlGn, RdYlGn_r, Reds, Reds_r, Set1, Set1_r, Set2, Set2_r, Set3, Set3_r, Spectral, Spectral_r, Vega10, Vega10_r, Vega20, Vega20_r, Vega20b, Vega20b_r, Vega20c, Vega20c_r, Wistia, Wistia_r, YlGn, YlGnBu, YlGnBu_r, YlGn_r, YlOrBr, YlOrBr_r, YlOrRd, YlOrRd_r, afmhot, afmhot_r, autumn, autumn_r, binary, binary_r, bone, bone_r, brg, brg_r, bwr, bwr_r, cool, cool_r, coolwarm, coolwarm_r, copper, copper_r, cubehelix, cubehelix_r, flag, flag_r, gist_earth, gist_earth_r, gist_gray, gist_gray_r, gist_heat, gist_heat_r, gist_ncar, gist_ncar_r, gist_rainbow, gist_rainbow_r, gist_stern, gist_stern_r, gist_yarg, gist_yarg_r, gnuplot, gnuplot2, gnuplot2_r, gnuplot_r, gray, gray_r, hot, hot_r, hsv, hsv_r, inferno, inferno_r, jet, jet_r, magma, magma_r, nipy_spectral, nipy_spectral_r, ocean, ocean_r, pink, pink_r, plasma, plasma_r, prism, prism_r, rainbow, rainbow_r, seismic, seismic_r, spectral, spectral_r, spring, spring_r, summer, summer_r, terrain, terrain_r, viridis, viridis_r, winter, winter_r

```
axis=plt.axes(projection='3d')
Z=np.linspace(0,20,200)
X=np.sin(Z)
Y=[z*z for z in Z]
axis.scatter3D(X, Y, Z, c=Z,cmap='Greens');
plt.show()
```

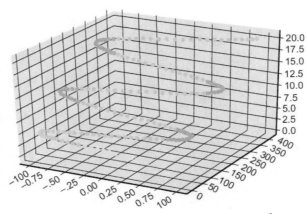

FIGURE 19.21 The X-axis is sine Z and Y-axis is Z^2

In the illustration that follows, the X and the Y have 20 values from -5 to 5. That is,

```
X= [-5,  -4.47368421,  -3.94736842,  -3.42105263,  -2.89473684,
-2.36842105,       -1.84210526,       -1.31578947,-0.78947368,
-0.26315789,0.26315789,  0.78947368,  1.31578947,  1.84210526,
2.36842105,2.89473684, 3.42105263, 3.94736842, 4.47368421,  5.]
```

Y is the same as X. Z contains the square root of the sum of squares of X and Y, that is,

```
Z=[  7.07106781,   6.32674488,   5.58242196,   4.83809903,
4.0937761 ,3.34945317, 2.60513025, 1.86080732, 1.11648439,
0.37216146,0.37216146, 1.11648439, 1.86080732, 2.60513025,
3.34945317,4.0937761 , 4.83809903, 5.58242196, 6.32674488,
7.07106781]
```

The label of the X axis can be set using the `set_xlable` function. Likewise, the `set_ylabel` and `set_zlabel` function sets the labels for the Y and the Z axis. The output of the plot has been shown in Figure 19.22.

```
X=np.linspace(-5,5,20)
Y=np.linspace(-5,5,20)
X,Y = np.meshgrid(X,Y)
Z=np.sqrt(X*X + Y*Y)
fig =plt.figure()
axis=plt.axes(projection='3d')
axis.contour3D(X,Y,Z,50,cmap='Greens')
axis.set_xlabel('X axis')
axis.set_ylabel('Y axis')
axis.set_zlabel('Z axis')
plt.show()
```

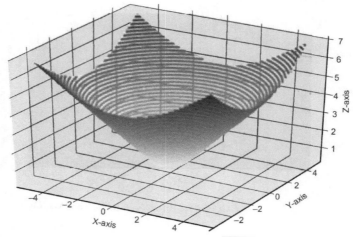

FIGURE 19.22 Plot of $Z = \sqrt{X^2 + Y^2}$

Note that the whole figure can be rotated by any angle along the XY plane and any angle counter clockwise about the Z axis. The `view_init` function of the `pyplot.axes` helps to accomplish this task. The function takes two arguments: the angle about the XY plane and that (counterclockwise) about the Z axis. The following code is same as the above except for the last but one line, which rotates the figure. Figure 19.23 shows the output.

```
X=np.linspace(-5,5,20)
Y=np.linspace(-5,5,20)
X,Y = np.meshgrid(X,Y)
Z=np.sqrt(X*X + Y*Y)
fig =plt.figure()
axis=plt.axes(projection='3d')
axis.contour3D(X,Y,Z,50,cmap='Greens')
axis.set_xlabel('X axis')
axis.set_ylabel('Y axis')
axis.set_zlabel('Z axis')
axis.view_init(60,30)
plt.show()
```

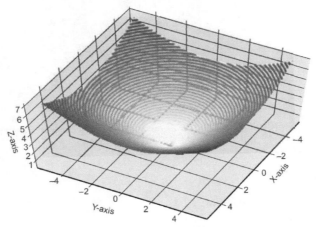

FIGURE 19.23 The rotated plot of Figure 19.22

The `wireframe` function helps with easy visualization of the plot. The following illustration plots a wireframe plot of the above example. Likewise the surface plot of the function can also be plotted using the `plot_surface` function. On the basis of the above discussion, the reader is expected to decode the output of the variants that follow (Figures 19.24 and 19.25).

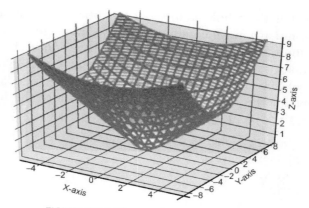

FIGURE 19.24 The use of `wireframe` function

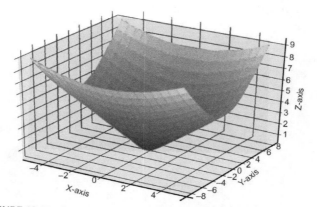

FIGURE 19.25 The axis.contour 3D (X,Y,Z,50,cmap='Greens') function plots
the above graph

Code

```
X=np.linspace(-5,5,20)
Y=np.linspace(-8,8,20)
X,Y = np.meshgrid(X,Y)
Z=np.sqrt(X*X + Y*Y)
fig =plt.figure()
axis=plt.axes(projection='3d')
axis.contour3D(X,Y,Z,50,cmap='Greens')
axis.set_xlabel('X axis')
axis.set_ylabel('Y axis')
axis.set_zlabel('Z axis')
```

```
axis.plot_wireframe(X, Y, Z, color='red')
#axis.view_init(60,30)
plt.show()
```

Code

```
X=np.linspace(-5,5,20)
Y=np.linspace(-8,8,20)
X,Y = np.meshgrid(X,Y)
Z=np.sqrt(X*X + Y*Y)
fig =plt.figure()
axis=plt.axes(projection='3d')
axis.contour3D(X,Y,Z,50,cmap='Greens')
axis.set_xlabel('X axis')
axis.set_ylabel('Y axis')
axis.set_zlabel('Z axis')

axis.plot_surface(X, Y, Z, rstride=1, cstride=1,
                       cmap='viridis', edgecolor='none')

#axis.view_init(60,30)
plt.show()
```

19.5 CONCLUSION

Plotting is important. It is important to be able to visualize the data to analyze the results and discover patterns. The popularity of MATLAB is partially attributed to its ability to present mesmerizing graphs. The same can be achieved in Python using `Matplotlib`. This chapter introduces plotting using `Matplotlib`. The chapter begins with the explanation of basic plots. The lines, sine curve, cosine curves and so on can be plotted easily using the `Matplotlib` package. `Matplotlib` allows the subplots also. This can be done manually by using the `Matplotlib.axes` function. The `subplot` function can also be used to create subplots. As stated earlier `Matplotlib` used to support only `2-D graphics`. The package now supports `3D graphics` as well. This has helped the package share the stage with MATLAB. In order to plot a 3D graph, an additional argument `'projection'` is set to `'3d'`.

GLOSSARY

Pyplot: The `pyplot` collection of the `matplotlib` provides a set of functions which help the programmers to perform various tasks associated with plotting.

POINTS TO REMEMBER

- Visualization gives an insight of the results and may help to uncover the underlying patterns.
- A plot created using pyplot can be saved as a `png` file using the `savefig` function.
- If one wants to plot only the points and not the lines, then an additional argument "*o*" can be passed to the plot function. Likewise, the plots indicated by a square and a triangle can be plotted by giving "*s*" and "^".
- The color of the plots can be changed by setting the `color` attribute to the requisite value.
- The `imshow` function of the `matplotlib` shows the image.
- The `hist` function can be used to accomplish the task.
- In order to plot a 3 dimensional plot, the `projection` attribute of the subplot function is set to "3D."
- To divide the given plot into two plots by creating another horizontal axis (that is dividing the graph, vertically, into two subplots), the `add_axes` function can be used.
- The horizontal and vertical spaces between the various subplots can be specified using the `subplots_adjust` function.
- The label of the *x*-axis can be set using the `set_xlabel` function.
- The `wireframe` function helps with easy visualization of the plot.

EXERCISES

MULTIPLE CHOICE QUESTIONS

1. Visualization is important because

   (*a*) It gives an insight of the results   (*b*) It helps to uncover underlying patters

   (*c*) It can be used for reporting   (*d*) All of the above

2. Which collection of MATPLOTLIB provides functions to plot functions, create a plotting area, etc.?

   (*a*) Pyplot   (*b*) PyPy

   (*c*) PIL   (*d*) None of the above

3. Which of the following can be an argument of the plot function of pyplot?

(*a*) [[1,2], [3,4], [5,6]] (*b*) [1,2,3,4]

(*c*) [[1,2,3,4],[4,5,6,7]] (*d*) All of the above

4.
```
X=[-5,-4,-3,-2,-1,0,1,2,3,4,5]
Y= [2*x*x-3 for x in X]
plt.plot(X,Y)
```
The above code would plot a

(*a*) Parabola (*b*) Ellipse

(*c*) Hyperbola (*d*) None of the above

5. Which of the following is used to show a curve?

(*a*) show (*b*) display

(*c*) Both (*d*) None of the above

6. Which function is used to save the plot using pyplot?

(*a*) savefig (*b*) save

(*c*) saveimg (*d*) None of the above

7. Which of the following cannot be passed as an argument in the plot function of pyplot?

(*a*) color (*b*) List

(*c*) Both (*d*) None of the above

8. The plot function can plot circles using which of the following arguments?

(*a*) o (*b*) s

(*c*) delta (*d*) None of the above

9. Which of the following is true with respect to plots in Pyplot?

(*a*) Multiple curves can be plotted on the same plot

(*b*) The plot can be divided into two subplots manually

(*c*) The subplot function can be used to see various plots in a single plot

(*d*) All of the above

10. Which function is used to plot a histogram in pyplot?

    (*a*) hist   (*b*) mist

    (*c*) jist   (*d*) None of the above

THEORY

1. Discuss the importance of visualization. How does visualization help with analyzing the results?

2. Name a package that helps to plot graphs in Python.

3. Explain how the values of a list can be plotted using pyplot.

4. Explain how multiple lines can be plotted in a single plot.

5. How is subplotting carried out in Python? Explain the splitting of axes and the subplot function.

6. Explain 3 Dimensional plotting in MATPLOTLIB.

7. How can you change the color of the graph in Pyplot? Also explain the importance of cmap.

8. Which package, other than pyplot, can be used to plot graphs in Python?

PROGRAMMING EXERCISE

1. Create a list having numbers in arithmetic progression. Ask the user to enter the first term, the common difference and the number of terms of the arithmetic progression. Plot the values using the plot function.

2. Create a list having numbers in geometric progression. Ask the user to enter the first term, the common ratio and the number of terms of the geometric progression. Plot the values using the plot function.

3. Create a list having numbers in harmonic progression. Ask the user to enter the values of "*a*," "*d*," and the number of terms and plot the curve.

4. Plot the point plots of the above curves.

5. Now, plot the above curves in the same plot and compare them.

6. Create subplots showing the curves of questions 1, 2, and 3.

7. In the above question, adjust the horizontal and the vertical distance between the subplots.

8. There are four types of parabolas: upward, downward, left facing, and right facing. The equations of the parabolas having vertex at the origin are as follows:

Upward: $\quad x^2 = 4ay$
Downward: $\quad x^2 = -4ay$
Right facing: $y^2 = 4ax$
Left facing: $\quad y^2 = -4ax$

If the values of x range from [10, 10] and the values of y are calculated using the appropriate equation, (you can use comprehensions to calculate the values of y), plot the above parabolas on a single plot.

9. Now create a subplot to plot each one of them.

10. Using plotting prove that $(\sin \theta)^2 + (\cos \theta)^2 = 1$.

11. Plot the curve of tan θ and identify the points of discontinuity.

12. Plot an ellipse having the length of major axis = 10 and the length of minor axis = 5.

13. Plot a circle having radius = 10 and center at (5,5).

14. Now plot 10 circles having radius 10 and center's x coordinate varying from 0 to 10. The y coordinate of the center should be 8.

15. Plot a hyperbola. Ask the user to enter a coordinate and display the coordinate on the plot. The program should display whether the point is inside the curve or outside it.

## CHAPTER 20

INTRODUCTION TO IMAGE PROCESSING

After reading this chapter, the reader will be able to

- Understand the importance of image processing
- Open an image, read it into an object, and write the object in a file
- Understand the concept of clipping
- Extract statistical information from an image
- Perform rotation, translation, and scaling

20.1 INTRODUCTION

The processing of an image and its manipulation has become more important with time. Image processing is important in not just identifying people and objects but is used in numerous fields like medicine, mining, networks, etc. The importance of image processing can be gauged from the fact that it is used in magnetic resonance imaging (MRI), X-rays, ultrasound, CT (Computer Tomography) scans, etc. In addition to the above, image processing is used in industries for surveillance, fingerprint recognition, face recognition, authentication, signature verification, etc. Image processing techniques are also used in areas like weather forecasting, remote sensing and in astronomical studies. Image processing is an involved and intricate task. Interestingly, humans are better at recognizing faces and objects. The marvelous network of neurons helps to recognize objects in a fraction of a second. The recognition of objects and their classification has always fascinated the computing fraternity. As a matter of fact the fraternity has lately been mimicking the human beings to develop such classifiers and recognizers.

The past few decades witnessed marked growth in both hardware and software. This was coupled with the advances in machine learning techniques. The combination played a pivotal role in the evolution of the field. The image processing field has since emerged as one of the most important and independent fields.

In digital image processing images are manipulated. To begin with, one needs to remove noise from a given image. The anti-aliasing, sharpening, and removing blurriness are some of the important tasks that are needed to make a given image better from our perspective (assuming we all are human beings). From the machine's point of view, converting the given image to binary, removing redundant information, and reducing the sampling rate, etc., are important. So there are two major goals of image processing: improving human perception and improving machine perception.

In addition to the above, the machine learning techniques have been successfully applied to identify diseases from various modalities like MRI (magnetic resonance imaging) and PET (positron emission tomography). Scientists have also been successful in making predictive models for the above. However, this requires some serious image processing. The images need to be segmented and subjected to various feature extraction techniques, etc., to carry out the above tasks.

Before processing an image, it needs to be stored. An image can be stored as a two dimensional array or a 3 dimensional array. If an image is stored as a two dimensional array, then a 512×512 size of image would require a 512×512 matrix and therefore 262144 units of memory. Now, if each pixel requires an 8 bit integer the total memory requirement will be 2097152 bits. In the case of a 3 dimensional array the value of the color intensity (say the values of R, G, B) will also be stored for each pixel.

This chapter discusses image processing using standard functions in `SciPy` and `NumPy`, though image processing can also be done in other ways.

The chapter has been organized as follows. Section 20.2 introduces the basics of image manipulation in Python. The next section discusses the contour function. Section 20.4 introduces clipping and Section 20.5 discusses basic transformations like translation, rotation, and scaling. The last section concludes the chapter.

20.2 OPENING, READING, AND WRITING AN IMAGE

All the homeless utilities have been included in `SciPy.misc()`. The following discussion uses an 8 bit greyscale, 512 × 512 image, which can be accessed by the `ascent()` function. The reader can also use the `face()` function for accomplishing any of the following tasks.

20.2.1 Opening an Image

In order to open and manipulate images, the `misc` and `pyplot` packages (the latter from `matplotlib`) need to be included. In the code that follows, the object 'a' will contain the image generated by the `ascent` image. The image can be saved using the `imsave` function. This function takes two arguments: the name of the file in which the image will be stored and object (in this case 'a'). The image can be shown by the `imshow()` function of `Pyplot`, followed by the invocation of the `show()` function (Figure 20.1).

```
fromscipy import misc
importmatplotlib.pyplot as plt
a = misc.ascent()
misc.imsave('ascent.png', a)
plt.imshow(a)
plt.show()
```

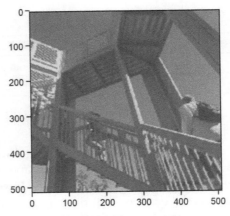

FIGURE 20.1 The ascent image

20.2.2 Reading

In order to read the above image, the `imread` function can be used. The `imread` function takes a `png` file as an argument and creates a two dimensional array. The shape and the `dtype` of the array can be displayed. The output is, as expected, (512, 512) and the data type is unit 8.

```
fromscipy import misc
ascent_array = misc.imread('ascent.png')
type(ascent_array)
print(ascent_array.shape)
print(ascent_array.dtype)
```

Output

```
(512, 512)
uint8
```

20.2.3 Writing an Image to a File

The array obtained in the above program can again be converted into a file. The `tofile()` function of the array (`ascent_array`, in the above example) converts the array into a raw file. The function takes a single argument, which is the name of the file to be created. The data of the file can be stored in an object (`sayascent_raw`). Note that the shape of the array obtained would be 262,144 in the given example.

Summary

`misc.imsave`	for saving an object as image
`misc.imread`	for reading an image and putting it in a two dimensional array
`tofile`	for converting a two dimensional array to a raw file
`fromfile`	to read data from a .raw file

20.2.4 Displaying an Image

The image can be displayed using the `imshow` function. The optional 'cmap' argument is not used when the image has shape $(m, n, 3)$. The values of the array in such cases are interpreted as RGB. However for a (m, n) array this argument depicts the color map of the image. In the following examples the value of `cmap` is set to 'grey' to display an image in the greyscale and it is set to 'jet' to display a colored image. The enumeration of the values of `cmap` has been presented in the chapter. The `imshow` function can also take the `vmin` and `vmax` argument. Figure 20.2 shows the output of the code. The image can also be displayed in greyscale (Figure 20.3).

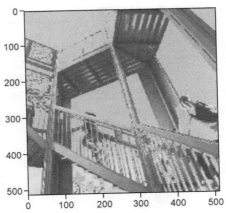

FIGURE 20.2 The ascent image with cmap = jet

FIGURE 20.3 The ascent image in greyscale

```
importnumpy as np
ascent_array.tofile('ascent.raw')
ascent_raw = np.fromfile('ascent.raw', dtype=np.uint8)
ascent_raw.shape
(262144,)
plt.imshow(a, cmap=plt.cm.jet)

plt.show()
plt.imshow(a, cmap=plt.cm.grey, vmin=30, vmax=200)
plt.show()
```

The axis can be removed by passing 'off' to the axis function of pyplot.

```
plt.axis('off')
plt.show()
```

20.3 THE CONTOUR FUNCTION

The edges of the polygon can be seen using the `contour` function. The `contour` function draws the contour lines and the `fcontour` function draws the filled contour lines. The next example shows the subplots created by varying the second argument of the `contour` function from [10, 20] to [200, 210]. Figure 20.4 shows the output.

```
plt.contour(a)
plt.show()
```

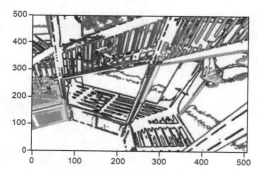

FIGURE 20.4 The contour of ascent

As a matter of fact, the reader can see the output at various arguments of `contour` and observe the differences. The following code passes (10, 20) in the first iteration, 20, 30 in the second iteration and so on. The output is shown in Fig. 20.5.

```
for i in range (1,21):
  plt.subplot(5,4,i)
  plt.contour(a,[10*i,10*i+10])
  plt.show()
```

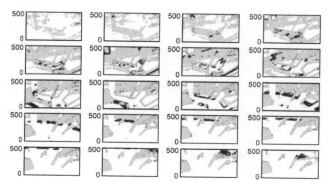

FIGURE 20.5 The plots for different values of contour

20.4   CLIPPING

A part of the image can be extracted by creating a mask and putting the values in the region as 0. For example if one wants to extract a circular area from a given image, the following steps must be followed. First of all a two-dimensional array corresponding to the image is created. This is followed by creation of the mask. Note that in the two examples that follow, the first excludes the area above the circle (Figure 20.6) and the second excludes the area inside the circle (Figure 20.7).

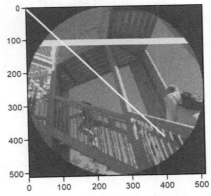

FIGURE 20.6 The region outside the circular region has been excluded

Code 1

```
ascent1 = misc.ascent()
ascent1[100:120] = 255
lx, ly = ascent1.shape
X, Y = np.ogrid[0:lx, 0:ly]
mask = ((X - lx / 2) ** 2) + ((Y - ly / 2) ** 2) > lx * ly / 4
ascent1[mask] = 0
ascent1[range(400), range(400)] = 255
plt.imshow(ascent1)
plt.show()
```

Code 2

```
ascent1 = misc.ascent()
ascent1[100:120] = 255
lx, ly = ascent1.shape
X, Y = np.ogrid[0:lx, 0:ly]
mask = ((X - lx / 2) ** 2) +((Y - ly / 2) ** 2) < lx * ly / 4
ascent1[mask] = 0
```

```
ascent1[range(400), range(400)] = 255
plt.imshow(ascent1)
plt.show()
```

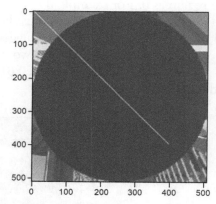

FIGURE 20.7 The region inside the circular region has been excluded

20.5 STATISTICAL INFORMATION OF AN IMAGE

The statistical information corresponding to a given image can be easily extracted using Numpy. The max() function returns the maximum value; the min() function returns the minimum value, the mean function returns the mean and finally the std function returns the standard deviation. Consider the code that follows and observe the output:

```
ascent2 = misc.ascent()
print(ascent2.mean())
print(ascent2.max(), ascent2.min())
print(ascent2.std())
```

Output

```
87.4798736572
255 0
48.7744598771
```

20.6 BASIC TRANSFORMATION

Consider any involved task in image processing. The task will require us to do something with the given image: to translate it, rotate it, or scale it, at the least. Moreover, in animations such transformations are also required. If the position or the shape of a given figure is to be changed, the transformation discussed in this section comes to one's rescue. The transformations, though, defined for a point are applicable to lines or curves. These are extensively used in the field of animation, games, etc. We begin our discussion with three basic transformations:

- Translation
- Rotation
- Scaling

20.6.1 Translation

Translation is the movement of a point or a curve. The operation can be accomplished by changing the x and the y co-ordinates by a fixed amount. Here, it may be stated that it is not necessary to change the x and the y co-ordinate by the same value. The translation of a point is easy to comprehend. The translation of a line has been shown in the following figure (Figure 20.8).

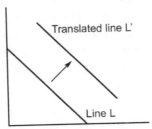

FIGURE 20.8 The line L is translated along a given direction. The translated line is L'

The movement of the line is shown in the above figure. Note that the shape and size of the line remains the same and only its x and y co-ordinates would change. That is, for each (x, y)

$$x' = x + t_x$$
$$y' = y + t_y$$

where x represents the old X co-ordinate
y represents the old Y co-ordinate
x' represents the new X co-ordinate
y' represents the new Y co-ordinate
t_x represents amount by which x is incremented
t_y represents amount by which y is incremented

The above operation can be described in terms of matrices as follows:

$$M = \begin{pmatrix} x \\ y \end{pmatrix} \qquad M' = \begin{pmatrix} x' \\ y' \end{pmatrix} \qquad T = \begin{bmatrix} t_x \\ t_y \end{bmatrix}$$

$$M' = M + T$$

In the case of more than one translation, the corresponding matrices are added to get the translation matrix. That is,

$$\begin{bmatrix} x' \\ y' \end{bmatrix} = \begin{bmatrix} x \\ y \end{bmatrix} + \begin{bmatrix} t_{x1} \\ t_{y1} \end{bmatrix} + \begin{bmatrix} t_{x2} \\ t_{y2} \end{bmatrix}$$

$$\begin{bmatrix} x' \\ y' \end{bmatrix} = \begin{bmatrix} x \\ y \end{bmatrix} + \begin{bmatrix} t_{x1} + t_{x2} \\ t_{y1} + t_{y2} \end{bmatrix}$$

$$M' = M + T'$$

Where
$$T' = T_1 + T_2$$

20.6.2 Rotation

Rotation is the movement of a line or a curve from a fixed point in a circular direction by a certain angle. The fixed point is known as the pivot point and through this pivot point, a line perpendicular to X-Y axis (in this case) is known as axis about which the line rotates. Note that the x coordinate and the y coordinate can be perceived as the projection of a given line along the x and the y coordinates. That is,

$$x = r \cos a$$
$$y = r \sin a$$

After rotation by the angle b, the angle becomes $(a + b)$ and hence the projections of the final coordinates become:

$$y' = r \sin (a + b)$$
$$= r \sin a \cos b + r \cos a \sin b = x \cos b + y \sin b$$
$$x' = r \cos (a + b)$$
$$= r \cos a \cos b - r \sin a \sin b = x \cos b - y \sin b$$

The above operation can be described in terms of matrices as follows:

$$M = \begin{bmatrix} x \\ y \end{bmatrix}$$

$$M' = \begin{bmatrix} x' \\ y' \end{bmatrix}$$

$$CIS = \begin{bmatrix} \cos\theta & -\sin\theta \\ \sin\theta & \cos\theta \end{bmatrix}$$

$$M' = M \times CIS$$

To apply translation and rotation at the same time, the following transformation is used:

$$X' = t_x + (x - t_x)\cos b - (y - t_y)\sin b$$
$$Y' = t_y + (x + t_x)\cos b + (y - t_y)\sin b$$
$$M' - T = CIS(b) * [M - T]$$

The `rotate` function, which takes the angle as an argument, can be used to rotate the figure. The following figures (Figure 20.9 and Figure 20.10) show the original image and that after rotation.

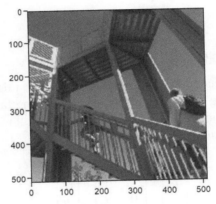

FIGURE 20.9 Figure before rotation

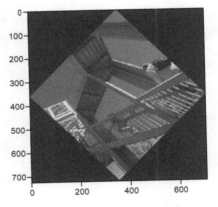

FIGURE 20.10 Figure after rotation

When you have to rotate the same figure twice, the task can be accomplished by rotating the figure by an angle $\alpha + \beta$ where α is the first angle and β is the second. The premise can be proved as follows:

$$\begin{bmatrix} x' \\ y' \end{bmatrix} = \begin{bmatrix} \cos\alpha & -\sin\alpha \\ \sin\alpha & \cos\alpha \end{bmatrix} \cdot \left[\begin{bmatrix} \cos\beta & -\sin\beta \\ \sin\beta & \cos\beta \end{bmatrix} \cdot \begin{bmatrix} x \\ y \end{bmatrix} \right]$$

$$\begin{bmatrix} x' \\ y' \end{bmatrix} = \left[\begin{bmatrix} \cos\beta & -\sin\beta \\ \sin\beta & \cos\beta \end{bmatrix} \cdot \begin{bmatrix} \cos\alpha & -\sin\alpha \\ \sin\alpha & \cos\alpha \end{bmatrix} \right] \cdot \begin{bmatrix} x \\ y \end{bmatrix}$$

$$\begin{bmatrix} x' \\ y' \end{bmatrix} = \begin{bmatrix} \cos\alpha\cos\beta - \sin\alpha\sin\beta & -(\cos\alpha\cos\beta - \sin\alpha\sin\beta) \\ \sin\alpha\cos\beta + \cos\alpha\sin\beta & \sin\alpha\cos\beta + \cos\alpha\sin\beta \end{bmatrix}$$

$$\begin{bmatrix} x' \\ y' \end{bmatrix} = \begin{bmatrix} \cos(\alpha+\beta) & -\sin(\alpha+\beta) \\ \sin(\alpha+\beta) & \cos(\alpha+\beta) \end{bmatrix} \cdot \begin{bmatrix} x \\ y \end{bmatrix}$$

$$M' = CIS(\alpha + \beta).M$$

20.6.3 Scaling

Scaling is changing the size of the curve or a figure by changing its X and Y axis by some factor. It's not necessary for the factor to be the same for both the X and the Y axis. In the formulas that follow, the scale along the X axis is s_x and that along the Y axis is s_y.

$$x' = x \cdot s_x, y' = y \cdot s_y$$
$$\begin{bmatrix} x' \\ y' \end{bmatrix} = \begin{bmatrix} S_x & 0 \\ 0 & S_y \end{bmatrix} \cdot \begin{bmatrix} x \\ y \end{bmatrix}$$
$$M' = S(s_x, s_y) \cdot M$$

In the case where translation is followed by scaling, the resultant matrix can be crafted using the following mathematical formulation.

$$x' = t_x + (x - t_x) \cdot s_x, y' = t_y + (y - t_y)s_y$$
$$M' - T = S(s_x, s_y) \cdot (M - T)$$

In case scaling is to be applied twice then the scaling by a factor, which is a product of the individual scaling factors, can be used. That is,

$$\begin{bmatrix} x' \\ y' \end{bmatrix} = \begin{bmatrix} S_{x1} & 0 \\ 0 & S_{y1} \end{bmatrix} \cdot \left(\begin{bmatrix} S_{x2} & 0 \\ 0 & S_{y2} \end{bmatrix} \cdot \begin{bmatrix} x \\ y \end{bmatrix} \right)$$

$$\begin{bmatrix} x' \\ y' \end{bmatrix} = \left[\begin{bmatrix} S_{x1} & 0 \\ 0 & S_{y1} \end{bmatrix} \cdot \begin{bmatrix} S_{x2} & 0 \\ 0 & S_{y2} \end{bmatrix} \right] \cdot \begin{bmatrix} x \\ y \end{bmatrix}$$

$$\begin{bmatrix} x' \\ y' \end{bmatrix} = \begin{bmatrix} S_{x1} \cdot S_{x2} & 0 \\ 0 & S_{y1} \cdot S_{y2} \end{bmatrix} \cdot \begin{bmatrix} x \\ y \end{bmatrix}$$

$$M' = S\ (s_{x1} \cdot s_{x2}, s_{y2} \cdot s_{y2})$$

Figure 20.11 shows the original image and Figure 20.12 shows the image after scaling.

FIGURE 20.11 The original image

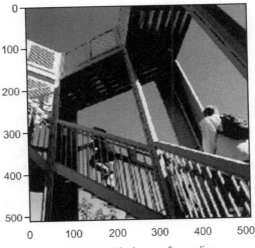

FIGURE 20.12 The image after scaling

20.7   CONCLUSION

The chapter introduces image processing in Python. To start with image processing, it is important to appreciate that an image can be stored as a multi-dimensional array. It is important to be able to store an image, to create an image from an array and to be able to save the image in a file. Also the reader must understand the concept of transformations before applying transformations to a given image. The underlying mathematics helps to untangle the intricacies and helps the programmer to devise a solution in the case of challenging situations. It is equally important to be able to clip an image and extract statistical information from it. The chapter discusses all the above and paves the way of the application of Python in diverse areas requiring image processing. The reader is expected to have a look at the references given at the end of this chapter for a clearer understanding.

GLOSSARY

Translation: Translation is the movement of a point or a curve.

Rotation: Rotation is the movement of a line or a curve from a fixed point in a circular direction by a certain angle.

Scaling: Scaling is changing the size of the curve or a figure by changing its X- and Y- axis by a factor.

POINTS TO REMEMBER

- In order to read an image from an object, the `imread` function can be used.
- The `tofile()` function of the array converts the array into a raw file.
- The edges of the polygon can be seen using the `contour` function.
- A part of the image can be extracted by creating a mask and putting the values in the region as 0.
- The statistical information corresponding to a given image can be extracted using `Numpy`. The `max()` function returns the maximum value; the `min()` function returns the minimum value; the `mean` function returns the mean and finally the `std` function returns the standard deviation.

- The `rotate` function, which takes the angle as an argument, can be used to rotate the figure.
- When you have to rotate the same figure twice then the task can be accomplished by rotating the figure by an angle $\alpha + \beta$, where α is the first angle and β is the second angle.

EXERCISES

MULTIPLE CHOICE QUESTIONS

1. Which of the following is used in processing images in Python?
   - (*a*) re
   - (*b*) Python Imaging Library
   - (*c*) Pillow
   - (*d*) None of the above

2. An image can be stored as a
   - (*a*) 2 dimensional array
   - (*b*) 3 dimensional array
   - (*c*) Both
   - (*d*) None of the above

3. In Python, the two dimensional array in which an image is stored can be manipulated by
   - (*a*) NumPy
   - (*b*) re
   - (*c*) Both
   - (*d*) None of the above

4. Which of the following constitute basic transformations in image processing?
   - (*a*) Translation
   - (*b*) Rotation
   - (*c*) Scaling
   - (*d*) All of the above

5. Which of the following functions can be used to rotate an image?
   - (*a*) rotate
   - (*b*) rot
   - (*c*) rota
   - (*d*) None of the above

6. Which of the following can be done using Python Imaging Library?
   - (*a*) Clipping
   - (*b*) Rotation
   - (*c*) Scaling
   - (*d*) All of the above

7. Image processing is used for
   (*a*) Medical diagnosis   (*b*) Weather forecasting
   (*c*) Animations   (*d*) All of the above

8. Which of the following has the rotate function or rotating an image in Python?
   (*a*) ndimage   (*b*) ndarray
   (*c*) Both   (*d*) None of the above

9. Which of the following can be obtained with the contour function?
   (*a*) Edges of the polygons in a given figure
   (*b*) Statistical information
   (*c*) Both   (*d*) None of the above

10. Which of the following can be used for plotting graphs (both 2D and 3D) in Python?
    (*a*) MATPLOTLIB   (*b*) NumPy
    (*c*) Scipy   (*d*) All of the above

THEORY

1. Explain some of the applications of image processing.

2. How is an image stored in an array? How is this array used to write an image to a file and then read it later?

3. Explain three basic transformations. Write the mathematical formulations involving matrices for carrying out the following tasks:
   (*a*) Rotation
   (*b*) Translation
   (*c*) Scaling

4. Prove that if two translation matrices are added, the resultant matrix would produce the same effect as individual translations.

5. What is pivot point rotation?

6. Explain clipping. How is clipping carried out in Python?

7. Explain the process of extracting the statistical information of an image.

8. What are contours? How are edges of a polygon extracted in Python?

9. Explain the importance of Python Imaging Library. Can the library be used with NumPy and SciPy?

10. What is the relation between PIL and MATPLOTLIB?

PROGRAMMING

Write a program to read an image and carry out the following tasks.

1. Store the image in an array and extract statistical information out of it.

2. Find the edges of the polygons in the image.

3. Rotate the image by 30 degrees in an counterclockwise direction.

4. Scale the image by a factor of 2 along the x-axis and 3 along the y-axis.

5. Translate the image by t_x and t_y (entered by the user).

6. Change the image to greyscale.

7. Reduce the image to half the size.

8. Clip the image by making a square of appropriate size.

9. Clip the image by making an ellipse of appropriate size.

10. Store a text in the image.

USEFUL LINKS

1. *http://www.scipy-lectures.org/advanced/image_processing/*

2. This chapter explains image processing using PIL. Open CV is also an important package dedicated to image processing. The introduction to Open CV can be found at *http://www.scipy-lectures.org/packages/scikit-image/*

3. This chapter explains image processing using PIL. Scikit-image also an important package dedicated to image processing. The introduction to the package can be found at: skimage 0.13.0 docs–skimage v0.13.0 docs.

4. The following link gives a brief overview of Pillow: *http://www.bogoto-bogo.com/python/python_image_processing_with_Pillow_library.php*

A

MULTITHREADING IN PYTHON

A1.1 INTRODUCTION

Modern systems can run many processes simultaneously. In the case of a multiprocessing system, various processes are allocated different memory space. However, these processes can share some memory space for purposes like communication. If a system has a single CPU (central processing unit), it can distribute the CPU time between these processes. The CPU hops between these processes and gives a slice of processing time to each process. There are many ways to carry out this scheduling like First Come First Serve, Shortest Job First, Round Robin, etc. Multiprocessing helps with achieving efficiency and results in better utilization of resources. At times a single process may have some portions that can run independently, provided that the problems like synchronization have been handled. This gives rise to the idea of multithreading. As per the literature *"Multithreading is the ability of a computer's operating system to run several programs or apps at what seems to be the 'same time' by a single processing unit or CPU."*

When a process is expected to process two or more parallel tasks, generally a thread is implemented. In fact, every process is a single thread of execution and a thread can give rise to many threads. Using multi-threading, a single program can perform several of its **sub-tasks** concurrently. One of the simplest examples can be the spell check, grammar-check and word count utilities in a word processor. The word processor here is a main process and the utilities can be the various threads, which run in parallel. Figure A1.1 shows the differences between a process and a thread.

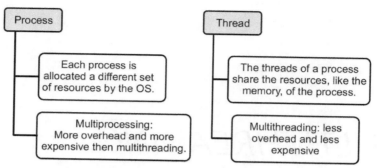

FIGURE A1.1 Difference between a process and a thread

Python supports multi-threading. In a multi-threading system, a thread is the smallest unit of execution. Threads of a process share the same memory space. Also, the state of a process is shared by a thread. Threads can also share global variables. If one of the threads is changed by the global variable, others can access the updated value. These threads are run in parallel by scheduling or by dividing the CPU time amongst the threads. In the first instance, these threads might appear to be just an extension of a function. However, a detailed look will reveal the difference, primarily in the return behavior.

Threads can be segregated into two classes. The threads can be created by the user or even created by a kernel. The latter are the part of the operating system. In any case different tasks are being done by different threads, resulting in better CPU utilization. That is, multi-threading is advantageous vis-a-vis resource utilization. The computers with many processors can use multi-threading to full advantage. Moreover, as explained in the above discussion, the time during which input, etc., is processed can be judiciously used. Figure A1.2 shows the advantages of multi-threading.

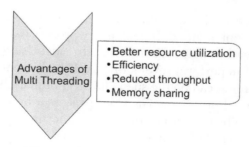

FIGURE A1.2 Advantages of multi-threading

A1.2   THE JAVA THREADING MODULE

The Python threading model is inspired by the Java threading model which has been explained in this section.

In Java, a thread is created using the **thread** class or the **runnable** interface. A new thread is born when it begins its life cycle. This state is referred to as "**New**." When a thread is born, it becomes "**Running**." That is, it becomes ready to accomplish the task for which it was created. During the execution, there might be a condition where it waits for some signals, perhaps IO. This state is referred to as the "**waiting state**." It may be stated here that this waiting can also be timed. Finally, a thread is "**terminated**." The states of a thread have been presented in the following diagram (Figure A1.3).

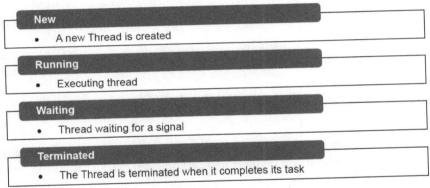

New
- A new Thread is created

Running
- Executing thread

Waiting
- Thread waiting for a signal

Terminated
- The Thread is terminated when it completes its task

FIGURE A1.3 States of a thread

A thread can be assigned some priority, based on which the operating system decides which thread to execute. In Java, the minimum priority that can be associated with a thread is 1 (MIN_PRIORITY) and the maximum can be 10 (MAX_PRIORITY). As a matter of fact we assign a higher priority to a thread when it is more important. However, the final decision in this regards is at the operating system's discretion.

A1.3   THREADING IN PYTHON

Python has two modules to facilitate the usage of threads: `threads` and `threading`, though `threading` is used and the former has been deprecated.

In Python 3, the former is called `thread`. The `thread` module comes with many functions to accomplish various tasks. A new thread can be started by using the `start_new_thread` method.

The `start_new_thread` method starts a new thread. The arguments of the method are `function`, `args`, and `kwargs`. `function` is the name of the function, the list of arguments is in `args` and `kwargs` is the dictionary of the keyword arguments.

The following listing shows the usage of the `start_new_thread` function. The function, first of all, needs to be imported from the `_thread` module. Then a function, say `fun1` is defined. This is followed by any number of invocations of the threads, as shown. Note that the exception is caught in the function and hence when a particular thread is invoked, the requisite exception is caught (or the invocation leads to a normal execution).

```
def fun(num):
    print('Hi there\n Number\t:' +    num)
from _thread import start_new_thread try:
    start_new_thread(fun,(1,))
    start_new_thread(fun,(2,))
except Exception:
    print('Caught exception')
```

The threads can be monitored using `counters`. A global counter can be created, which can be incremented on each call to the `start_new_thread` function and decremented when the thread exits. As stated earlier, the `thread` module has been deprecated so the `threading` module provides various interfaces for accomplishing different tasks. The important points regarding the creation of threads are as follows:

- The number of thread objects that are currently active are displayed by the `active_count()` function.
- The current thread object is returned by the `current_thread()` function of the caller's thread.
- The thread identifier can be seen using the `get_ident()` function. As per Python.org
  "This is a nonzero integer. Its value has no direct meaning; it is intended as a magic cookie to be used e.g. to index a dictionary of thread-specific data. Thread identifiers may be recycled when a thread exits and another thread is created."

- The complete list of all threads running can be viewed by the `enumerate()` function. The list contains the main thread and all other threads.
- The main thread can be seen using the `main_thread()`. In order to set the trace for all threads `settrace()` can be used.
- The size of the stack can be set using the `stack_size` function.

A thread can have its local data as well. The data specific to a thread can be stored in an instance of the local class. An instance of the `threading.local` can be created as follows:

```
data = threading.local
data.x = 1
```

A1.4   IMPORTANT METHODS OF THE THREAD CLASS

This section briefly introduces some of the most important methods of the `thread` class and paves the way for their usage in the requisite code.

`_init_()` and `run()`

A thread in Python can be created by instantiating the `thread` class. The activity that a thread would initiate can be represented in two ways. The first is to pass the object to the `_init_()`, that is the constructor of the `thread` class, in which case other methods of the thread class should not be overridden. The other way to initiate the activity is to override the `run()` method.

`start()` and `isalive()`

After creating a thread the requisite activity can be started by calling the `start` method. The calling of the `start()` invokes the separate thread of execution. The thread initiated would be in the live state. The `is_alive()` method checks whether the thread is alive.

`join()`

If the `join()` method of another thread is invoked by a thread, the calling thread is blacked until the thread whose call has been invoked is terminated.

`name` Attribute

The `name` attribute of a thread is used to see or change the name of a thread.

A1.5 TYPES OF THREADS

A thread can be a daemon thread, dummy thread or a normal one. A brief description of the types of threads has been presented as follows.

If a thread is a "`daemon thread`", then the program exits if it is left with only `daemon threads`. The flag can set through the `daemon` property. That is they can be abruptly shunted. The main thread corresponds to the initial thread of control in Python program. The `main` thread cannot be a `daemon thread`.

Then there are `dummy` threads. These threads are `daemonic` and are always alive. These threads cannot be joined with any other thread.

```
class threading.thread(group=None, target=None, name=None,
args=(), kwargs={}, *, daemon=None)
```

The arguments of this constructor are as follows:

- `group` should be none; It is reserved for future extension when a `threadGroup` class is implemented.
- `target` is the callable object to be invoked by the `run()` method.
- `name` is the thread name.
- `args` is the argument tuple for the target invocation.
- `kwargs` is a dictionary of keyword arguments for the target invocation.

A1.6 CONCLUSION

This appendix introduces multi-threading. The importance of threading and the difference between a thread and a process was explained in the first section. It has been argued that multi-threading is good, both in terms of resource utilization and efficiency. The Python threading model is largely based on the Java threading model. The appendix, therefore, gives a brief introduction of the Java threading model as well. The threading class and its important methods have been discussed so as to give an idea of how threading is implemented in Python. The reader is requested to visit the references at the end of the book for a detailed insight into the topic. It may also be stated here that the purpose of the appendix is not to discuss each and every aspect of threading but to briefly introduce it.

EXERCISES

1. What is multitasking?
2. State some conditions where multi-threading cannot be used.
3. Differentiate between a thread and a process.
4. What are the advantages of multi-threading?
5. In case of a uni processing system, what is the use of multi-threading?
6. Name three languages which support multi-threading.
7. Explain the Java threading model.
8. Explain how threads are implemented in Python.
9. Name the libraries which help to implement multi-threading in Python.
10. Name a technique via which thread safely can be implemented.
11. Which exception must be handled for a multi-threading code?
12. What is the function of the `join()` method?
13. All the threads are waiting for a signal. Which method would notify all of them?
14. How is a thread stopped in Python (name the method)?
15. What are the various types of threads?

APPENDIX B

REGULAR EXPRESSIONS

The functions studied in strings and the procedures studied in the third section of this book helped us to search a pattern from a given text or extract it. However, searching, finding patterns, and extracting a text are common tasks—so common that a whole module of Python is dedicated to these tasks. The `re` module helps the user to extract or search a pattern from a given text. It is a bit complex and therefore has not been included in the main text. However, it is important and has therefore been introduced in this appendix. The aim of this appendix is not to cover the topic comprehensively and analyze every aspect of the topic. However, a brief introduction paves the way of the use of the module for simple tasks. Regular expressions are powerful and can be used to search patterns like e-mail IDs, phone numbers etc., from a given text. Also, their use in parsing and the development of compilers is well known.

B1.1   INTRODUCTION

Python provides the users with the `re` module to deal with the regular expressions and search requisite texts. Writing a complex regular expression is an intricate task which requires practice. However, simple expressions can be written right away. In fact, just by reading this section!

First of all, let us consider the characters in a regular expression. The types of characters in a regular expression are as follows:

- Literal characters
- Character class
- Modifiers

The literals represent the class that has a single character: upper and lower case, digits and special characters. The special characters require a backslash (/) to be placed before the character itself.

Character class has one or more characters in square brackets. The expression will be matched by the occurrence of any character from the class. As a matter of fact, one can even mention a range in the class. The following symbols depict some of the standard matches:

- Alphanumeric characters are represented by \w,
- The non-alphanumeric characters are represented by \W
- The digits are represented by \d
- The non-digits are represented by \D
- The white spaces are represented by \s
- The beginning of a string is represented by ^. The end of a string is represented by $
- In a regular expression the dot (.) depicts a single character
- The asterisks (*) represent zero or more occurrences of the preceding character
- The + represents 0 or more occurrence of a string and
- ? represents 0 or 1 occurrence of the preceding character
- In order to match exactly n occurrences of a regular expression, use {n}.
- To match n or more occurrences, the {n,} is used.
- To match any number of occurrences between *n* and *m* {n, m} is used.

A regular expression is generally compiled before being used to accomplish the said tasks. The comparisons are done only after the given regular expression is compiled. As a matter of fact, even if a function is accepting an un-compiled regular expression, then also it is better to use a compiled regular expression as this greatly reduces the time taken for searching.

A regular expression is written in single quotes, preceded by *r*. For example, the name of a website can be any number of alphanumeric characters followed by a dot and then a domain. This regular expression can, therefore be written as:

```
sitename= re.compile(r'[\w.]+@[\w.]+')
```

The presence of a regular expression can be searched in a string using functions like search and match. These functions can be called as per the expression whether it is compiled or not:

- `match`: looks for the expression at the beginning of the string
- `search`: looks for the expression everywhere in the string

Each function takes the `pos` and `endpos` arguments indicating the beginning and the end position to be searched in the expression. If the expression is found in the given text, a match object(s) is returned. If the match is not found then `None` is returned. Let us consider the following example:

```
import re
mailid=re.compile(r'[\w.]+@[\w.]+')
```

Here, `import re` is for importing the re module. `mailid=re.compile (r'[\w.]+@[\w.]+')` is for creating a regular expression called `mailid`. Note that it starts with *r* and the expression is in '_'. The email ID can have any number of alphanumeric characters followed by a . and then @, which should be followed by any number of alphanumeric characters and (any number of times). After being compiled, it can be used to search the requisite string.

```
text = 'The site of the university if harsh@jnu.ac.in'
mailid.search(text)
```

The output of the above follows:

```
<_sre.SRE_Match object; span=(29, 44), match='harsh@jnu.
ac.in'>
```

Having seen the basics, let us now dwell into the regular expressions with a newer and easier perspective.

B1.2 THE SEARCH FUNCTION AND POWERFUL REGULAR EXPRESSIONS

In a program that uses regular expressions, the `re` module must be imported. One of the simplest tasks that can be performed using the module is to use the search function of the module to find a given pattern. For example, the following code finds the occurrences of the string "Harsh" in the text from the file "file1.txt".

```
f = open ('Text1.txt')
i = 1
str = "
for line in f:
      line.strip()
    str+ = line
    if re.search ('Harsh', line):
          print (i)
          print (line)
```

```
else:
          print ('hi')
i+ = 1
```

The power of `re`, however, is immense. It can be used to perform rather complicated tasks like that of finding all the lines that begin with the string "`har`". The following code uses the ^ to accomplish this task:

```
f=open ('Text1.txt')
i= 1
str="
for line in f:
```

The above tasks could also be accomplished by using the existing string functions. Now, if a little difficult task, say, that of finding all the words that begin with a "*h*" followed by 4 symbols followed by a "*h*" are to be searched using the `re` module, first of all the module needs to be imported.

In a regular expression ? matches any character. This is one of the most commonly used special characters used to match an expression. For example, a H...*h* would match any word that starts with a "H" and ends with a "*h*." That is "H...*h*" would match \

Harsh
Haaah
H123h
H@12h
and so on.

The following code implements the above logic.

```
import re
f = open('text1.txt')
for line in f:
      line=strip()
      if re.search('H...h',line):
            print(line)
```

Output

```
I am Harsh.
```

Moreover, we can also specify if the character can repeat. The symbols "*" and "+" in regular expressions indicate that in place of matching a single instance of the given character, zero or more instances for a "*" and one or more instances for a "+."

```
import re
f = open('file.txt')
for line in f:
        line = line.strip()
                if re.search('^From:.+@', line) :
                print(line)
```

Note that there is a "+" after "." indicating that any number of symbols may be there between a From and a @

If one wants to extract all the strings that match a regular expression, the findall() function can be used.

B1.2.1   Extracting data using regular expressions

If we want to extract data from a string in Python we can use the findall(). For example to find all the email IDs from a given string the expression '\S+@\S+.com' can be used.

That is, writing

```
list = findall('\S+@\S+.com',str)
list
```

would generate a list containing all the email IDs that end with a .com.

Note that \S is a non-whitespace character and \S+ indicates any number of non- whitespace characters. The @ must follow. After the @ symbol, there can be any number of non-whitespace characters followed by a .com.

Likewise one can craft a regular expression for finding all .edu emails and so on.

Strictly speaking an email ID starts with a capital or a small letter, followed by any number of non-whitespace symbols and then a @ sign. The @ follows any number of non-whitespace characters. The regular expression for e-mail id would therefore be

```
[a-zA-Z0-9]\S*@\S*[a-zA-Z]
```

One of the most common examples that is encountered in literature is that of substrings that start with a single lowercase letter, uppercase letter, or number "[a-zA-Z0-9]", followed by zero or more non-blank characters ("\S*"), followed by an at-sign, followed by zero or more non-blank characters ("\S*"), followed by an uppercase or lowercase letter. The code follows:

```
import re
f = open('File1.txt')
```

```
for line in f:
    line = line.strip()
      emaillist = re.findall('[a-zA-Z0-9]\S*@\S*[a-zA-Z]',
                                                        line)
    if len(emaillist) > 0:
          print(emaillist)
```

The regular expressions can also be used to find all the expressions that follow a particular pattern. For example, if we want to extract patterns that begin with a H followed by a _ and then a colon followed by any number of digits, then a dot and then any number of digits, the following re would suffice.

Sample O/P

```
H-ABCD-lefthanddrive: 0.1234
H-XYZT-righthanddrive: 0.1111
H-NMOP-lefthand: 0.0101
H-KLMN-righthand: 0.0001
H-AAAA-leftdrive: 0.01010
H-C DCD-rightdrive: 1010.90990
```

We say that we want lines that start with "H-," followed by zero or more characters (".*"), followed by a colon (":") and then a space. After the space we are looking for one or more characters that are either a digit (0-9) or a period "[0-9.]+". Note that inside the square brackets, the period matches an actual period (i.e., it is not a wildcard between the square brackets).

Code

```
import re
f = open('File1.txt')
for line in f:
line = line.strip()
if re.search('^H-\S*: [0-9.]+', line) :
print line
```

The execution of the above code would throw up the string we are exactly looking for. Actually the reason for splitting a given text into lines was to spare the need for parsing and searching at the same time. Parentheses are special characters in regular expressions. Adding parentheses to a regular expression helps us to ignore while matching the string.

However, when we use findall() parentheses to indicate that we want the whole expression to match, we are only interested in extracting a portion of the substring that matches the regular expression.

```
import re
f = open('File.txt')
for line in f:
        line = line.strip()
pattern = re.findall('^H-\S*: ([0-9.]+)', line)
if len(pattern) > 0 :
        print(pattern)
```

The output from this program is as follows:

```
['0.8475']
['0.0000']
['0.6178']
['0.0000']
['0.6961']
['0.0000']
```

At times we need to search the characters which are actually special symbols in a regular expression. In such cases it must be indicated that the characters are normal and not that with a special meaning. We can indicate that we want to simply match a character by prefixing that character with a back-slash. The examples follow.

As stated earlier, the purpose of the appendix was to give an introduction of the topic. Actually, using the regular expressions we can construct strings that are to be searched/matched with some of the string in the given text.

B1.3 CONCLUSION

At times, big text needs to be searched for a particular pattern. The strings to be searched can be of various types. For searching for a given pattern, Python provides us with regular expressions via the re module. For example, in searching the email IDs from a given document or in finding the names that end with "*a*," regular expressions can be used. Regular expressions, as a matter of fact, are not just used to find patterns but can also be used to define or modify a pattern. For example, if you are required to find "all the TV series whose names begin with a K followed by a *k*" the task can be accomplished by defining the requisite re, compiling it and then using it to find the pattern. This appendix introduces the package and explains its use.

SYMBOLS TO REMEMBER

Some of those special characters and character sequences are as follows:

^:   The beginning of the line.

$:   The end of the line.

. :   Any character (a wildcard).

\s: A whitespace character.

\S: A non-whitespace character (opposite of \s).

*:   Indicates to match zero or more of the preceding character(s).

*?:   Indicates to match zero or more of the preceding character(s) in "non-greedy mode."

+:   Indicates to match one or more of the preceding character(s).

+?:   Indicates to match one or more of the preceding character(s) in "non-greedy mode."

[abcde]:   The example would match "*a*", "*b*", "*c*", "*d*", or "*e*", but no other characters.

[a-z0-9]:   Single character that must be a lowercase letter or a digit.

[^A-Za-z]:   Single character that is anything other than an uppercase or lowercase letter.

():   Ignored for the purpose of matching, but allows you to extract a particular subset of the matched string rather than the whole string when using findall().

\b: Matches the empty string at the start or end of a word.

\B: Matches the empty string, but not at the start or end of a word.

\d: Matches any decimal digit; equivalent to the set [0-9]

\D: Matches any non-digit character; equivalent to the set [^0-9]

EXERCISES

THEORY

1. What are regular expressions? How are they useful?

2. Are regular expressions better then string functions?

3. What is the difference between a compiled and a non-compiled regular expression?

4. Can we use regular expressions to find patterns from a web page?

5. Name three functions used for finding a string from a given text.

PROGRAMMING

1. Take a text of around 2000 words from a news web site. From this text find

    (i) The email IDs of all the people who have their mail at the Yahoo server

    (ii) The phone number of people living in Jordan (the phone number starts from 011-)

    (iii) The code that begins with an "H," has two digits after "H" and any number of characters after the digits.

    (iv) All the occurrences of the names that begin with an "H" and ends with an "h."

    (v) "Ashish" followed by three digits from the given text.

C

EXERCISES FOR PRACTICE: PROGRAMMING QUESTIONS

SECTION I: PROCEDURAL PROGRAMMING

Conditional Statements

1. Ask the user to enter a four digit number and check whether the second digit is one more than the third digit.

2. In the above question if the given condition is false, swap the digits at the third and the second places and increment the digit at the units' place by one, if it is not 9. If the digit at the units place is 9, then do not change the digit.

3. Ask the user to enter a three digit number and find the characters corresponding to the digits. Create a string out of these characters and find whether any letter of this string is a capital letter.

4. Ask the user to enter his monthly salary, his house rent (or home loan), his car, newspaper subscription, the amount he spends on food in a month. Now find if the amount left is sufficient enough to start a 401K. Note that a 401K can be started with even $500.

5. Ask the user to enter his total savings. If the savings are above $1,000,000, then the person need not to pay any tax. Also this person is entitled to get a subsidy from the Government. If the savings are above $1,000,000 but below the above specified amount, he is liable to pay 30% of his savings as tax, plus a surcharge of 2% on the tax. Calculate the total amount paid by the person as this tax.

6. Ask the user to enter a three digit number and find the largest digit of the number. Also find the sum of the digits and find if the sum of the digits is the same as twice the largest digit.

7. Ask the user to enter the marks obtained by a student in 5 subjects. If the person scores more than 90% in a subject he gets an A+. If the score is less than 90% but greater than 85%, he gets an A. If the score is greater than 80%, he gets an "A-." Likewise if the score is greater than 75%, he gets a B+ and B is awarded to a person scoring more than 70%. A person getting more than 65% but less than 70% gets a "B-" and the one getting more than 60% but less than 65% gets "C+." A person getting more than 55% (and less than 60%) gets a "C" and the one getting more than 50% (and less than 55%) gets a "C-." Furthermore, for each grade the corresponding CGPA is as follows.

Grade	cgPA
A+	9
A	8
A–	7
B+	6
B	5
B–	4
C+	3
C	2
C–	1

Find the average CGPA of the student.

8. Find whether the year entered by the user is a multiple of 7, without using the mod operator.

9. Find whether the number entered by the user is a multiple of both 5 and 7, without using the mod operator.

10. Ask the user to enter a string and find the number of occurrences of vowels in the string.

Looping

11. Ask the user to enter a number and find the number obtained by reversing the order of the digits.

12. Ask the user to enter a decimal number and find its binary equivalent.

13. Ask the user to enter a decimal number and find its octal equivalent.

14. Ask the user to enter a decimal number and find its hexadecimal equivalent.

15. Ask the user to enter an n-digit number and find the digit which is the maximum amongst them.

16. Ask the user to enter any number of numbers (he must enter 0 to quit) and find the maximum number.

17. In the above question find the minimum number.

18. Ask the user to enter n numbers and find their standard deviation and mean.

19. In the above question, find the mean deviation.

20. Write a program to generate the following pattern. (Refer to the link of cellular automata at the end of this appendix).

Functions

A piece of data is given to you. The data has many features (columns) and the last column states the class to which it belongs (0 or 1). Each feature's data can be segregated into X and Y, where X is the data that belongs to class 0 and Y is the data that belongs to class 1. The relevance of a particular feature can be calculated by numerous methods, one of which is the Fisher Discriminate Ratio.

The Fisher Discriminate Ratio of a feature (a column vector) is calculated using the following formula

$$FDR = (\mu_X^1 - \mu_Y^1)^2 / (\sigma_x^2 - \sigma_Y^2)$$

Where μ_x is the mean of the data X, μ_y is the mean of the data Y. The standard deviation of X is σ_x and that of the Y data is σ_y.

Ask the user to enter the elements of two lists - feature and label.

21. Create a function, segregate, which takes the feature and label as input and find the vectors X and Y.

22. The calculate_mean function should calculate the mean of the input vector.

23. The calculate standard_deviation function should calculate the standard deviation of the input vector.

24. The FDR function should calculate the FDR of a feature.

25. Finally write a program that takes 2D data as input and calculate the FDR of each feature.

The relevance of a particular feature can also be calculated by the coefficient of correlation.

The coefficient of correlation of a feature (a column vector) is calculated using the following formula.

$$CC = \frac{X.Y}{|X| \times |Y|}, \text{ where } |X| \text{ is } \sqrt{x_1^2 + x_2^2 + \ldots + x_m^2}. \text{ For } X = [x_1, x_2, \ldots x_m].$$

Likewise, $|Y|$ is $\sqrt{y_1^2 + y_2^2 + \ldots + y_m^2}$. For $Y = [y_1, y_2, \ldots y_n]$.

26. Create a function, "segregate" which takes the feature and label as input and find the vectors X and Y.

27. The calculate_mod function should calculate the $|X|$ for the input vector, X.

28. The calculate_dot function should calculate $X.Y$.

29. The CORR function should calculate the correlation coefficient of a feature.

30. Finally write a program that takes 2D data as input and calculate the coefficient of correlation of each feature.

File Handling/ Strings

31. Create a file called data and insert data from a text file containing 5 news articles from a news site.

32. Now open the file and find the words beginning with vowels. Make 5 lists of words beginning with each vowel.

33. Draw a histogram of the above data.

34. Make the first letter of each word capital and write the words in 5 separate files.

35. Now, from each file find the words that end with a vowel and place the words in 5 separate files.

36. Check which of these words begin and end with a vowel.

37. From the original file find the word which is repeated the maximum number of times.

38. Do the above task for all the words and plot the frequency of each word in a graph.

39. From the original file find which alphabetic character is used the maximum number of times.

40. The reader is expected to read about Huffman code from the following link and encode the file using Huffman code.

    https://users.cs.cf.ac.uk/Dave.Marshall/Multimedia/node210.html

41. From the original file, find the string that has the maximum length.

42. From the original file find the string that has "cat" as the substring.

43. From the original file find the strings which are substrings of some other strings in the file.

44. From the original file find the strings which begin with a capital letter.

45. From the original file, find all the email IDs.

46. Find the email IDs which are on the Yahoo server.

47. Create a regular expression for the land line number in India and find all the landline numbers from the file.

48. From the above list find the phone numbers which belong to a particular area.

49. Find the words which are in all five articles.

50. Find the words which end with a consonant and contain a vowel.

SECTION II: OBJECT-ORIENTED PROGRAMMING

Classes and Objects

You are required to develop software for a car wash company. The company wants software that can store the details of a car and generate invoices. After due deliberation, it was decided that a class called car with the following members would be created.

Data members

(*a*) Registration Number   (*b*) Model
(*c*) Make   (*d*) Year
(*e*) Name of the owner

Methods

(*f*) `getdata()`	: Takes data from the users
(*g*) `putdata()`	: Displays data
(*h*) `__init ()`	: Initializes members
(*i*) del	: Destructor
(*j*) capacity	:

1. Create a class called car to facilitate the development of the said software.

2. Make two instances of the class and display the data. The first instance should display the data entered using the `putdata()` function and the second should display the data assigned using the `init ()` method.

3. Create an array of cars. Ask the user to enter the data of *n* cars and display the data.

4. Find the cars whose registration numbers contain "HR51."

5. Find the cars which are manufactured by "Maruti."

6. Find the cars which were manufactured before 2007.

7. Find the car whose owners are named "Harsh."

8. Find the cars whose owners names begin with "A" and are manufactured after 2014.

9. Find the cars which have a certain type of engine (entered by the user).

10. Find the car with the maximum engine capacity.

Operator Overloading

11. Create a class called vector, which has three data members

    (*a*) $x1$: The x component of the vector

    (*b*) $y1$: The y component of the vector

    (*c*) $z1$: The z component of the vector

    The class should have a method called `getdata()`, which takes data from the user; `putdata()`, which displays the data; `init`, the constructor.

12. Create a class called vectors and make two instances of vector: v_1 and v_2. Display the data of the two objects.

13. The mod of a vector can be defined as follows. If $v_1 = x_1\hat{i} + y_1\hat{j} + z_1\hat{k}$, then $|v_1| = \sqrt{x_1^2 + y_1^2 + z_1^2}$. Create an array of vectors. Ask the user to enter the data of n vector and find the vector that has the maximum mod.

14. From the above vectors (Question 13) find the vectors which have the y component 0.

15. Two vectors v_1 and v_2 can be subtracted by subtracting the corresponding components of the two vectors. That is if $v_1 = x_1\hat{i} + y_1\hat{j} + z_1\hat{k}$ and $v_2 = x_2\hat{i} + y_2\hat{j} + z_2\hat{k}$ then
$$v_1 - v_2 = (x_1 - x_2)\hat{i} + (y_1 - y_2)\hat{j} + (z_1 - z_1)\hat{k}.$$
Using the above concept, overload the + operator for the class.

16. Two vectors, v_1 and v_2 can be added by adding the corresponding components of the two vectors. That is if $v_1 = x_1\hat{i} + y_1\hat{j} + z_1\hat{k}$ and $v_2 = x_2\hat{i} + y_2\hat{j} + z_2\hat{k}$ then
$$v_1 + v_2 = (x_1 + x_2)\hat{i} + (y_1 + y_2)\hat{j} + (z_1 + z_2)\hat{k}.$$
Using the above concept, overload the + operator for the class.

17. The dot product of two vectors can be obtained by adding the products obtained by multiplying the corresponding components of the two vectors. That is, if $v_1 = x_1\hat{i} + y_1\hat{j} + z_1\hat{k}$ and $v_2 = x_2\hat{i} + y_2\hat{j} + z_2\hat{k}$ then
$$v_1.v_2 = (x_1.x_2)\hat{i} + (y_1.y_2)\hat{j} + (z_1.z_2)\hat{k}$$
Using the above concept, overload the . operator for the class.

18. A hypothetical operation can increment can be defined as follows. If $v_1 = x_1\hat{i} + y_1\hat{j} + z_1\hat{k}$ then
$$v_1 + + = (x_1 + +)\hat{i} + (y_1 + +)\hat{j} + (z_1 + +)\hat{k}$$
Using the above concept, overload the ++ operator for the class.

19. A hypothetical operation can increment can be defined as follows. If $v_1 = x_1\hat{i} + y_1\hat{j} + z_1\hat{k}$ then
$$v_2 - - = (x_1 - -)\hat{i} + (y_1 - -)\hat{j} + (z_1 - -)\hat{k}$$
Using the above concept, overload the $--$ operator for the class.

20. For the vector class, overload the unary (−) operator.

Inheritance

21. Create a class called Book that has the following members.

    (*a*) Name of the book   : String
    (*b*) Author(s)   : List
    (*c*) Year   : Year of publication
    (*d*) ISSN   : String
    (*e*) Publisher   : Name of the publisher

    The class should have `getdata()`, `putdata()` and `init ()` as its methods.

22. Create two subclasses: TextBook and ReferenceBook having requisite data members. Demonstrate the use of overriding in the above hierarchy.

23. Now create three subclasses of the TextBook class, namely SocialScience, Engineering and Management. Each class should define its version of `getdata()` and `putdata()`. Make instances of these subclasses and call the method of the derived classes.

24. Create a class called XBook, which is a subclass of both TextBook and Reference Book and demonstrate how this can lead to ambiguity.

25. Create a class called ABC and craft a class method and an instance method of the class.

Exception Handling

26. Create a class called array which contains an array and max which is the maximum number of elements the array can have and methods `getdata()` and `putdata()`, which perform the requisite tasks.

27. Now create a class to raise customized exceptions. The exception should be raised if the user enters more elopements than the max allowed.

28. If the user enters anything except for integer, an exception should be raised and the requisite message should be displayed.

29. Now ask the user to enter two indices and divide the numbers at those positions. If the number at the second position is 0, an exception should be raised.

30. Ask the user to enter three indices. These three indices contain the values of "*a*," "*b*," and "*c*" of the quadratic equation $ax^2 + bx + c = 0$. Find the discriminant and the roots of the equation. If the value of $b^2 - 4ac < 0$, an exception should be raised.

SECTION III: DATA STRUCTURES

Sorting and Searching

1. Implement linear search and binary search. Compare the time for searching an element from a list of 500 random numbers.

2. Repeat the experiment for a list of 5000 integers and compare the time for searching for an element with the two algorithms. Does increasing the number of elements 10 times increase the running time 10 fold?

3. Implement counting sort. (Reference at the end of this appendix)

4. Implement bucket sort. (Refer to the links at the end of this appendix)

5. Implement selection sort which takes $O(n \log n)$ time.

6. Now take a list of 500 integers and compare the time for selection sort and bucket sort.

7. Which of the two - bucket sort or counting sort - takes less time? Are they really comparable?

8. Implement quick sort and merge sort using lists.

9. Take an array of 5000 random integers and compare the time of running of quick sort and merge sort.

10. Can the average case complexity of quick sort be bettered?

Stacks and Queues

11. Refer to the chapter on stacks and queues and implement a dynamic stack in which a single placeholder is added when overflow occurs.

12. Refer to the chapter on stacks and queues and implement a dynamic stack in which the number of placeholders is doubled when overflow occurs.

13. Implement a dynamic stack in which the number of placeholders is randomly increased when overflow occurs.

14. Using a stack convert an infix expression into a postfix expression.

15. Using stacks convert an infix expression into a prefix expression.

16. Using stacks find the nth Fibonacci term.

17. Using stacks find the number obtained by reversing the order of digits for a given number.

18. Using queues implement priority scheduling.

19. Using queues implement First Come First Serve scheduling.

20. Using queues implement First Come First Serve with time slice.

Linked List

21. Write a program to find whether a given linked list has a cycle.

22. Write a program to join two linked lists.

23. Write a program to merge two linked lists.

24. Write a program to remove duplicate elements from a given linked list.

25. Write a program to find the second maximum element from a given linked list.

26. Write a program to find the element greater than the mean (assume that the linked list has only integers in the data part).

27. Write a program to find the common elements from two given linked lists.

28. Write a program to find the union of elements of two linked lists.

29. Write a program to arrange the elements of a linked list in descending order.

30. Write a program to partition a linked list as per the algorithm in the following reference.

Graphs and Trees

A graph can be represented using a two-dimensional array. The array will contain 0's and 1's . If the element at the ith row and the jth column has 1, it indicates the presence of an edge from vertex i to j. Ask the user to enter the number of vertices of a graph and create a two dimensional array depicting the graph.

31. Find the number of edges in the graph. (Note that the number of 1's in the 2-D array is not same as the number of edges in the graph).

32. Find the vertex connected to the maximum number of edges.

33. Find if the graph has a cycle.

34. Ask the user to enter the initial vertex and the final vertex and find if there is a path from the initial to the final vertex.

35. In the above question find whether there is more than one path from the initial to the final vertex, in which case find the shortest path.

36. Now, in place of 1's ask the user to enter a finite number representing the cost of the edge from the vertex i to the vertex j. Find the shortest path from the source vertex to all other vertices.

37. Write a program to find the spanning tree of the graph.

38. Write a program to find whether the graph is a tree.

39. A tree can be represented using a two dimensional array having n rows and two columns. In each row the first column is i and the second column is j, which means that there is an edge from i to j. Ask the user to enter the requisite data and display the tree (just the list of vertices and edges associated with them).

40. Create a binary tree using a doubly linked list. For this tree accomplish the following tasks.

41. Write a program to implement the post order traversal of a binary tree.

42. Write a program to implement the pre order traversal of a binary tree.

43. Write a program to implement the in order traversal of the tree.

44. Check if the given tree is a binary search tree.

45. In a given binary search tree, find the leftmost node of the right sub tree of a given node.

46. In a given binary search tree, find the rightmost node of the left sub tree of a given node.

47. Write a program to insert an element in a binary search tree.

48. Write a program to delete a given node from a given binary search tree.

49. Write a program to create a heap from a given list.

50. Implement heap sort.

APPENDIX D

PROBLEMS FOR PRACTICE: MULTIPLE CHOICE QUESTIONS

SECTION 3: INTRODUCTION TO DATA STRUCTURES

Introduction

1. In linear data structures, the elements are

(*a*) Stored in a linear fashion

(*b*) Elements are accessed in sequential order

(*c*) Both

(*d*) None of the above

2. In non-linear data structures

(*a*) Elements are stored and accessed in a non-linear fashion

(*b*) Elements are accessed in a non-linear fashion

(*c*) Elements are stored in a non-linear fashion

(*d*) None of the above

3. An ADT consists of

(*a*) Declaration of data

(*b*) Declaration of operations

(*c*) Definition of data

(*d*) Definition of operations

4. The time complexity of inserting an element at a given position, in an array, is

(*a*) O(*n*)

(*b*) O(n^2)

(*c*) O(log *n*)

(*d*) None of the above

5. The time complexity of deleting an element at a given position, from an array, requires
    (*a*) O(*n*)   (*b*) O(*n*^{2})
    (*c*) O(log *n*)   (*d*) None of the above

6. Which of the following is not a type of algorithmic analysis?
    (*a*) Worst Case   (*b*) Best Case
    (*c*) Average Case   (*d*) Boundary Case

7. The time complexity of linear search is
    (*a*) O(*n*)   (*b*) O(*n*^{2})
    (*c*) O(*n*^{3})   (*d*) None of the above

8. The time complexity of linear search is
    (*a*) Ω (*n*)   (*b*) Ω (*n*^{2})
    (*c*) Ω (*n*^{3})   (*d*) All of the above

9. The time complexity of linear search is
    (*a*) θ(*n*)   (*b*) θ(*n*^{2})
    (*c*) θ(*n*^{3})   (*d*) All of the above

10. If *f*(*n*) = 3*n*^{2} + 5*n* + 2, Then *f*(*n*) is
    (*a*) θ(*n*^{2})   (*b*) Ω(*n*^{2})
    (*c*) θ(*n*^{2})   (*d*) All of the above

11. Which one of the following is the most essential attribute of an algorithm?
    (*a*) Correctness   (*b*) Finiteness
    (*c*) Definiteness   (*d*) All of the above

12. Which of the following is recursive, but a non-recursive algorithm can be created using stacks?
    (*a*) Merge sort   (*b*) Quick sort
    (*c*) Bubble sort   (*d*) Insertion sort

13. Which of the following is iterative?
    (*a*) Merge sort   (*b*) Quick sort
    (*c*) Bubble sort   (*d*) Insertion sort

14. Which of the following data structures cannot have a cycle?
    (*a*) Directed graph   (*b*) Undirected graph
    (*c*) Tree   (*d*) None of the above

15. On which of the following data structures does NumPy rely on?
    (*a*) Array   (*b*) Trees
    (*c*) Stacks   (*d*) Queues

Stacks and Queues

16. Given an expression: $(a + b) - (c/d) \times f$. The postfix form of the expression is _____.

17. Given an expression: $(a + b) - (c/d) \times f$. The prefix form of the expression is _____.

18. Given an expression: $(a/(b + c)) - d$. The corresponding postfix expression is _____.

19. Given an expression: $(a/(b + c)) - d$. The prefix form of the expression is _____.

20. Given an expression: $a + ((b/c) \times (d / f))$. Which of the following is the postfix form?

21. Given an expression: $a + ((b/c) \times (d / f))$. The prefix form of the expression is.

22. In dynamic stacks if one of the elements is added at the time of overflow, what would the time complexity of copy operations be?
    (*a*) O(n)   (*b*) O(n^2)
    (*c*) O(log n)   (*d*) None of the above

23. In the dynamic stacks if the number of the elements are doubled at the time of overflow, what would the time complexity of copy operations be?
    (*a*) O(n) time   (*b*) O(n^2) time
    (*c*) O(log n) time   (*d*) O(n log n) time

24. When reversing a string which one of the following data structures can be used?
    (*a*) Array   (*b*) Trees
    (*c*) Stacks   (*d*) Queues

25. In case of linear queue what is the initial value of FRONT and REAR?

(*a*) FRONT = 0, REAR = 0

(*b*) FRONT = 0, REAR = – 1

(*c*) FRONT = – 1, REAR = Not Defined

(*d*) FRONT = –1, REAR = –1

26. Which one of the following is not possible in linear queues?

(*a*) FRONT = 0, REAR = 1

(*b*) FRONT = 3, REAR = 2

(*c*) FRONT = 2, REAR = 3

(*d*) FRONT = – 1, REAR = – 1

27. In which of the following cases value of FRONT and REAR are same?

(*a*) Empty queue   (*b*) A single element

(*c*) Both   (*d*) None of the above

28. In FIFO algorithm for scheduling in operating system which data structure is used?

(*a*) Array   (*b*) Trees

(*c*) Stacks   (*d*) Queues

29. In spooling which one of the data structures is used?

(*a*) Array   (*b*) Trees

(*c*) Stacks   (*d*) Queues

30. Recursion requires which of the following data structures?

(*a*) Array   (*b*) Trees

(*c*) Stacks   (*d*) Queues

Linked List

31. In implementing stacks using linked lists which of the following operations are used?

(*a*) Insertion at beginning   (*b*) Insertion at end

(*c*) Deletion from beginning   (*d*) Deletion from end

32. In implementing queues using linked lists which of the following operations are used?
    (a) Insertion at beginning
    (b) Insertion at end
    (c) Deletion at beginning
    (d) Deletion at end

33. For a circular linked list which of the following is true?
    (a) Pointer of last node points to first node
    (b) There is no NULL pointer in a non-empty queue
    (c) Pointer of the first node may point to the last node
    (d) All of the above

    While storing polynomial in a linked list a special node is created which has two data members and a next pointer. The data members store the coefficient and exponent of a given term.

34. Using the above representation what would be the complexity of addition of polynomials?
    (a) O(n)
    (b) O(n^2)
    (c) O(log n)
    (d) O(n log n)

35. In the above question, what would be the complexity of subtraction of polynomials?
    (a) O(n)
    (b) O(n^2)
    (c) O(log n)
    (d) O(n log n)

36. What would be the complexity of multiplication of polynomials?
    (a) O(n)
    (b) O(n^2)
    (c) O(log n)
    (d) O(n log n)

37. Which of the following strategies is the most efficient for reversing a linked list?
    (a) Recursion
    (b) Creating a new linked list in the order of the elements is reverse of that of the original linked list
    (c) Creating two pointers
    (d) Using a temporary array

38. What is the complexity (best case) in reversing a linked list using above strategy?

(a) O(n)

(b) O(n^2)

(c) O($\log n$)

(d) O($n \log n$)

39. What is the strategy for finding a cycle in a linked list?

(a) Recursion

(b) A new linked list

(c) Using two pointers

(d) Using a temporary array

40. What would be the complexity of the above?

(a) O(n)

(b) O(n^2)

(c) O($\log n$)

(d) O($n \log n$)

Trees

41. What is the height of a complete binary tree which has n nodes?

(a) n

(b) $n \log n$

(c) $\log n$

(d) $\sqrt{n}$

42. What is the number of nodes of a complete binary tree which has n levels?

(a) $2n$

(b) $n \log n$

(c) n^2

(d) 2^n

43. What is the complexity of searching in a complete binary tree which has n nodes?

(a) O(n)

(b) O(n^2)

(c) O($\log n$)

(d) O($n \log n$)

44. What is the worst case time complexity for searching in a skewed binary tree?

(a) O(1)

(b) O(n)

(c) O($\log n$)

(d) O($n \log n$)

45. What is the best case complexity for searching an element in a skewed tree?

(*a*) $O(n)$ (*b*) $O(n^2)$

(*c*) $O(\log n)$ (*d*) $O(1)$

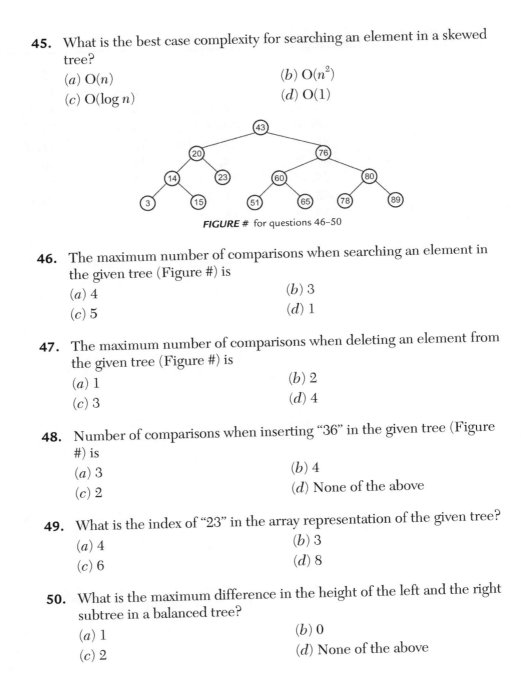

FIGURE # for questions 46–50

46. The maximum number of comparisons when searching an element in the given tree (Figure #) is

(*a*) 4   (*b*) 3

(*c*) 5   (*d*) 1

47. The maximum number of comparisons when deleting an element from the given tree (Figure #) is

(*a*) 1   (*b*) 2

(*c*) 3   (*d*) 4

48. Number of comparisons when inserting "36" in the given tree (Figure #) is

(*a*) 3   (*b*) 4

(*c*) 2   (*d*) None of the above

49. What is the index of "23" in the array representation of the given tree?

(*a*) 4   (*b*) 3

(*c*) 6   (*d*) 8

50. What is the maximum difference in the height of the left and the right subtree in a balanced tree?

(*a*) 1   (*b*) 0

(*c*) 2   (*d*) None of the above

ANSWERS TO THE MCQ'S

1. (*a*)	**2.** (*a*)	**3.** (*a*, *b*)	**4.** (*a*)	**5.** (*a*)
6. (*d*)	**7.** (*a*, *b*, *c*)	**8.** (*a*)	**9.** (*a*)	**10.** (*d*)
11. (*a*)	**12.** (*a*, *b*)	**13.** (*c*, *d*)	**14.** (*c*)	**15.** (*a*)
22. (*b*)	**23.** (*d*)	**24.** (*c*)	**25.** (*a*)	**26.** (*b*)
27. (*c*)	**28.** (*a*)	**29.** (*a*, *d*)	**30.** (*c*)	**31.** (*b*, *d*)
32. (*b*, *c*)	**33.** (*a*)	**34.** (*a*)	**35.** (*a*)	**36.** (*b*)
37. (*c*)	**38.** (*a*)	**39.** (*c*)	**40.** (*c*)	**41.** (*c*)
42. (*d*)	**43.** (*c*)	**44.** (*b*)	**45.** (*d*)	**46.** (*a*)
47. (*d*)	**48.** (*a*)	**49.** (*b*)	**50.** (*a*)	

ANSWER TO THE MULTIPLE CHOICE QUESTIONS

Chapter 1

1. (c)	**2.** (b)	**3.** (b)	**4.** (c)	**5.** (c)	**6.** (c)
7. (b)	**8.** (c)	**9.** (b)	**10.** (a)	**11.** (d)	**12.** (d)
13. (d)	**14.** (d)	**15.** (a)			

Chapter 2

1. (a)	**2.** (b)	**3.** (b)	**4.** (d)	**5.** (a)	**6.** (b)
7. (b)	**8.** (b)	**9.** (d)	**10.** (b)	**11.** (d)	**12.** (d)
13. (a)	**14.** (a)	**15.** (a)			

Chapter 3

1. (a)	**2.** (a)	**3.** (b)	**4.** (a)	**5.** (b)	**6.** (a)
7. (a)	**8.** (b)	**9.** (b)	**10.** (b)		

Chapter 4

1. (b)	**2.** (d)	**3.** (c)	**4.** (c)	**5.** (d)	**6.** (a)
7. (d)	**8.** (a)	**9.** (a)	**10.** (b)		

Chapter 5

1. (d)	**2.** (a)	**3.** (a)	**4.** (c)	**5.** (d)	**6.** (a)
7. (c)	**8.** (c)	**9.** (a)	**10.** (d)		

Chapter 6

1. (e)	**2.** (a)	**3.** (a)	**4.** (a)	**5.** (b)	**6.** (a)
7. (d)	**8.** (d)	**9.** (d)	**10.** (a)		

Chapter 7

1. (c)	**2.** (a)	**3.** (d)	**4.** (a)	**5.** (c)	**6.** (c)
7. (b)	**8.** (c)	**9.** (a)	**10.** (b)	**11.** (c)	**12.** (a)
13. (b)	**14.** (a)	**15.** (b)	**16.** (a)	**17.** (a)	**18.** (b)
19. (c)	**20.** (a)	**21.** (b)	**22.** (c)	**23.** (b)	**24.** (d)
25. (d)					

Chapter 8

1. (a)	**2.** (a)	**3.** (c)	**4.** (a)	**5.** (b)	**6.** (a)
7. (b)	**8.** (a)	**9.** (b)	**10.** (b)	**11.** (b)	**12.** (c)
13. (a)	**14.** (c)	**15.** (b)	**16.** (d)	**17.** (d)	**18.** (b)
19. (b)	**20.** (b)	**21.** (a)	**22.** (a)	**23.** (a)	**24.** (b)
25. (b, c)					

Chapter 9

1. (a)	**2.** (d)	**3.** (a)	**4.** (a)	**5.** (a)	**6.** (a)
7. (a)	**8.** (b)	**9.** (a)	**10.** (a)	**11.** (b)	**12.** (a)
13. (d)	**14.** (d)	**15.** (a)	**16.** (d)	**17.** (b)	**18.** (b)
19. (b)	**20.** (d)				

Chapter 10

1. (a)	**2.** (d)	**3.** (a)	**4.** (c)	**5.** (a)	**6.** (c)
7. (b)	**8.** (a)	**9.** (a)	**10.** (a)	**11.** (a)	**12.** (a)
13. (a)	**14.** (c)	**15.** (b)	**16.** (a)	**17.** (a)	**18.** (a)
19. (a)	**20.** (b)				

Chapter 11

1. (a)	**2.** (c)	**3.** (b)	**4.** (b)	**5.** (a)	**6.** (a)
7. (a)	**8.** (c)	**9.** (a)	**10.** (b)	**11.** (a)	**12.** (a)
13. (c)	**14.** (b)	**15.** (a)			

Chapter 12

1. (a)	**2.** (a)	**3.** (d)	**4.** (b)	**5.** (b)	**6.** (a)
7. (b)	**8.** (b)	**9.** (c)	**10.** (b)	**11.** (a)	**12.** (a)

Chapter 13

1. (c)	**2.** (b)	**3.** (c)	**4.** (d)	**5.** (d)	**6.** (d)
7. (c)	**8.** (c)	**9.** (a)	**10.** (a)		

Chapter 14

1. (d)	**2.** (d)	**3.** (a, b)	**4.** (c)	**5.** (a)	**6.** (b)
7. (d)	**8.** (d)	**9.** (b)	**10.** (a)	**11.** (d)	**12.** (d)

Chapter 15

1. (a)	**2.** (a)	**3.** (a)	**4.** (a)	**5.** (c)	**6.** (b)
7. (a)	**8.** (a)	**9.** (b)	**10.** (a)	**11.** (b)	**12.** (b)
13. (a)	**14.** (c)	**15.** (d)			

Chapter 16

1. (b)	**2.** (c)	**3.** (a)	**4.** (c)	**5.** (d)	**6.** (b)
7. (a)	**8.** (a)	**9.** (b)	**10.** (b)	**11.** (a)	**12.** (b)
13. (b)	**14.** (a)	**15.** (a)			

Chapter 17

1. (a, c, d)	**2.** (a)	**3.** (b)	**4.** (a)	**5.** (d)	**6.** (a)
7. (b)	**8.** (c)	**9.** (b)	**10.** (c)		

Chapter 18

1. (a)	**2.** (a)	**3.** (a)	**4.** (a)	**5.** (a)	**6.** (c)
7. (c)	**8.** (c)	**9.** (a)	**10.** (a)	**11.** (c)	**12.** (d)
13. (a, b, c, d)		**14.** (d)	**15.** (b)		

Chapter 19

1. (*d*)   **2.** (*a*)   **3.** (*d*)   **4.** (*a*)   **5.** (*a*)   **6.** (*a*)
7. (*c*)   **8.** (*a*)   **9.** (*d*)   **10.** (*a*)

Chapter 20

1. (*b*)   **2.** (*c*)   **3.** (*a*)   **4.** (*d*)   **5.** (*a*)   **6.** (*d*)
7. (*d*)   **8.** (*a*)   **9.** (*a*)   **10.** (*a*)

BIBLIOGRAPHY

Python

1. Mark Lutz, *Learning Python*, Fifth Edition, O'Reilly, 2013.

2. Stef Maruch and Aahz Maruch, *Python for Dummies*, John Wiley & Sons, 2006, ISBN:9780471778646.0020

3. David Beazley, *Python Essential Reference*, Third Edition, Sams Publishing, USA, 2006.

4. Allen Downey, *Think Python, How to Think Like a Computer Scientist*, Version 2.0.16, Green Tea Press, Needham, Massachusetts.

5. Wes McKinney, *Python for Data Analysis*, Wes McKinney. USA, 2013, ISBN: 978-1-449- 31979-3.

6. Andrew Johansen, *Python, The Ultimate Beginner's Guide*!

7. Wesley J. Chun, *Core Python Programming*, First Edition, Prentice Hall PTR, 2000, ISBN: 0-13-026036-3, 8.

8. Peter Harrington, *Machine Learning in Action*, Manning Publishing Company, 2012.

9. Richard L. Halterman, *Learning to Program with Python*, Copyright © 2011 Richard L. Halterman.

10. Willi Richert, Luis Pedro Coelho, *Building Machine Learning Systems with Python, Building Machine Learning Systems with Python*, Packt Publishing, 2013.

Web resources

11. *http://www.python.org*
12. *http://www.cheeseshop.python.org/*
13. *http://www.wiki.python.org*

Data Structure and Algorithms

14. Cormen, Leiserson, Rivest, Stein, *"Introduction to Algorithms,"* Second Edition, Prentice Hall of India,

15. Kleinberg, Tardos, *"Algorithm Design,"* Pearson, 2011.

16. Dave and Dave, *"Design and Analysis of Algorithms,"* Pearson, 2008.

17. Neapolitan, Naimipour, *"Foundations of Algorithms,"* Fourth Edition, Jones & Barlett, 2013.

18. Horowitz et. al., *"Algorithms,"* Second Edition, University Press, 2007.

19. Levitin, *"Introduction to Design and Analysis of Algorithms,"* Perason, 2009.

20. Rajeev Motwani and P. Raghavan, *"Randomized Algorithms,"* Cambridge University Press, New York (NY), 1995.

21. Williamson and Shmoys, *"The Design of Approximation Algorithms,"* Cambridge University Press, 2012.

22. Christos Papadimitriou, *"Computational Complexity,"* 1st ed., Addison Wesley, Chapter 11: Randomized computation, pp. 241–278, 1993.

23. Tenenbaum et. al.,*" Data Structures Using C,"* Pearson, 2006.

24. Horowitz, Sahini, *"Fundamentals of Data Structures,"* Galgotia Booksource, 1999.

25. Weiss, *"Data Structure and Algorithm Analysis in C++,"* Pearson, 2013.

26. Sharma, *"Data Structures Using C,"* Pearson, 2013.

27. Kanitkar, *"Data Structures Through C,"* BPB Publications,

28. Arora, Sanjeev, Barak, Boaz, *"Computational complexity—A Modern Approach,"* Cambridge University Press, ISBN 978-0-521-42426-4, 2009.

29. Sipser, Michael, *"Introduction to the Theory of Computation,"* PWS Publishing, ISBN 0-534- 94728-X, Section 8.2–8.3 (The Class PSPACE, PSPACE-completeness), pp. 281–294,1997.

30. Papadimitriou, Christos, *"Computational Complexity,"*1st ed., Addison Wesley, ISBN 0-201- 53082-1. Chapter 19: Polynomial space, pp. 455–490, 1993.

31. Sipser, Michael, *"Introduction to the Theory of Computation,"* 2nd edition ed., Thomson Course Technology, ISBN 0-534-95097-3. Chapter 8: Space Complexity, 2006.

32. Jones and Pevzner, *"An Introduction to Bioinformatics Algorithms,"* MIT Press.

33. Attwood, Parry Smith, Phukan, *"Introduction to Bioinformatics,"* Pearson, 2009.

34. Bishop, C.M., *"Neural Networks for Pattern Recognition,"* Oxford University Press, Oxford, England, 1995.

35. Bishop, C.M., *"Pattern Recognition and Machine Learning,"* Springer-Verlag, New York, 2008.

36. Goldberg, D.E., *"Genetic Algorithms in Search, Optimization and Machine Learning,"* Addison- Wesley, Reading, MA, 1989.

37. Goldberg, D.E., *"The Design of Innovation: Lessons from and for Competent Genetic Algorithms"*, Addison-Wesley, Reading, MA, 2002.

38. Stuart J. Russell and Peter Norvig, *"Artificial Intelligence: A Modern Approach,"* 2 ed. Pearson Education, 2003.

39. Rich, E., Knight, K, *"Artificial Intelligence,"* McGraw-Hill, 1991.

40. Strang, Gilbert, *"Introduction to Linear Algebra,"* 4th ed. Wellesley, MA: Wellesley-Cambridge Press, February 2009.

41. Va˘sek Chv́atal, *"Linear Programming,"* W. H. Freeman & Co., 1983.

42. G. B. Dantzig, *"Linear Programming and Extensions,"* Princeton University Press, 1963.

43. David Gale, *"The Theory of Linear Economic Models,"* McGraw-Hill, 1960.

44. Samuel Karlin, *"Mathematical Methods and Theory in Games, Programming and Economics,"* Volume 1, Addison-Wesley, 1959.

45. James K. Strayer, *"Linear Programming and Applications,"* Springer-Verlag, 1989.

46. Brigham, E. Oran, *"The Fast Fourier transform and its applications,"* Englewood Cliffs, N.J.: Prentice Hall, 1988.

47. Oppenheim, Alan V.; Schafer, R. W.; and Buck, J. R., *"Discrete-time Signal Processing*. Upper Saddle River, N.J.,*"* Prentice Hall.

48. Smith, Steven W., *"Chapter 8: The Discrete Fourier Transform,"* *The Scientist and Engineer's Guide to Digital Signal Processing,"* Second ed., San Diego, Calif.: California Technical Publishing.

49. P. Duhamel, B. Piron, and J. M. Etcheto, *"On computing the inverse DFT,"* *IEEE Trans. Acoust., Speech and Sig. Processing* 36 (2): 285–286, 1988.

50. Knuth, Donald, *"Sorting and Searching—The Art of Computer Programming,"* Volume 3 (Second ed.). Addison–Wesley, 1998.

51. Bhasin, Harsh, *Algorithms: Design and Analysis*, Oxford University Press, 2015.

INDEX